The Woman Who Brought Matisse Back from the Dead

Alison Leslie Gold

ISBN-13: 978-1495916724

ISBN-10: 1495916723

Oneiro Press Edition, U.K., 2014

Author's website: www.AlisonLeslieGold.com
https://www.facebook.com/AlisonLeslieGold

PEARLS MELT IN VINEGAR

The studio on the Boulevard du Montparnasse was not far from the Boulevard Raspail crossing. The door to the concierge's loge was ajar. The husband of the concierge was urinating into the sink when he noticed the full-bodied woman framed in the door as she entered the building and walked toward the lift. These chalk-faced women who came and went all had the same effect on him. This one was not pretty per se. Her legs were too short, her grape-gray dress belonged to another season and gave off the scent of mildew. Though he was not a rutting dog, she aroused him. Something leaked from her like juice from a too-soft peach. The concierge saw her and turned to get a better look at her. It was the time in the morning for brioche and milky coffee and she had just spread a coral and gray striped cloth over the table. She clucked to her husband, "Of course she's the new little model. Monsieur Matisse will make use of her for a while, then, when he's through with her, as with the rest, he'll order a fresh one and another after that."

The new model stepped out of the lift-cage at the sixth floor. She contained the bun of red-brown-green hair with one hand, removed two long eggshell-white hairpins with the other. She held the pins with the strongest teeth that remained in her mouth before plunging each one deeply into the unruly nest. She was not concerned when a few wiry curls escaped nor that the smear of lemon-yellow lipstick across her lips had rubbed into the corner of her mouth. After she made the sign of the cross, she tapped on the door.

Inside, the shutters were drawn. The artist's Russian assistant, rumored to be his slavish mistress, told her to wait at the door near a woman's torso done in the Greek style. Once invited to enter, rather than looking toward the grizzled artist when he greeted her from his wheelchair, the model's cocoa-gray eyes were drawn over his head to the large charcoal drawings of the Seven Stations of the Cross that had been drawn/redrawn/erased/drawn/rubbed. Because she was Catholic, she experienced the urge to get down on her knees before the brash drawings.

*

Scattered through the studio were broken shards of china and crockery, bolts of colored cloth, embroidered tapestries, canvas, bottles of turpentine, linseed oil. Henri Matisse sat in a wheelchair beneath the drawings of the Seven Stations. He was shriveled and white. He wheeled over, shook her hand. Though she did not need to, she reminded him that they had met before. He looked at her with friendly eyes. She leaned toward him, heard him say, "Of course I remember you."

6

She was 36, wore down-at-heel shoes and her feet hurt. She could not resist saying, "I prayed that God would give you more time ... and he has."

"You did. And you have given me nine extra years."

A rose tint spread across the part of his face that was visible above his white beard, behind his thick glasses.

"I see you left your order."

"Temporarily."

"Will that be possible?"

"If God wills it."

He was ready to work. Not sure if she had also shed her Catholic modesty, he gave instructions to disrobe. When she willingly obliged, he saw that inhibitions had been shed. He pointed to a chair. A bouquet of orange marigolds stood in a vase on the table at which she was seated. He told her to keep her legs uncrossed, to lean into the tabletop. He instructed her to look away from the orange flowers that gave off an appealing smell of wet earth. When an hour had passed and he was deep in concentration – two thick pencils in hand – she glanced at his blissful face. Magnified through gold wire eyeglasses, his unblinking eyes were several shades of blue and even gray – intense, steady and steadying eyes that appeared to change color – as she remembered them. He wore a black wool hat, a cigarette dangled from his lips.

Her body and face spilled over him until his senses were wet. About his models he had many times said: "I've got to be so penetrated, so impregnated by my subject that I could draw it with my eyes closed." People who knew nothing presumed that it was he who did the penetrating, did not realize it was the subject that pierced and flooded all of him.

She had been doing this work for Alice Hoska and other artists since the war and could keep a pose even if it became tiring or painful. She did not mind suffering. Fortunately a fat black stove heated the room. If she had one souvenir beside intimidation and hunger from the past, it was that she could never seem to shake off the cold. The artist worked until 12 then sent her away, instructed her to return after lunch. She took the lift-cage down, crossed the street and sat on a bench in a small square. She ate two yellow-ochre pears, two brown buns, and swallowed a garlic clove to purify her blood. She was still hungry when her sack was empty. Nearby was a kiosk that had pots of white carnations for sale though it was winter. While she sat, the sky went from dusky gray to gunmetal gray. At a few minutes before two, she pushed back the grill of the lift.

When she was naked once again, she awaited his instructions. The strong smell of fresh garlic was steeping through the room. He positioned her, told her he would stop work at five but did not. At six the émigré assistant, Lydia Delectorkaya – blamed

8

for his marital break-up – urged him to save his eyes for the following day. It was not possible to tell if Lydia's concern was amorous or practical. He worked for another hour before he put down the pencil, then wheeled the wheelchair away and turned his attention to twittering turtledoves. Lydia put an envelope into the model's hand. The money in it would pay for a pair of nylon stockings with dark seams down the back that she had been coveting at Printemps.

"Monsieur would like to book you for the week. Is Sunday a problem for you? Do you need to go to Mass? Do you have a man friend to see on Sunday? And ... what shall we call you?"

"I was baptized Paule Boule although you knew me as Sister Paule. My name was changed during the war to Claude. I do go to church on Sunday, do have a man friend," then added as an afterthought, "It's an honor to sit for Monsieur. I would work through the night with pleasure if he requests."

"You will be paid double for Sunday."

Matisse began to cough. An off-white bird flew across the room and landed on the back of a fringed lampshade. The bird stretched its wings. When the coughing stopped, he caressed the bird's neck. As soon as Lydia showed the new model out, he loosened his corset, had his nurse help him with his personal needs, then stretched out on his bed for a rest.

9

To make some point about temptation, Father Clutier in his homily told the small group who had pushed through the dark, sticky rain to attend Mass that pearls melted in vinegar. The moment mass was over, after lighting a candle for her dead mother stranded for all eternity in purgatory, Sister Paule, a nursing nun, age 28, born in Marseille, orphaned as a young girl, walked back to the hospital. She was weary; the gluey wetness in the air made the gray fabric of her habit even heavier.

Sister Paule had been attending a dying matron from Nice, Madam Alberes, for more than a month. Round-the-clock attention was needed. Earlier, when the nurse whom she had been assisting, Sister Lameijer, noticed Sister Paule's lagging amethyst eyelids, she had sent her to Mass rather than to bed because she believed in the energizing power of prayer. Sister Lameijer nursed all manner of patients like Madam Alberes. Though Sister Paule showed willingness to serve, to make herself useful with soaked sheets and chamber pots, she lacked a healing touch and wished Reverend Mother had chosen other work for her to do. Her hands were rarely clean. Because of this, Sister Lameijer kept her at a distance from the patient. When Sister Paule asked if she could rub the patient's feet, Sister Lameijer told her not to lest she infect one of the many suppurating sores.

When blood mixed with raw mocha and pink chunks poured from Madam Alberes's mouth, a porter was summoned. He was a small foreigner wearing broken, putty-colored shoes who carried a slop bucket and a mop. Sister Lameijer sent him away because she did not want the woman to die hearing the sound of a sloshing mop. Madam Alberes's time was coming to an end. She sent Sister Paule to fetch the priest who would offer Madam Alberes extreme unction.

The end came with a quiver. Sister Lameijer rolled down Madam Alberes's amber eyelids. She stretched the coarse white sheet over her head and said the rosary. Neither the priest nor Sister Paule had returned when she began preparing the body for removal.

*

Sister Paule walked along rue de la Buffa. She was hungry so she took the route through the market, passing pink fish, ochre hams, bloody cuts of meat hanging from hooks. Burlap sacks of muddy potatoes and hard fruit hung from stalls. She had no money of her own, could look but could not taste except for a mashed apple fallen onto the ground that she picked up and bit into. There were a few local fishmongers and workers in blue overalls, but it seemed that Nice was becoming clogged with foreign faces.

The walk to Cimiez was uphill. When she noticed a piece of sapphire-green silk cloth lying on the sidewalk, she reached down and picked up a man's dirty handkerchief that had grape-colored stains. Four cherries were embroidered with crimson thread with cross-stitches in white thread decorating the edges. Her swollen eyelids stung, her empty stomach cramped.

Back in convent, in her mirror-less partitioned cell, she poured water from the pitcher into the porcelain basin. She was rubbing the little handkerchief with green soap when a novice from Collioure came to tell her that Reverend Mother wanted her. She squeezed the wet handkerchief and went along the corridor to the convent's office. Reverend Mother was sealing an envelope when she entered. After licking it with her tongue, she turned her attention to Sister Paule.

"I'm sending you to another patient."

"Will I be helping Soeur Lameijer once again?"

"No. You'll administer medicines to a new patient and help with washing and attending to. It is an easy assignment, like a holiday. He is an old man returned from surgery, living out his last days."

Reverend Mother's milk-blue eyes never softened around Sister Paule. Because of the sinful death of Sister Paule's mother by her own hand, she never could warm to her. She would not let Paule forget that if the convent that Mother ruled with an iron fist had not taken her in, Sister Paule would be warming her hands with homeless people and foreigners beside the hearth of one church or other.

"And you must remember to wash your hands both before and after you attend to the patient."

While they ate bread and potato soup, Sister Louise told her that the dying patient in question was a 70-year-old man who lived in the Régina next door, the old artist who did not wear a coat in winter. Sister Paule knew whom she meant. The man in question had a white-flecked beard and very often strolled in the convent's garden. Sister Louise said that she had been temporarily nursing him because his private nurse had gone to tend to a dying aunt in Toulouse. She was needed elsewhere and could not continue, which was why Sister Paule was being sent.

While Sister Paule chewed bread, Sister Louise explained that the old man had returned from a long hospital stay in Lyons following two heart attacks brought on by surgery for abdominal cancer. The doctor had urged that those watching over him do what was possible to keep him comfortable but not stop him from working. Since it was doubtful he would last very long, why not let him have his way? Seeing how hungry she was, Sister Louise offered Sister Paule her own bread. She added that the artist was a non-believer.

Of course Sister Paule knew the Régina from outside, had lived in its shadow since coming to convent. All who resided in and around Nice knew the Hotel Régina at the top of the hill looming over the convent. Once the Grand Hotel Excelsior, where royalty and the very rich and other personages of high place stayed, had had the radiance of a castle. But no more. Not only had it gotten shabby, it was in the midst of renovation. Because there was talk that the Côte d'Azur would be bombed, makeshift shelters were being prepared and the exteriors and roofs of all prominent buildings like the Régina were splashed with black and avocado-green paint that added a frightening look to the mess of renovation.

Since the war, hundreds of common soldiers, perhaps Moroccans, certainly heathens, were being housed at the Régina. Day and night these small brown men sat on curbs, eating, playing cards and other games, talking in their language, washing their underclothes using rainwater and no soap, hanging them to dry in the street. Once dried, their clothes were as dirty as they had been before.

*

The old artist was sitting up in a bed cluttered with books and paper eating goose liver when Sister Paule was brought to him. She could not imagine how his doctor would approve of goose liver. He noticed her disapproval, said, "Though I have lost a

14

meter of intestine, my digestion is fine. And, since I have been given a temporary reprieve from death, why not eat what I please?"

His words were not challenging. She smelled eau de cologne. His eyes swallowed her eyes, something she was not used to, since she had been taught not to make eye contact. His looked into, rather than at, her until his housekeeper came to take her to a little room that had a window overlooking her Franciscan convent and attached garden. Seeing the garden from above was strange; whoever looked could watch the sisters and novices going about their daily lives.

Sister Paule sat for a long time in a plum-colored chair that was upholstered with soft furrowed fabric. Because cubicles in convent had no doors, she had rarely been alone behind a closed door as she was now. She did not like it. When she rested her head against the wall, she dozed. It was dark when she was summoned to where he was sitting on the side of his bed wearing blue and white striped pajamas. It was time to dole out medicines. He was in acute pain, doing his best to override it. Again he looked hard at her.

"So that you know my routine, I wake up at eight. My work schedule has been abbreviated from about 9:30 or 10 to 2:30 or three when I stop for lunch and a rest until four. You should know that I'm an insomniac and, doubtlessly, will call you in the middle of the night."

After Matisse swallowed what she poured into a spoon, she noticed that the wastebasket was filled to the brim with crumpled paper. He asked her to empty it when she went, so she carried the caramel-colored wicker basket to the kitchen. Curious, she picked out a few of the crushed sheets of paper and smoothed them out. She saw that Matisse had many times begun a letter. It was beyond her to resist reading what he had written, and she read two snippets from the various versions of the oft-started, oft-discarded, letter:

... As you may know, my operation must have been the same one that Bignou endured when they fitted him with an artificial anus. Between you and me, I, too, have one now. Not everyone who has drawn that particular ticket in the lottery likes to talk about it ...

She had not been told this; it shed quite another light on her responsibilities. The second said something about dark blue shadows and the colors red and white like a barber pole, and:

Now I feel as if I had come back from the dead. It changes everything. Time present and time future are an unexpected bonus.

Reading these private writings lengthened the list she would have to give up at confession. Now, as well as the sin of nosiness, she would have to add the sin of stealing. Had it been a love letter from him to his assistant, there would have been the sin of lasciviousness to add.

*

He finished drinking café au lait while Sister Paule poured additional doses of glassy-gold fluid into a metal spoon. She noticed the bread thick with butter left uneaten on a plate decorated with gold geese. She looked to see if her hands were clean, decided they were. He sat surrounded by pillows. The housekeeper was dusting. He said, "I can't imagine that rat poison tastes any more unpleasant."

He swung his feet onto the floor. When he tried to stand up, she reached out to assist him.

"Are you suffering, Monsieur?"

"Cramps. But so what, the pain will ease once I shuffle around the room a few times. If this is the price of living on borrowed time, I'm happy to pay in full."

And this he did while the housekeeper turned down his white-on-white bedcovers for airing. His sheets had daisies embroidered with sand-colored thread. Sister Paule washed him and serviced his intimate needs. He appreciated quickness in these matters. She laced the stiff corset he was forced to wear, helped him dress and suggested he add something under his shirt to keep the chill from his kidneys. He picked an undershirt, one that was apple-green. The pressed shirt he had chosen to wear that day was bright pink. She who had spent most of her life in black and white and gray was surprised to see colors like these. His trousers were burnt brown wool and it pained him to bend to ease them on. She held up the beige jacket that had been hanging on the back of a chair so that he could slip his arms into its sleeves. Where did one find clothing in such colors? The fabrics were soft to the touch, the colors were like she imagined God might have used in the Tabernacle in the Wilderness in the Book of Exodus.

"Your shoes and socks! I will help you ... "

He shrugged and shuffled away on bare feet. Through the course of the morning she moved freely through the apartment bringing medicines at the allotted times, checking his pulse, his temperature, adding numbers to his chart, washing and rewashing her hands in between. He drank café au lait with a small blond woman who smoked one cigarette while lighting another from the end of the first. Sister Paule wondered if this was his daughter until the blond woman was introduced as Madam Lydia.

A charcoal-gray cat brushed against his calves, back and forth many times. He did not mind. He smoked a forbidden cigar during the brief time he was able to stand up among bright green cactuses and blood-orange jungle-like plants in pots arranged on the open balcony, bracing himself with a hand on the railing. Nothing of the city could be seen because the rooftops were shrouded in fog. Sister Paule came up behind him, looked out, too. His eau de cologne was appealing. He quietly laughed, "We live above the fogs."

With great difficulty he walked to the aviary, told her to follow, picked up and held a white turtledove on two fingers to show her and brought the subdued bird to his lips. If it had been anyone else she would have shaken a finger and reminded him that birds were carriers of vermin and germs, but since he was not long for the world, why reprimand? And, dirty as her hands often got, who was she to shake her finger?

After breakfast he inched his way through the apartment half-bending despite the pain it caused, retrieving things that had been discarded in the various trash bins. It seemed that he enjoyed collecting all manners of discards like she did. Of course there was no one to stop him from hoarding whatever he liked. Madam Lydia prepared the workroom. At 9:30 he sat on the side of the cushion-filled Empire bed in his studio. His bare feet were placed side-by-side flat on the floor. He smoked a second cigar. The screams and whistles of his birds in their cages were ear-splitting. Sensing that he was suffering, Sister Paule administered a dose of pain medication.

A visitor arrived at 9:45. As Sister Paule greedily ate bread, butter and salty cheese, she got a glimpse of a dark-haired, foreign-looking girl. The cook told her, "She is his model. These days he uses film extras."

Sister Paule saw the girl remove her clothes and saw Matisse begin a drawing using charcoal. His face and the girl's entirely naked body were very close. The girl's hair-covered private part was directly in his line of vision so that he could easily have looked inside if the girl widened the space between her thighs. If she got any closer, Sister Paule could easily have looked as well. In all her life, she had never seen a naked woman in a state of shame-free repose.

Later, when the day had cooled, Sister Paule brought a blanket for his lap, also his pills. He was sitting on a chair, his easel facing the window. The gray Angora cat had curled up against a bolt of golden fabric, fast asleep; Matisse's coloring had gone from pinkish to biscuit-colored. The model was gone and the assistant was standing on a ladder pinning a drawing to the wall. Matisse was complaining that he needed canvas and pigments, but the assistant reminded him, "There's a war going on, nothing can be found anymore."

Sister Paule watched him wrap the blanket she had brought around his shoulders, heard him say, "It's prostate cancer Rouault has. Pin that a little higher, Madam Lydia."

*

20

Late in the afternoon the fog dissolved. On unsteady feet, he prepared for a walk. Sister Paule asked if she should accompany him so that he had an arm as ballast.

"Thank you. No!"

A little later, she looked down from the balcony into the garden she knew so well and saw him taking slow steps among the postulants who strolled in pairs in the shade of the eucalyptus trees. How unfamiliar the trees were from above, flat, bushier, not green, more a blend of black and the blue of morning glories. The roof of the convent was not what it seemed from below either. Rather than angular, it was flat with red sloping tiles. Twenty minutes later he returned and took a nap. Afterwards, he called Sister Paule into his room and asked her to help with his intimate needs.

Because he was feeling strong, he and Lydia went into Nice to go to the cinema. Sister Paule thought it strange that he would take his employee out for an evening of pleasure. When she was alone, she glanced into the receptacle in his studio, picked up and smoothed out a few sheets and saw false starts at drawings of a foot, bits of broken charcoal, dirty rags grown stiff. She threw them back into the receptacle, did not notice that her hands had gotten smudged black.

She wandered through his studio and looked at and touched everything. There was much that caught the eye: Profusions of fabrics. Broken bits of ceramics. Tapestries. Women's blouses, hats. Plants everywhere, paintings, drawings, paints, brushes. There were vases filled with flowers – mimosa, white carnations, white roses – mostly dried, also dried-out oranges and lemons, three rotting green apples, pencils, pens, charcoals, a humidor. It was pleasant that the rooms were full of things to look at. How much nicer than living in an austere convent.

Thumbtacks held sketches and drawings on the walls, pinned in straight lines. There was a painting of three green apples, a coffee pot, a shell from the sea, a blue flowerpot and a teacup. All the while, the birds screeched. Soon Cook served some kind of fish coated with mayonnaise in the kitchen with a full liter of *vin rouge*. Sister Paule ate like royalty, could not stop until the serving plate was empty. Cook was soaking her feet in hot water because she had bunions. She was Polish but her French was not hard to understand. She speculated that Matisse was suffering from gallstones, also diverticulitis, which he had had before.

"Do you think his end is near?"

Not wanting to doom him, Sister Paule replied with false modesty.

"I know little beside emptying slops. But I've been praying for him."

When Cook dropped an additional chunk of bread onto her plate, she ate it. Suddenly sleepy, she got up to go to her room.

"Keep your ears open, his voice isn't strong when he calls out in the night."

An hour before dawn he called out her name. Quickly, forgetting to wash her hands, she went to him. He confessed that his eyes ached – would she read to him? Haltingly but with feeling, she read a chapter from the book he handed her by Pearl Buck, called *The Patriot*.

*

Every night Sister Paule read a chapter of this book to him. Sometimes while she read he made quick pencil sketches of her face. One night, after nine days and nights, he asked her questions. He asked if she had a hero.

"Yes. Several."

"Who?"

"Jeanne d'Arc, the saint?"

"Oh."

"And Napoleon."

"How old are you?"

"I was born in 1916."

"Where were you born?"

"In Marseille."

"Do you have parents?"

"My mother died by her own hand when I was four ... " she hesitated, then whispered,

" ... after my father was sent to prison for debt."

23

"Do you believe in the possibility of resurrection after death?

"Of course, wasn't Christ resurrected?"

"I don't mean Christ. I mean human resurrection? Do you believe that it is possible?"

Remembering that she was speaking to a non-believer with one foot in the grave, she was cautious.

"I've no way of knowing, Monsieur Matisse. It would be a good idea if you would try once more to sleep. But I have been praying for you to live on."

Without warning, Matisse explained that his regular nurse, Monique Bourgeois, was returning. He stood shoeless in his usual blue and white striped pajamas and upright, holding onto the wall. Sister Paule's services were no longer required.

"How soon is she coming?"

"Very soon. In two hours."

She helped him clean up, dress and lace his corset. She would never know how *The Patriot* ended. That this was the last time she would have to endure the grating noise made by the birds was a relief. He thanked her for her service. She bent her knee in a curtsy of respect. He apologized for being difficult. His face flushed a lemony shade, purple and black bruises circled his eyes. She assured him he had been an easy patient and encouraged him to keep faith and that – of course she was lying – his health would surely improve.

"Keep me in your prayers."

"I have been and always will."

When she returned to her room to gather her things she found an aromatic bouquet of violets laying on the pillow. Also a note:

Dear Soeur Boule: You have well-meaning hands and you are caring and you read with sweetness. I won't forget the kind help you've given me, your prayers for my survival, and your expressive face. If ever you have a free moment and would enjoy doing so, let Madam Lydia know and she'll arrange for you to model for me. You would be paid for your time, of course. H. Matisse

How had Lydia scrounged up a bunch of violets in Nice during wartime? They smelled sweetly but she left them in the room because it would not be correct to bring them into the convent for the others to envy.

*

Right away Mother sent her to a rich house outside of Nice to care for a high police personage. She worked days only, had to travel back to convent at night, a hardship indeed as it was a long, uphill walk to the tram. The policeman had been blinded while performing his duties. Sister Paule helped him to fasten and unfasten his black suspenders, to eat, dress, undress, make pee. He hardly spoke, did not care about the weather or the war, had no way of knowing if she had washed her hands or not, was only interested in descriptions of food. He ate *paté* with *cornichons* while she guided his hand. He complained that the coffee was ersatz, burned barley that tasted like swill. While he chewed and harangued, she fed herself forkfuls of his food.

She was leaving for the night when the air raid siren sounded. There was no time to take him down into a shelter at the end of the street, so she did not go either. It was as if she were losing her mind when a heart-stopping explosion came close and sent her down on her knees to beg God for help. A second, even louder detonation caused her to cower like a dog behind a door. The policeman thought her terror was funny. She felt a sharp pain deep inside her ears from the ensuing explosions that muffled the sound of his laughter. She saw his lips open wide. What she heard sounded like a dry pen scratching paper.

Lyon, 1941

Finally the many days of bombing came to an end. She received instructions to return to convent. The hearing in her right ear was not what it had been – all sounds were heard as if through a wad of cotton. After Mass to celebrate the feast day of St. Adelaide, she went for a walk in the frosty garden of the convent. For a moment she stood under the eucalyptus tree and looked up toward Matisse's

26

windows and saw that all the shades were tightly drawn. She asked Sister Danielle when the old artist had passed away.

"He hasn't. Monsieur and his illicit Russian mistress have gone inland to Vence to get away from the bombing."

She was surprised that he had not died and that he had had the strength to move residences. It seemed wrong for him to die in Vence rather than looking out over Nice. Irate, she said, "I doubt that Mademoiselle is his mistress," unsure if she was right or not but determined to protect his reputation.

After two days, she was told to prepare for a journey. She and Sister Susanne were going to Lyon where neither had ever been. Before they left, Mother Superior summoned them to her office that had been fitted with blackout shades.

"You are going into the eye of the storm, the worsening war. I shall pray for your safety. Despite recent setbacks, the Germans will prevail. Remember what I say."

They left after vespers, went on foot to the train station in which people were sleeping on the floor. In the crowded second-class car they were joined by a group of nursing sisters from a different order. There was a shortage of hospital help in Lyon. The train passed hillsides of pale lavender that would probably freeze and die because of the unseasonable snow. They passed through a small city. Shocking ruins from the recent bombings were seen through the window until the glass became frosted by fat gray snowflakes that fell and pasted themselves onto the glass.

In Lyon street signs had been removed; clothes were drying on poles outside the Cathedral where hungry dogs foraged. It took various turnings until they found a church for Mass. They had eaten nothing so they would be allowed to receive communion. After Mass, Sister Paule lit a candle for her mother and father, one for the dying artist. Both flickered in front of a statue of the Virgin. Afterwards, she unwrapped and ate some cheese.

To find the hospital they went from nameless street to nameless street, were often wrong. The sewers had backed up and the smell was rank. From the moment they reached the hospital that was overcrowded with people injured from the bombings there was not a moment to think. Sister Paule and Sister Susanne were assigned to a young doctor named Antoine Robaud who told them the Partisans had shot two German soldiers and, in reprisal, the Germans had executed twenty-two Frenchmen by firing squad. Christmas-green spots of anger crossed his face. Sister Susanne was shocked.

"That's eleven French for one German."

Through the winter, there was not a moment for Sister Paule to catch her breath. There was no gas or coal, little soap to keep underclothes clean. Snippets of war news were passed around but no one knew what was and was not true. In August, information came that the Americans were on French soil in Toulon or maybe Cannes. The doctor gleefully told her that the Fritzes were enraged like wild bees. He predicted the Allies would free all of France soon. Did his glee mean that he was looking forward to France's defeat? Didn't he know that the Germans, as Mother Superior had promised, would prevail? They all despised the bombs and airplanes of the Allies.

*

There were days and weeks of continuous rain. No one knew that Dr. Robaud was working with the Maquis until two men from the Gestapo arrested him. Because Sister Susanne and Sister Paule were at his side, they, too, were herded into the police van though neither would have known a Partisan if they had seen one. Because it was not their duty to ask about the loyalty of patients, they had not. Those arrested were crammed into a stone jail cell along with 20 others.

On the afternoon of the second day soldiers herded those arrested into trucks – men mixed with women. Sister Jeanne, Sister Susanne, Sister Paule, Dr. Robaud and a priest, Father de Fleur, who had done nothing but administer last rights to the dying, were bunched with unknown others. In two open trucks were 80 prisoners, mostly ordinary French people, a few from the country who wore muddy wooden clogs.

The trucks bounced through the oily rain past a river that was swollen on the verge of overflowing to a place in St. Genis Laval that was once a fort. The soldiers ordered the captives down from the trucks, pushed men and women into a tangled group. Sister Susanne gripped Sister Paule's shoulder. The Gestapo officers stood, watched all, leather gun pouches dangling from leather belts. When all prisoners were gathered, the soldiers shouted for everyone to go down on their knees. As one they did so. Soldiers passed among them hoisting jerry cans. At a signal from an officer, soldiers flung gasoline from the cans over heads and shoulders. A second group of soldiers stood at the back of the crowd holding truncheons. Sister Susanne crunched the words to Hail Mary but Sister Paule could think of none of the hundred prayers she had learned through the years in convent.

The soldiers wielding flame-throwers encircled the group and bright red, peach and yellow streams of fire shot out. The smoke was mixed with screams, begging prayers. Forceful licks of flame touched everyone while machine guns tattered. One by one people were alight with spreading flames while crumbling from bullet wounds. Sister Susanne's habit and coronet blazed. Sister Paule pulled away because her own sleeve was flaming. A short woman with frizzled mint-green hair wearing a brown coat caught fire from head to foot at once.

Sister Susanne pushed Sister Paule so hard she fell away, was spared, as the roaring gasoline-fueled conflagration melted cloth, hair, flesh and leather. Sister Susanne's black habit, coif headpiece, large black beaded rosary with the hanging metal cross with crucified Jesus became a fiery furnace until a hot flood of smoky sapphire-red drenched everything.

*

The old rampart led past a black statue of the virgin. Hand in hand, the farmer dragged her.

"Faster! Faster! Before it gets light."

She could see nothing, had lost her shoes, her feet were like cold potatoes. First light of dawn illumined drizzle that was darkly silver, a misted mirror because for an instant she thought she saw her face in it until her forehead punctured the reflection when the farmer pulled her through it into a vast expanse of sunflowers that cut her feet as they ran. Clusters of colorless grapes hung heavy and low in a vineyard they passed. How luscious a handful of grapes would have tasted. He veered toward, then passed around, a row of bending trees to a dark farmhouse on the other side of the trees where he jerked her through a door.

The farmer told her to sit right there, left and came back with his sister. The farmer sat down at a table and began eating cooked fish. He spoke with food in his mouth.

"The smuggler comes to Lyon every Thursday at noon. The Germans have checkpoints all over the city but no one suspects a shabby farmer. Have you any money?"

She did not hear so he shouted the same question and she answered, "I have nothing."

"Too bad. We'll have to find another way to pay for false papers."

She smelled of kerosene mixed with smoky sewage. She looked over at the woman, spoke timidly.

"I'm hungry and thirsty."

"First you must be cleaned."

It was not easy to remove the stinking half-burnt habit, which had attached itself to her skin. The woman brought her to a stone room that had a low ceiling filled with oak barrels all the while complaining that she had varicose veins that were hurting terribly. The woman took a knife and peeled at the stiff cloth as she would skin an apple; the underclothes were even more wretched. Everything dropped on the dirt floor. She left brown soap and a stiff brush soaking in a pan of vinegar, told Sister Paule to scrub herself as she scooped up what had been dropped on the floor.

"Stay here. Don't make noise. I'll tell you when the young priest arrives."

Confined to the windowless room, naked, shameful, hungry and shivering, unable to clear her mind in order to think, she looked at the vinegar and brush and sat on the edge of a cot that was against the cold, wet stone wall. Why clean herself? Even strong soap could not remove what had dirtied her.

*

When the woman returned with a gray dress over her arm, Sister Paule was deeply asleep, dangling over the edge of the cot. The woman had to pinch her cheek to wake her. She laid the shabby dress on the cot.

"You haven't cleaned yourself."

She picked up the brush, rubbed it with soap, dipped it in vinegar.

"I'll try to clean you up."

Aggressively, the woman brushed at the grime coating Sister Paule's body, brushed so hard that the brush scraped through her skin. Each time she dipped it into the vinegar, Sister Paule whimpered. Finally, she put down the brush.

"It's impossible to get you clean. Make yourself as pretty as you can."

Sister Paule pulled the stiff fabric over her head, down along her stinging skin. Whose dress was it? She realized that her undergarments had not been returned with the dress, then sat on the cot. She smoothed the skirt over her knees, pressed her thighs together, prayed for her virginity. Because she had only two hairpins, she slid one through the hair above her right ear, one above the left. A mouse ran from under one cask up the side of another, stood staring at her with red eyes.

A little later the woman brought a husky young priest who had an old leather case under his arm. When they were alone, the priest looked down at her, asked her to stand because he was shortsighted. He brought his face toward hers, examined her cheekbones, nose and forehead with his fingertips. Then, he got down on his knees and felt her feet, ankles, up her calves and thighs.

"Lift your skirt, I need to know that you're not pregnant."

"I'm a virgin, Father."

"I need to know that you're not lice-ridden before I can issue a certificate."

Terrified not to, she closed her eyes and lifted the fabric of her skirt so that his face was level to her pubic hair. She could not get out words that would tell him that, like him, she belonged to God. He moved his face closer until his nose and mouth were pressed into the sticky tapestry. He reached his arms around her thighs. With his fingertips, he touched along and under her buttocks until he groaned, then he stood up. He shuffled through the folio.

"Do you prefer the name Claude or Ginette?"

"Not Ginette."

He made a notation with a pen, handed her a certificate and an identity card. She noticed the mouse again and began to cry, but bent her knee.

"Thank you, Father."

Vienne, 1942

Backtracking through the expanse of sunflowers, the smuggler took her by night along the lower Loire, past a large château. Every step she took with potato feet was an effort. Reaching a village, he brought her upstairs to a room above a café that had drawn willow-green curtains. The village was Vienne, not far from Lyon but far enough, the smuggler told her. Already hiding in the room was a young woman, Marlena, and her mother, Alice Hoska. Both looked like vagabonds. The smuggler told Alice that he would take this new woman elsewhere if Alice did not want her to remain.

"Who is she?"

"Mademoiselle Claude, a nurse."

"She can stay."

Claude and the smuggler were given bowls of fish soup. After the smuggler went on his way, Alice left to wash plates in the back of the café below; Marlena told Claude that her father was a famous painter who, after suffering horribly with lung cancer, had succumbed the previous October. Her family had been hunted by the Nazis. She told how she, her father and mother had fled south from Paris to Cusset. After that they went to Marseille until it became too dangerous. In November it had been necessary to flee again and they had been brought here by the maquis. They had been on the run for two and a half years.

Claude said, "I owe my life to your mother. She could have refused me."

"How could she say no? Sometime you might be in the same position and, you will see, you would do what she did. You must be someone special to have been brought here. Only God knows how long this place will be safe. We might have to flee again."

Marlena passed her the bowl of stew and shared her glass of wine. The room in which they were had a clock, a window, a small table, two chairs, a three-legged stool, two beds for the three of them to share. The glass that covered the clock-face served as a mirror of sorts for Marlena, reminding her of her degraded condition.

Two cats, both fat because of the wealth of mice in the café, came and went. The female was in heat causing the male to spray the walls, the bedding, Marlena's valise. Because the army had requisitioned all the coal and the room was entirely without heating, the cats were sources of heat and were invited to share the beds. After her shift at the café, when her daughter had gone down to replace her, speaking with a Polish accent, Alice asked, "Are you with the maquis?"

"No. I'm a Catholic nun."

"I would never have guessed it. My husband was a Catholic convert. It didn't help us."

Claude had never met a convert. Alice had never met a nun.

"I'm surprised you had to go into hiding."

"We were taken from the hospital. All of us, even doctors and nurses, were taken to a deserted place and incinerated. I don't know if anyone else besides me escaped."

"God help us all!"

Alice lay down on the bed. After a few minutes she got up.

"I hope we don't corrupt you, Mademoiselle. We are worldly people. Like my husband, I'm an artist. I'm from Krakow, Poland. I came to Paris when I was 19, I married Louis. He was 16 years older than me. Appolinaire, Braque, Degas, Max Jacob, André Salmon, Picasso were his friends then became mine. We knew everyone, had many exhibitions in Parisian salons. That didn't help us either."

"I don't know who those people are."

Claude spooned up the last dregs of ochre broth in her bowl.

"I nursed an artist for a short time in Cimiez ... Monsieur Henri Matisse."

"We all know Matisse. Early on, both he and Louis painted in Brittany, at the seaside. Did he paint you? You'd be his type."

"I was his nurse, he was gravely ill. But, a few times while I read to him at night, he did drawings of me with a pencil in a little book ... "

" ... sketches?"

" ... sketches. He said I should come back and pose for him."

"You must. His wife left him because of a young model, you know."

"I doubt he's alive. He was fatally sick."

"Perhaps you'll model for me? I have a pen and a little ink. It would pass the time in a pleasant way ... for me. I can't pay you in money but I can pay you with food. I've no appetite anymore."

"If it would please you, madam. I owe my life to you. I'll do whatever you wish."

"Perhaps I could ask you to pose for me before the church swallows you again."

"I would not turn down more food. If you, by chance, could find underclothes for me, I would be very grateful. I'm ashamed that I'm naked under my dress."

Chamonix, 1943

In spring Vienne was no longer safe. By night, Alice's contacts took her into hiding in the mountains in Chamonix near the Swiss border. Though there was space only for two, because Alice insisted, they agreed to take Claude along. A black car with a white cross painted on its roof and hood drove part of the way. At a glassy river, the car turned back and a trail guide, who had been paid by someone unknown, took charge. He led them by foot through villages set between forests and snowy mountain crags. Still icy lakes lay among Alpine meadows strewn with flowers, pale blue in the moonlight. The spring thaw had just begun.

None of them had proper shoes and by the time they reached the chalet in which they would be hidden their makeshift shoes and stockings were crusted with dirty ice. Claude suffered from dysentery. Alice was fearful that she would lose all strength in her wobbly legs. The only thing she could find to fortify them was a bottle of treacle for which she had traded six drawings with the trail guide.

A bulldog was tied outside of the chalet day and night. It frightened Claude who could not look at it because it seemed as if its red eyes could see into her soul, something she did not want even a dog to do. On the snowy night that Alice took Marlena for a walk, Claude laid down flat on the floor in penance, whispered, "*In nomine Patris ...*"

One morning their trail guide returned and asked Alice if he could take Marlena out to look at

Mont Blanc. Alice told him, "Claude is of age. Take her."

The guide said to Claude, "I would bring fresh cow milk for everyone in the morning if I could convince you to accompany me."

By way of reply, Alice wrapped Claude in her dirty milk-blue shawl. She had traded two drawings for it. The guide smiled, told Alice, "Don't worry about her."

Alice was not pleased.

"She's not worldly. She's religious. She may look a mature woman but she's not. I beg you to bring her back safely. I won't ask any questions if you do."

The trail guide led Claude through an intricate web of trails to Lac Blanc, bright turquoise beneath the snowy peaks of Mont Blanc. Along the trail, half in and half out of a cloud beside a deep gorge was a wooden refuge. Inside, a cold hearth of ash under half-burned branches, 10 bare cots, a wooden table and wooden chairs. Claude sat heavily on one of the chairs while the guide went to gather fresh branches and she watched him through the open doorway.

Arms full of firewood, he returned and lit a fire. As the refuge warmed, he showed her a slab of real butter wrapped in brown paper that had left oil on the cloth of his jacket pocket.

"Would you like to taste this butter?"

"Oh yes please. I've hardly tasted real butter in my life."

"Have you ever seen a grown man without his clothes on?"

"When would I, unless he was ill? I was brought up by nuns."

"Don't play me for a fool."

"It's true. I lived in a Catholic convent for my whole life. I've never seen a male child without his clothes either. Why would I want to?"

"It's not that you would want to ... it would please me if you would remove my clothes and look at me unclothed. Wouldn't you like to please me? I risked my life to protect you from the Nazis hunting you and your kind."

"I'm very grateful."

"I want you to realize that Christ was a man and what he looked like."

With a penknife he cut a nub of butter and fed it to her. Emboldened by the lure of more, she unbuttoned his jacket. As she removed each article of clothing, he placed a pat of butter on her tongue. When he was naked, revealing hairy sacks and upturned organ, she did as he had suggested and examined every thistly hair on his blue-veined body – with her eyes, then her hands, and finally – after he fed her the largest pat of butter so far – with her buttery mouth. When the fire had burned down and the chill was returning to the refuge, he put his clothes back on, emptied his pockets, made a pile of broken chocolate bits and fed them to her bite by bite.

The next day when he carried a bucket of fresh milk to the chalet, he also carried an auburn wool coat that had a fur collar and gave it to Claude. Quite soon, Chamonix was no longer safe so Alice's contacts took them by foot twenty miles away to Sallanches where they remained, until the day of liberation, in a tiny room made of rotting beams of black wood.

As Alice and Marlena began preparing to make their way to Paris to find out who was alive and who was dead, Marlena asked Claude, "Where will you go?"

"I don't know what I should do. My mind is not clear anymore."

"Since God has cast you here, perhaps he wants you to live a secular life. Once you know what you've been missing, if you don't like it, you can rejoin your order."

"I've never taken care of myself. What could I do?"

"You could pay your way by modeling for artists like Mama and Monsieur Matisse."

"For money?"

"You wouldn't get rich but you could earn enough to pay for bread and a bed. You'll need lipstick and rouge, though. You're doughy and bland."

Paris, 1944

When she arrived in Paris, Claude had nothing except the coat with the fur collar and the stiff gray dress. Parisians spoke rapidly. Although she could not always understand what was said, she was curious to walk the boulevards of the city. Alice secured a bed in an attic for her. Jam was rationed, the only way to get lipstick was on the black market. The room in which she slept had paisley wallpaper. It was occupied by an old servant lady who was even deafer than she was. The old lady heated a kettle full of hot water and poured it into a gray metal tub. She told Claude she needed to bathe herself and she would prepare the bath. When Claude stepped in she burnt her feet. To correct the situation the old woman poured too much cold water into the tub. Claude was not much cleaner when she stepped out of the tub.

Alice directed her to Le Dôme in Montparnasse where, on Mondays, artists were again coming to find models. Finding Le Dôme, she remembered what Alice had told her, "Be bold. Go and sit at a table where you see the experienced models." The place was crowded with painters, writers, drinkers, models, streetwalkers. She did not have to make the first move because one of the seasoned models called Kiki saw her and invited her to join her table. When Claude told her the

43

circumstance of her arrival in Paris, Kiki touched her cheek.

"Living in perpetual adoration of Christ is no life. No one should give themselves to God after this war. After the mess God made, He doesn't deserve it. You did the right thing. If I were you, while you still can, find yourself a rich boyfriend who will take you to America. Wait until you have to stand naked for hours in an unheated studio."

Kiki had a husky voice and was known to have no pubic hair. Because she seemed to know everything and everybody, Claude asked, "When did Monsieur Henri Matisse die?"

"He's as alive as you are."

Kiki was not much older than Claude. She looked like a country girl. She kept a string bag stuffed with dresses, brown stockings and scraps of rope. Seeing Claude's threadbare clothes, she gave her a black dress decorated with white dots. Kiki had a boyfriend who played the accordion. An underfed model wearing all black, Bebe Vriesman, got Claude her first paying job modeling for a class of American and Canadian GIs who had stayed on in Paris after war's end. Fuel was still rationed, the studio was icy. The teacher held out a brown bathrobe to her.

"I know it's cold, Mademoiselle. After you've taken off your garments, keep this on until I tell you."

Claude looked for somewhere to go where she could undress and leave her clothes. In the corner of the room was a chair. She turned her back to the class. Modeling for Alice had been easy, but Alice had warned that a day would come when a roomful of art students would be gaping at her exposed body. As she removed her dress, she worried about whether or not the teacher would ask her to open her thighs, and, if he did, whether or not the GIs would look inside. And if they did, would she go to hell?

In winter a "Gooseflesh Bonus" was announced in the newspaper: If goose pimples appeared, the model was entitled to a bonus of 36 francs an hour. Despite the decree, no one paid Claude this bonus. Many whom Alice knew before the war, especially refugees and Jewish artists, had not returned to Paris.

Kiki told Claude to come to her room so that she could give her more hand-me-downs and a taste of absinthe. When she did, Kiki filled two glasses with oily fluid, strained water through a lump of dissolving sugar. The liquid in the glasses turned sapphire-green. The bitter, licorice taste was like nothing Claude had ever tasted. While they drank, Kiki told stories of better days, how an artist painted her with a pineapple rather than a head, how another painted her with a fish instead of a stomach, and still another had a studio that had a terrible odor because he was doing a portrait of lamb chops using real

45

meat. Though the lamb chops had rotted, he had not thrown them away because the painting was not yet finished.

"But that happened before the war. I wonder if he's dead or alive?"

Claude saw a yellow saint's halo above Kiki's head. When Kiki's boyfriend arrived with a jazz musician – Pierre Poppie – they, too, had yellow halos encircling their heads. Everyone's features appeared blurred, murky, as if she was staring at a reflection through a dirty window, like saints on icons in a candle-lit church. A church gave protective comfort, a second skin, but she had never been hugged by such a pleasure as the drink was causing now.

Because there was no more absinthe, bottles of wine were opened and drunk. Before she knew it, Poppie's halo glowed like young Christ newly arisen. Claude's arms and hands shimmered with heavenly colors when she held them out to Poppie, who took her by the arm and led her to Kiki's bed. He laid himself on top of her, pushed up her dress. He lowered his cherry lips onto hers, pushed something hard but slippery inside her and let it stay there until, from nowhere, came an eruption of pleasure so overmastering she wet herself. After repeated eruptions, the pleasure subsided, left burning and stinging. She realized she was no longer a virgin.

No one had taught her how to clean herself afterwards and she was ashamed for Kiki to know how inexperienced she was. She did not ask what she should do, did nothing. A month later she feared that she was pregnant and borrowed money to go to the doctor, who gave her a rabbit test. When she returned for the result, the doctor told her, "The rabbit lived. You're not pregnant."

What she wanted was clothes, as many as she could get. One model she knew at the café gave her a pair of shoes with high heels. Another gave her a stove for cooking, but she was ashamed for her to know that she had never cooked, had not been taught, and, hoping the model did not find out, traded it for stockings. She ate bread, sausage or rabbit prepared at the cafe. Fabric was not easy to come by but when she found some remnants, she sewed a dress, making good use of the skills she had learned in convent.

Paris, 1948

Claude's reputation for holding her solid body in a pose as long as was needed kept her in demand. On Mondays, when artists or their helpers came to Le Dôme to see who was available for work, she was often chosen. In the cafés she heard a tidbit or two about Matisse – that he had remained in Vence after the war, that he had not done a painting in several years, that he would probably never paint one again, that, despite ill health, his lasciviousness was not curtailed because the Russian woman remained. In summer she heard that the heat of Vence had gotten to him and he had come to Paris to settle his family affairs. She would have liked to send him a note, remind him of their encounter, tell him what she was doing, but was afraid that if he remembered her at all, he would disapprove of the choice she had made.

When she had saved enough, Alice helped her find an apartment at 1 rue de Téhéran in the 8th arrondissement. It had an engulfing bed, a chair. She could not adjust to so much solitude, so she left the door to her apartment ajar in order to hear human sounds. When Alice hired her to model, she sorted through the pile of old clothes she kept on the chair and found a white dress that had salmon-gray cabbages on it. Diego Giacometti, a Swiss, hired her. A Pole named Henri Hayden, whose studio had been vandalized during the war, hired her. A Russian, Ossip Zadkine, used her once, never used her again. And more. Within the year she was hired to sit for three different life drawing classes on three different evenings and was able to buy butter for her bread.

STRING OF PEARLS

Paris, 1950

A young model upset Matisse, who had, as usual, come to Paris for the summer. The young model reminded him of his first lover, Camille Jobland. After he paid her for an extra day he let her go. The model promised to find a replacement for him and asked Claude if she would like to replace her. Claude said she would try. The girl wrote down the address – 132, Boulevard du Montparnasse. Claude's teeth had been giving her trouble, four back teeth had been extracted and she had recently moved into a hotel room near Sacré Coeur with an American man named Roy Foot, who mopped up juice with bread when he ate meat.

Roy was 27 years old, was studying art in Paris on the GI Bill. On consecutive Tuesdays she had been the model for his life drawing class. After both classes, the teacher told him he had just done his best drawing. When he learned the names of some of the important artists for whom she had posed, he invited her to his hotel for a drink. He told her that he was destined to become a consequential painter. She didn't contradict, let him seduce her. She was passive but experienced, wanted to please and be molded to his likes and dislikes. After a few weeks he invited her to move in with him.

Once she had pushed the brown and tan suitcase and sack of collectibles under Roy's bed and draped her auburn wool coat with the fur collar across the chair, she made love to him, as he had taught her to. Afternoons, if she was not working, while she waited for him to return from class, she sat by the hotel window that looked out on the garden watching cats prowl. One gray, black and oyster-white tiger cat that looked Egyptian, with front legs that were shorter than its back legs, often sat on its haunches and returned her stare.

Home from class, Roy stretched out on the bed wearing big chestnut-brown shoes and watched her watching the cat. On the day that she was preparing to sit for Henri Matisse, he watched her dress, then undress, then dress once more. That his mistress was about to model for such an important artist, he knew, would give him special status with the other GIs. She finally chose the grape-gray dress and left for the sitting with Matisse. She was fraught, forgot to close the hotel room door. She left a clutter of lipsticks and rouges strewn across the dressing table. The glasses that held the dregs of rum from the night before remained unwashed, hers had a Chinese-red imprint of her lips on it.

She was the first to return to the room that evening. When he arrived, to celebrate, he brought absinthe with him, made her describe every moment of her sitting with Matisse and, while he mixed the sapphire-green liquid into the unwashed glasses, repeat everything he had said to her. Because the bedding was beginning to give off a sour smell, she had crushed sage and rosemary into the sheets.

52

Though it irked him that she was not much on personal hygiene, his desire usually overrode his disgust. Now, because she had modeled for Matisse, he could barely contain himself, wanted her naked so he could gloat over what the great Matisse had seen.

Since arriving in Paris, he had concluded that French women had funny ideas about cleanliness, but that aside, lacked nothing in bed. Weighing the two, hygiene came second. After Babette, he had needed a dose of disinfectant for *papillons d'amour* – crab lice. He enjoyed conventional intercourse but preferred oral love to any other kind. He liked having French be the language used in lovemaking but his French was so-so; if he tried to think in it he came away with a headache. Roy pined for the tropical heat of Florida, where he grew up. Paris was beginning to lose its tang; he was becoming homesick. If it were not that he made his best paintings when Claude posed for him, that he was sharing her with the colossus Matisse, he would have gotten on the next ship and sailed home. In a sublime moment he had asked her to marry him thinking it might be good for his career.

Paris, 1952

She was sitting for Matisse, and no one else. In the morning he could not settle on how he wanted her to pose. He was in pain and exhausted because of insomnia, had changed her pose around again and again. Finally, earlier than usual, he sent her away to have lunch so that he could have his siesta and Lydia could play a few rounds of Patience.

After walking, Claude sat on a bench in the Jardin du Luxembourg until hunger ruined the pleasure and she went looking for ham with bread and strong coffee. The hawthorn trees that were filled with white blooms in springtime were bare. She crossed out of the park, walked through the small streets looking for a café that might not be cold as ice. When the time came, she went back to work.

He cut the session short. After she had changed back into the mushroom-gray dress, she told the painter and Lydia, "I am going to get married."

He said, "Eh bien."

Lydia did not look pleased.

"I thought you planned to return to convent."

"It's not easy for me to decide things since the war. My husband-to-be is American. He wants to take me to America."

The radio was playing. India ink drawings were scattered across various surfaces. Matisse was lining up his pens.

"My son lives in New York. Once I sailed into New York. The gold and black building blocks in the night reflected in the water. A gentleman beside me at the railing said, 'It's a spangled dress,' but to me it wasn't a spangled dress, it was a gold nugget. Will you remain in New York?"

"No."

"If I were younger I would join you and your husband in your travels. It would not hurt you to have an old father to watch over you, make sure you're treated well. But ... I've no time left for the luxury of travel. It would please me if you would think of me as one who, in spirit, accompanies you and bolsters you whether you need bolstering or not."

"It would be a blessing to have your protection. As I have always done, I will keep you in my prayers."

"After New York, what?"

"We will travel on by train for two days and nights to reach his village."

"Where is that?"

"Florida, in the south. It is the tropics in Florida."

"Do you want this?

She hesitated, then flatly replied, "I want a warm life even though my habits are French. I have not given up thoughts of returning to convent."

"Then why marry? If you marry, I doubt your order will take you back. Modern girls don't always marry the men they love."

"I will marry in his Protestant church, so it will not be recognized by the Pope. In God's eyes I still belong to Christ. My man is an artist. He says I am his model, his muse, and, because of me, he does better work. He says that Florida is like Tahiti. He'll paint. We will be like Gauguin in Tahiti. I'm tempted. Also, I have strong feelings for this man."

The word "Tahiti" conjured the blue in Gauguin's *Blue Horse*. Tomorrow, if he were strong enough, he would think about doing something in that particular blue.

"And his feeling for you?"

"He's given me a string of pearls."

Hesitantly she added, "Perhaps you would do him the honor of looking at one or two of his paintings? Give a critique? *Vous voulez bien?*"

"Of course, as a favor to you."

When she was gone Matisse and Lydia examined the day's work. It was scanty indeed because his eyes had burned all day. The cook brought in a plate of skate in black butter. Lydia began to eat but he only picked because he did not like to eat at night.

"Must Claude go so far away? I do not have a good feeling about her going so far away. Renoir once told me, 'On an uninhabited island, no one is going to take up painting.'"

*

When Claude arrived with her American, Matisse was cutting paper with a long scissors, he was wearing an old gray sweater on top of his old

56

blue and white striped pajamas, had bare feet. The shape of a leg in an arabesque emerged from the heavy paper that had been painted jet black. He was in the wheelchair, his lap covered with a wooly throw that was sprinkled with snippets of black paper. Cuts of black painted paper lay scattered on the floor around the chair.

He shook hands and looked closely at Claude's man – Roy Foot. What a strange name, a man named after a body part, a man with full, wine-red lips, lime-green eyes carrying paintings strung together with brown rope. Something about him was like a Great Dane. His hair was chrome-yellow, had been cropped close to a flat skull.

Roy's eyes scanned the walls. Pinned on the one that faced the bed were works in progress. Among them two drawings of his future wife wearing a Russian blouse. In the drawing she was ravishing. Claude looked up at it, too. She had no idea she looked like that. She had never thought of her eyes as distrustful before. Gazing at herself, seeing herself through Roy's eyes, she understood why men wanted to take her to their beds. But did they not see how bad her teeth had become? Roy took in the room, the plants, the knick-knacks. He walked over to the wooden cage belonging to the turtledoves and saw the great drips of yellow-green slime on their wooden perches.

Lydia explained that the household would be leaving Paris shortly to travel south because Matisse must work on designs for the famous chapel that contained St. Veronica's kerchief with Christ's face imprinted on it. Lydia asked Claude, "Would you like a glass of *eau de Vichy*?"

"Yes, thank you."

"And you?"

"Beer, please."

Large incomplete drawings for the chapel were pinned on the opposite wall. Matisse had been able to work life scale because the two rooms in Paris corresponded to the interior size of the chapel in Vence. He commented, "I'm not yet sure of what I will design for the window."

A nurse crossed the room carrying a metallic tray on which various medicines were laid out. Matisse swallowed one after the other. He uttered, "*Merci*, Denise."

He examined each of Roy's paintings. After scrutinizing the final painting, he wheeled his chair over to the table, took pen in hand and scribbled a letter of recommendation on a sheet of off-white paper.

"*Eh bien*."

He folded the letter in thirds, slid it into an envelope. Roy's lime-green eyes leaked glee. Matisse said, "I think you might find it helpful to go to the Louvre and study the Egyptian antiquities."

At that moment, Matisse's face went deathly white. Shutting his eyes, he whispered "I'll be myself in a moment or two."

After a while he opened his eyes.

"I've got much work to do."

Relieved that he had not died during his visit, Roy asked, "How do you make yourself work if you're so ill, Monsieur?

"Nothing interferes with my work. I don't have much time left and there's more to do. I dearly hope your wife will not forget me in her prayers. Perhaps it is she who has been keeping me alive. Do you have another question?"

"How many colors did you use on your pallet when you paint?"

"Never more than 12 but I can't really paint anymore because of my health.

"Do you make much use of black?"

"Yes ... I use it to cool the blue."

*

Roy and Claude stopped at Le Dôme for a drink. The news was that Kiki had died from drugs and liquor. When her decomposing body was discovered, her bed was crawling with vermin. Under the mattress were found 20 paintings and 28 charcoals given to her by the artists for whom she had posed. Walking home after their drink they passed a dark man selling the first oranges that had come from Spain since the war. Roy bought a few.

In their room Roy admitted, "I was surprised by the clutter of junk in his studio ... rolls of cloth, empty jars ..."

She asked him to speak more loudly and he repeated what he had said.

"Before he became an invalid, Monsieur Matisse went to secondhand markets and picked things up that caught his fancy for a few *sous*. Same as me."

She bit into the orange, made a tear, peeled off chunks and curls of pocked orange skin. These she held in the palm of her hand and Roy saw she loved oranges more than she loved him. He opened a penknife and sliced his orange in eighths with a sharp blade, put the slices on the table beside the bed and sat on it.

" ... I was shocked that ash from the stove coated the room. It can't be good for his health."

"No, Roy.

It was not easy to know if Roy was being derisory. His French was clear but the tonality was confusing. Roy patted the lapel of his gray jacket. The letter was in the inside pocket. He removed the jacket and hung it on the back of the chair, pulled off his shoes and stretched out on the squawking bed. He looked greedily at the Catholic woman he had been sharing, and now was stealing, from the great Henri Matisse.

The light was draining away. Claude wiggled the single light bulb that hung from the ceiling. It

60

flickered but would not light. She felt her way to the window, releasing moist orange rinds from her hand as she opened the shutters. The street lamp outside was not yet lit. She felt her way back across the room and knelt beside the bed. She unbuttoned the belt on his trousers and pushed the buttons out of the buttonholes of his fly. He lifted his hips so that she could roll the trousers down to his thighs. She wanted him naked, wanted to examine every hair follicle, every orifice, but the smell from the orange juice on her hands tempted her to eat another orange first, sleep for an hour.

Port of Genoa, 1953

Once the ship left the Port of Genoa, Roy behaved more like a boy and less like a man. Among the other passengers in Cabin Class were Italians, an Australian, a Belgian priest, one French woman with a small violet-faced child who was journeying to America to take her child to a special doctor. Roy had booked an inside room but had wangled it so they were able to visit First Class. As soon as the ship was undulating gently, Claude wanted to sleep for an hour but he convinced her to stroll with him before dinner. They passed the card room, the ballroom, the reading room.

In one foyer was a bronze statue of an admiral in armor and cape, a bronze hand resting on his lizard-green sword. Eight paintings hung on the walls in the art gallery in First Class – scenes of old sailing ships on black roiling seas. When the bell signaling the first seating for dinner tolled, they hurried toward the restaurant but kept ending up at dead ends.

They located the dining room assigned to cabin class; the others at the table had already ordered appetizers. Because their table was full of Americans, Roy spoke English during the meal. No one spoke French except for the banker – Bill Moore – whose teeth were so white Claude could not take her eyes off them. To her left was a single man who smelled like sour red wine, who had been studying in Rome. He was returning to New York because his mother was dying. He directed his conversation to the Americans.

"I will be glad to drink American beer again. It will be a miracle if the doctors can keep my mother alive until I arrive. It's grand to leave the Old World. The war may be long over but European air, European people, are still tainted by its bad odor that will probably never go away."

She understood almost nothing. When she did not reply to a question the banker put to her, he spoke in Italian, then, realizing she spoke only French, turned to speak with the woman on his other side. After Roy announced to the table that he was an artist, there was a discussion about how someone had once painted the portrait of a woman with a pineapple instead of a head.

The sound of the English language was not piercing, was not like some foreign tongues that could be grating. Conversation was a violin bow that was sliding along strings, then back, or one finger on a piano key, one note repeating. She was able to get the gist when Roy told the group that she, his new wife, had modeled for the French painter Henri Matisse. Everyone turned their eyes in her direction, though, from their faces, it was not clear whether or not the name meant anything.

The dining room provided a vast choice of food and drink including daffodil-yellow butter in the shape of seashells. When she ordered two entrées, Roy thought it funny and ordered three. As much as she ate, he could eat more. The first words she learned were words for food, drink – butter, potatoes, beef, sprouts, chocolate, ice cream. After he ordered, "Chocolate ice cream," she would say, "Another portion please."

When she said this, Roy laughed, kissed her in front of everyone. His elation was infectious. After dinner he guided her back to their cabin so she could lie naked for him while he recorded her body. Seeing her like that brought out his talent. After four or five slow sketches he put down the charcoal and let her examine what he had drawn, then waited until she said, "*Très bien*. Very good."

Gleeful, he told her, "Matisse's praise has bolstered me."

"He said he would have enjoyed traveling to New York but that he was too old and sick. He promised that his spirit would hover."

"Good."

"Keep him as your touchstone."

When she reached for the quilted bed cover to cover herself, he put the pad aside.

"Don't!"

He pulled her pliant thighs apart with his hands.

Cimiez, 1935

Bruised because Cubists were shunning him, Matisse nursed his irritability while painting in the studio all morning. He expected to draw in the afternoon. Every time he stopped, he went into the apartment and sat beside his wife to smoke a cigarette or drink a cup of tea with her. No longer laced into a bodice, Amélie rarely got out of bed anymore. Today, because he had no one else, he had sketched his wife's Russian companion cum nurse, Lydia Delectorskaya, whose blond braid intrigued him. When he asked Lydia if she minded, she told him that, in the past, when she was desperate, to earn bits of money, she sat for several artists.

"Frankly, it's detestable work," she told him, and added, "But ... I did not even know you were drawing me, so it wasn't work at all."

A few days later he asked her to sit for him. He made light of the choice of the word "detestable." She did not dare to refuse since he and his wife had been very good to her at a time of neediness – after an older lover, who gambled her savings away, had left her for the roulette table. She was glad to earn a few extra francs as well. When, as he instructed, she undressed and stood before him, she saw the bliss on his face, understood what he meant when he commented that it was his model who penetrated, impregnated him, not the other way around.

Lydia found that being naked for Matisse was not a strain, especially when he saw the color of her skin as lilac. He asked her to sit again. And again, after that. He was taking her away from his wife's bedside so often, his wife hired a new helper. If he kept Lydia sitting for longer than usual, he paid double and told her, "Please have a good steak in the restaurant on the square."

At first his wife did not mind, in fact often was the one who told Matisse to pay her extra. Because Madam Matisse had hired another woman in need of work to care for her needs, she did not miss Lydia. She insisted that Lydia allow them to buy her a new dress. It was the first new piece of clothing Lydia had gotten since her gambler-lover spent all she had on roulette.

65

One bright blue day after Lydia sat for him, because his joints were suffering with neuritis, he asked if she would please scrape strontium yellow and lilac from a painting that did not satisfy him. She did this very well. Another day he asked her to scrape a section of white shaded with cadmium red, then, she watched with curiosity as he replaced the newly scraped area with madder and some white. The cushion shown in the painting was outlined with black. When she watched him repaint the darker part of the cushion Prussian blue, pure, applied with a finger of viridian, she understood what was meant when it was said that he was a "great man."

Cimiez, 1936

After the doctor left, Amélie went back to her embroidery. Had it really been six years since she had taken to her bed? When, still wearing his work smock, her husband took a break from his work to check on her, he was carrying a book. He kissed her with his usual tenderness, sat on the carved straight-backed chair beside her bed. When he asked for the thousandth time if the doctor had come to any conclusions about her condition, she shook her head. Although Gertrude Stein had published *The Autobiography of Alice B. Toklas* in 1933, the bits written about him had just come to his attention. He shook the book in the air, read:

66

Miss Stein called me and said she wanted to have me meet Matisse. She was talking to a medium sized man with a reddish beard and glasses. He had a very alert although slightly heavy presence and Miss Stein and he seemed to be full of hidden meaning.

He looked at his wife who always listened with concentration.

"Heavy presence! I'd say there was an even heavier presence beside me. Wasn't it 1905 ... '08 ... somewhere in there?"

"08."

He read more:

You know how painters are, I wanted to make them happy so I placed each one opposite his own picture, and they were happy so happy that we had to send out twice for more bread, when you know France you will know that that means that they were happy, because they cannot eat or drink without bread and we had to send out twice for bread so they were happy. Nobody noticed my little arrangement except Matisse and he did not until just as he left, and now he says it is a proof that I am very wicked, Matisse laughed and said, yes I know Mademoiselle Gertrude, the world is a theater for you, but there are theaters and theaters, and when you listen so carefully to me and so attentively and do not hear a word I say then I do say that you are very wicked.

He gazed at his wife for her response. The chrome yellow that coated her face had cracked because she was smiling. Under it was the pale peach and primrose orange of Collioure days when it was she, not Lydia, who undressed for him, took notes on the work in progress. For Amélie, note-taking had come naturally; Lydia was making do, learning from scratch. It was just like Amélie to pass Lydia along, to make sure he had the help he needed with his work since she no longer helped him. He kissed her again.

Back in the studio, Lydia kept looking up at *La Blouse Bleue* with fascination. When he dictated, she wrote:

Background: Ultramarine Blue and white. Foliage: Strontium Lemon Yellow and Viridian. Back of armchair: Ivory Black.   Collar, which was, if you remember, gray before, has been redone with Ivory Black and some white. You see it's become rose pink because the shadowing is done with Viridian and white. Understand?

"I'm beginning to understand."

"The corsage is painted somewhat more opaque: ultramarine with a dash of black, white and occasionally cobalt blue. Skirt: Venetian red. Arm of the chair ... with Venetian red. Hands: white, shaded with cadmium red light."

"Do you mean the bit of background between the arm of the chair, my ... the model's ... arm and the blouse?"

"Yes. Viridian, black and white. Near the head. As you can easily see, I've applied a layer of white, a layer of viridian. As you can also see," said with humor, "the head, neck and hair are not yet done."

His eyes burned. He removed his glasses and began cleaning them with his handkerchief.

"After my nap ... we'll continue."

Florida Everglades, 1954

Roy and Claude lived on a small floating houseboat in a mangrove swamp anchored near Ponce de Leon Bay. All day Roy wore a khaki hat that had a peaked brim. When he painted, he wore white overalls splashed with drips of color. In Paris he had painted in what he called a semi-abstract style. He continued this style in Florida but it was becoming more abstract with the passing of time. His dominant colors were Mars green, cobalt blue and umber. He rarely used the color red or any variety of red. Sitting for Roy was not what it had been with Matisse and with Alice. It was something else, a wifely chore. What he painted did not always flatter her. Sometimes what he painted wasn't even recognizable as human. After what had, for him,

69

been a particularly fruitful sitting, he told her, "I've never enjoyed you more. For once, I got under your sour nature."

As he wished, she made oral love to him after the sitting. He did not always return the favor because the so-so sanitation that went with Parisians' life did not go well with American life. He could not fathom why it had not bothered him before. He bought her a packet of douche powder. He also brought home a large bottle of ammonia, a bucket, a mop, and gave her a lesson in adding ammonia to hot water in order to sanitize their living quarters.

That he thought she did not know how to use ammonia was an offence to her. She said, "If you only knew how many hours I spent on all fours scrubbing floors in convent years with lye and brown soap even stronger than your American ammonia. Why do you harp on whether or not the dishes are washed, or whether or not stains remain on the toilet bowl? You should be painting and thinking about art, not armpits. Aren't you destined for greatness?"

*

Their bay was usually calm and green, rich with clusters of mangrove thickets. Because Matisse loved birds, Roy became curious about birds, learned to identify storks that flew in flocks – a lonely cormorant, wading birds, turkey vultures. Everything was in miniature on the houseboat –

70

small bed, minute sink, minute cooker in which Roy cooked stews and soups while she cleaned as best she could with a sponge dipped in hot water into which a drop, just a drop, of ammonia had been dropped. She did not complain that he rarely made love to her because, having discovered that if she rubbed her groin against the chair or bed leg as she mouthed him, she felt pleasure, too.   Around the room Roy had speared pithy quotations by admired artists with pushpins. Pinned on the bathroom door:

When he took his exercise by walking the gritty streets of Paris he was often alone but sometimes accompanied by a lady friend. He described an experience he had had to one of his female companions: "I entered my studio and was struck by an indescribably beautiful painting, all irradiated by an interior light. I could only distinguish ... forms and color and meaning. Suddenly I realized that it was one of my own paintings turned on its side. The next day in daylight I tried to recapture my previous impression ... with the painting on its side but I could always find the object, the blue light of dusk was missing. I felt a terrifying abyss opening under my feet." In 1910 Wasilly Kandinsky was 44.

Pinned beside his shaving mirror:

I remember a man standing on Broadway. The lights kept changing and he seemed lit up, as if abstracted by the reflection of the neon lights. It would suddenly turn from red to green. Then the idea of color outside of the drawn image came to me. And the idea of bodies hurling through space came to me on a crowded American beach when I saw 60 or 80 people simultaneously diving and jumping. During his exile in New York, Fernand Léger said.

In the water surrounding the houseboat, ginger shard-like shapes glinted. For seven months the temperature was oven-hot. Because of the humidity, insects, spiders, lizards inhabited the houseboat. At night mosquitoes whined in her good ear. Because she was deprived of the color red, her great joy became the tropical sunset that turned the entire world a mix of claret and crimson.

Fernandia, Florida, 1955

Their dog, part Alsatian, part Belgian water dog, licked its underside while Claude folded her clothes by color. The dog had appeared in their humidity-soaked yard shortly after they moved inland so Roy could be closer to his mother. One day the dog came over and smelled her bare feet. Roy named him Toby, a strange name. Because Claude had never lived with closets, she used wooden shelves held up by brass brackets for the small mountain of clothes – mostly secondhand – she had gathered, alternating dark fabric with light.

Everything that was red or shades of red – papaya, brick, cherry, clay, poppy – went into one pile. On one wall of their bedroom was a picture window. When she begged Roy for drapes to darken the room while they slept, he laughed at her, said, "This is America, my dear. Europeans pull drapes when they sleep. Americans like moonlight. We're extraverted, not closed and sealed up. I've come around to favoring American artists, too. I'm no longer interested in the old, tired European art standards."

At certain times of day the trees and Spanish moss were reflected in the glass. Twice a low-flying bird crashed into it. In low spirits, she resisted the urge to lie down, went into the kitchen. Toby trailed behind. Perhaps this would be the day that Roy would return from Birmingham? She ate a biscuit from the tin of arrowroot biscuits Roy's mother baked that smelled like wood and tasted like sawdust. Because of his mother, her English was improving. When Claude had refused to go to the Baptist church where Roy, his mother, father and other family members went, his mother understood, told Roy not to push her; he must remember that she would always be too foreign for them to understand.

Roy had loaded up the larder before he went away but she had, by now, eaten almost everything. She prayed to the Virgin Mary. She could live with hunger but fear was fatal. She walked into Roy's studio in which she had made a ring of loose bricks around the area where they planned to build the fireplace. In preparation, dusty pomegranate-colored bricks were piled floor to ceiling along the chestnut-brown wall. It was up to her to design the hearth and she had cut three designs out of cardboard with her scissors. She put on a blue smock and decided to organize the shelf full of jars of color, lining them up – light to dark – removing the jar of yellow.

She sat on the floor. She dipped a brush with a long handle into the bright yellow poster paint and decorated a sheet of paper with drawings of coconut palm trees. From the vantage of the floor she could see that a spider had fastened magenta threads on the underside of Roy's worktable and was weaving its web. She practiced her English, "Yellow spider." And ran the wet paintbrush across the spider before setting it in a glass of water. She went into the bathroom to wipe the mirror with ammonia. The smell of ammonia, reminiscent of caustic lye, brought her back to the long hallway that led to the sacristy at convent in Cimiez.

Because Roy had removed the clippings that quoted European artists and replaced them with quotes by Americans, she feared that he was away looking for a Jackson-Pollock-type of American woman to replace her. After cleaning the bathroom mirror, her eyes burned. The ammonia must have also affected Toby who lay shivering on the white tiles. Panicked, she splashed her eyes with water. Toby's water bowl smelled strongly of ammonia. She dipped her finger in and put the tip between her lips, burning them, brought the bowl up to her nose, burned her nostrils. Somehow it had gotten filled with ammonia. Being this anxious about Roy was making her stupid. The back of the bottle instructed:

Give water or milk immediately. Do not induce vomiting.

She picked Toby up, carried him inside, laid him on the bed. There was no milk, had not been in a week, so she filled a glass with water, got a soup spoon and tried to get Toby to open his mouth and take the spoon – but his teeth would not part. She got on her knees, closed her eyes, bent forward and kissed the floor. She said *Gloria* then recited *De profundis*. His breathing stopped. She contemplated drinking what remained in the bowl.

It was a long walk to Lady of Angel's church. As usual, there was no wind. She had disregarded Mother Superior's dictum that she was meant to take nothing and give everything. How stupid to listen to Alice's daughter. Why had she not listened to Matisse and stayed in France? He was the only person beside her mother who saw what was worthwhile about her. Was this what life had been for Matisse's wife? She saw a red car coming down the road toward her and moved to the side of the road, into the soggy swamp holly. Quickly mosquitoes were biting, and she let them. The local green and white taxi was coming up the road behind the red car. When it got close, she saw that Roy was in the front seat with the driver. She thanked the Virgin Mary.

Gainesville, Florida, 1956

It was old Mr. Foot who found her doubled over, foaming at the mouth, and drove her in his station wagon, in agony, to the nearest hospital 68 miles away. She was made to drink salt water until she vomited up the caustic cleaning fluid as well as the entire bag of jellybeans she had eaten. They found Roy in Atlanta preparing for a show of 14 paintings. He refused to return until he had attended the opening, had the promised interview with the local paper. The hospital – unwilling to accept the liability in case she tried it again – medicated her heavily and transferred her to the state hospital in Gainesville. When Roy arrived, they had already begun a series of 17 shock treatments. She gazed at him through soupy eyes, was wearing a hospital robe that showed food droppings along its neckline. He took her home.

The next time he left, she drank from a bottle of Mr. Clean. This time her stomach was pumped. More shock treatments along with thorozine treatment followed. Two more teeth were extracted. After six months, her doctor suggested she go home with Roy for a week's trial.

"Our dog is dead," she told the doctor, "I'm not needed there. I'm needed here to help with laundry and feeding catatonics and halfwits. Why go back? He no longer wants me there."

New York, 1957

The porter watched the bewildered woman with painted pink nails whose red-brown-green hair was falling away from its pins. She was the last person to get off the overnight train that arrived on Track Six. She wore a cornflower-blue stretch halter top over peach-colored pedal pushers, stood beside a brown and tan suitcase. A porter noticed her and took hold of her luggage. He climbed the steps and she followed him into the big waiting room of Pennsylvania Station where he put the suitcase on the floor, looked her up and down. She held up the backside of a letter on which was an address, and he pointed to a stairway. The steps reached a door that opened onto a street filled with lively, hurrying people, automobiles, activity. At the curb waited a line of yellow and black taxis. She noticed a gentleman walking a dog very much like Toby. Perhaps New York was not as heartless as Roy's mother had told her it would be.

A taxi driver saw her, got out and loaded her suitcase into the trunk of his cab while she got in. This taxi had red checks painted along its side. She handed the cabbie the envelope and he pulled down a black flag, put foot to gas, veered around a green bus. On 22nd Street was a row of brick brownstone houses. He stopped the cab. Claude counted money from a coral cloth change purse that clipped shut, and got out. The driver put the suitcase on the sidewalk and she handed him the fare. His eyes were glued to her breasts until she turned away, then he got back into the driver's seat, drove away. When the cab turned the corner, the back door on the passenger's side flew open because she had not shut it properly.

The number on the building matched the number on the envelope. Bringing the suitcase into the foyer, she scrutinized the row of metal mailboxes. When she found what she was looking for – R. FOOT – she left the suitcase standing against the wall, beside two black bicycles. She climbed to the second floor and knocked on door 2B. Her back was soaked with sweat. A small, dark American woman came to the door. There were moist cherry pits in the palm of her hand. When Claude showed her the back of the letter, the woman called out, "Roy!"

"Yes, Rosemarie?"

Claude looked into the room. Its walls were covered with messy purple and pink portraits of this woman. Roy was throwing a dart into a board; there were two cages filled with green parakeets. Wearing blue and white pajamas, scratching at his scraggly chrome-yellow beard and moustache, Roy came to the door. He slapped her hard after she had spat in his face.

*

It was a studio apartment. On the small coffee table was the lease Claude had signed with a Paper Mate pen. Beside the table were two brown Klein's shopping bags. Inside, fluffy white terrycloth towels and washcloths and sheets. She sat on the convertible sofa cutting out advertisements from magazines with pinking shears, refusing to reply when Roy spoke to her. Over a burnt-orange stretch halter, she wore a too-large man's jacket that was midnight blue and had chalk stripes, found in a thrift shop bin selling for 20 cents. She was waiting for him to leave so she could close her eyes and sleep. She was dead tired, her lips were chapped.

He reached into the bag and took out a set of sheets that were striped white and hunter green. He tore off the cellophane wrapping, removed cardboard, pins, tags, and spitefully made up the bed. From the other brown bag he removed several white towels and piled them neatly on the shelf in the closet. He dropped onto the coffee table a roll of five-dollar bills that were held together with a thick pink rubber band. Claude hissed, "You can look at a Rosemarie for 500 years and you'll never see what Matisse saw in me in an instant. Go home and paint plain vanilla Rosemarie. *Au revoir*."

He put on his champagne-white raincoat.

"Roy?"

"Yes."

"*S'il te plaît, mon chéri* ... why did you leave Florida?"

"I tried to bring you home from the hospital. It was you who didn't want to leave. I waited for you as long as I could. It was *you* who left *me*. I'm meant for success and New York is where it matters. I couldn't waste my talents caring for an unstable woman. If you're well enough to travel to New York, no doubt you can make a new life. I've paid your rent for three months. I'll give you more money when I can. Are you taking your medication?"

"I threw the pills away. They made hair grow on my face. What I want is a ticket to France."

"I'll need time to save for that."

"Rosemarie can get a job. Seeing the paintings you're doing, you don't need a model at all. You behaved like Joseph in Egypt."

He was going to take her by the shoulders and shake her. Instead, he buttoned the raincoat, took a pair of sunglasses from the pocket, covered his scornful lime-green eyes, walked out the door. As soon as the door closed, Claude picked up the cellophane from the floor, folded it and laid it beside her; she put down the shears, curled up. Still wearing chalk-white pumps, she slept.

New York, 1958

She went to six o'clock Mass at the Church of the Sacred Heart near Chinatown and sat at the back, listened to the priest whose eyebrow hair was as red as the harvest moon. His sermons were about the recognition of sin one day, about souls on fire the next Sunday, about the wonders of God the Sunday after that. She often watched the back of a diminutive, black-clad nun who sat close to the altar, building up courage to approach her as a sister, to ask for sanctuary. She examined the people who came to six o'clock Mass – old and young Puerto Rican ladies and men, old Irish and Italian ladies, some with the moth-eaten faces of martyrs. She prayed that God would send someone to take charge of her; she prayed that Matisse would not forget her, would send her a sign about how to come home.

It was the nun who approached her, took her aside and told her that the priest was aware that she was taking from the collection plate rather than giving. The message from the priest was to either come to confession or find herself a different church. The nun explained this with a gentle rather than scolding voice, clicking the black beads on the necklace from which a metal cross hung.

Roy regularly put money in an envelope and pushed it under her door. It was never enough for all the secondhand clothes – in thrift shops, on pushcarts on Orchard Street – she craved. Soft fruit and vegetables that were put out at night behind the A & P made for filling meals. She was good at finding half sandwiches, bits of donuts and buttered rolls left in crumpled paper bags tossed into wicker garbage cans. She was doing her best but she was going nowhere. She needed to sleep, needed to think straight, needed a plan.

She walked the neighborhoods until she found another church in another parish, St. Ann's, that had a massive Parochial School attached, a more robust congregation. It was in Little Italy. Large silver collection plates that held generous numbers of coins and bills were passed down one pew and up the next. When she was able to palm enough she could walk home past the meatpacking neighborhood to a Cuban sandwich shop on 14th Street. If she did not have enough to buy a sandwich, she would admire the dripping carcasses.

New York, 1959

Every sunny day after Mass, wearing her old coat whether the temperature was warm or not, Claude sat on the bench in the tiny park around the corner from where she lived. Instead of a pocketbook she carried a paper grocery bag with her. In the park was a leafy maple tree, a ring of gray cobblestones went around it. The bench was painted with high gloss tomato-red paint. There was a water fountain on top of a stone pillar at which wild birds drank. A Belgian newsagent on University Place, near N.Y.U., saved a day-old French newspaper for her that she would read while sitting in the park. There was a church a few feet away. It was not a Catholic church, but an Eastern Orthodox church.

One morning an old woman wearing glasses and a floral headscarf from which stiff platinum hair stuck out, labored down the street toward the church in black shoes. She was carrying a shopping bag from the A & P. It looked like the woman had just arrived from Eastern Europe. She was waving a copy of *Life Magazine*, shouting, "Look!" wiggling the magazine in Claude's face. It was open at an article written about a fashion illustrator and it included drawings. Claude read the article as well as she could and looked carefully at the illustrations.

"You like?"

"Why ask me?'

"You like the pictures?"

"I know nothing about shoes for rich people."

"I taught him. It's my son. He draw good, yes?"

She brightened

"If your son needs a model, think of me. I've modeled for important artists."

"Important artists? You think he good at drawing?"

From the brown bag the woman removed a package wrapped in butcher paper and twine. She tore off the wrapping, shook out a thick cotton shawl decorated with red and green patterns and waved it in front of Claude's face.

"Take."

Claude was more interested in the brown wrapping paper than the shawl, reached out and took hold of the paper. The woman understood.

"Take. Take. Good again."

Claude folded the paper into eighths and pushed it into her bag. The twine slipped to the ground. Claude eyed it. The woman bent down and picked it up.

"Missus. Good string."

She wound the twine around two very white fingers into a little ball.

"Take."

Claude pulled a magenta-blue bottle she had gotten from the FOR FREE table at the thrift shop out of her bag. It resembled a Milk of Magnesia bottle. She held it up to catch the sunlight.

"Like a diamond ... look. Here, take it, *chérie*."

The woman liked it, laid the shawl on Claude's lap.

"Missus, you want sandwich? You like bologna? I bring ... tomorrow ... before Mass? You come to Mass with me?"

"I'm a Catholic. I go to Mass at St. Ann's Catholic Church."

"Missus, want a cat? I bring you a cat for company. Cats good company. You want? Just tell and I bring. Just say yes."

A half smile meant to hide her missing back teeth twisted Claude's painted lips.

"Let me think about it, *chérie*."

IT IS POSSIBLE TO LEAD A COW UPSTAIRS, BUT
NOT DOWN

Pittsburgh, 1953

Julia Warhola held the brown glazed cookie jar in her lap. In it, bank book, last supper commemorative card, dog-eared Slavonic prayer book, packet of letters from Mikova tied with red and green Christmas ribbon, crumbling ebony peanut butter cookies. Shopping bags were squeezed together onto the floor of the front seat at her feet, also a sloshing pot of kapushta. Her son John was driving. Faster cars sped past John's white Good Humor truck since it could not go faster than 35 miles an hour. She had been prattling non-stop from the moment they left Pittsburgh. At home she usually spoke in Ponasemu, the language of Mikova (once part of the Austrian–Hungarian Empire) from where she had immigrated to America after the First World War. Of course John understood Ponasemu.

" ... In Mikova we make a costume out of rags that looks like a wolf, and my brother Yurko dress me. I scare the little children. They think I a real wolf. Ha. Your sister Justina die. My Matsuka die. The priest die. The cottage burns."

Tears rolled down Julia's cheeks. They passed: Latrobe. Altoona. Tyrone. Harrisburg. Rolling farmland. Middletown. Elizabethtown. Mount Joy. Lancaster. John kept to the right lane on the turnpike.

" ... I carry bags filled with potatoes on my back. I tie the legs of goats together and carry over

89

my shoulder. Ah. Smell. Can you smell, John? Manure. Like Mikova."

Coatesville. Paolli. Trenton, New Jersey.

" ... They tell us that my best brother Yurko died. Everyone cry. But Yurko come back from the dead. Resurrected like Christ our Lord. Someday you meet your Uncle Yurko."

When the truck entered the Holland tunnel she clutched at her son's shoulder.

"How come the big river no burst through the tunnel? A big river is heavy."

It was almost evening when they emerged from the tunnel; the sky had turned shades of raspberry and violet. John drove up and down. He was looking for Third Avenue. He turned onto a wide street that had an elevated subway train above it. The blue street sign told him he was in luck – Third Avenue. When he found the number there were no parking places near it, so he rolled up at a fire hydrant at 75th Street. Immediately children sprang from nowhere, nickels and dimes gripped in their fists. Seeing the children, Julia urged, "Go sell. Go."

She adjusted the black nylon scarf on her head and gathered her things while John sold toasted almond bars and vanilla pops. She lined up the bags and pots on the sidewalk as a subway train clamored on the track overhead. She patiently held the cookie jar against the cotton housedress that was dappled with pale blue and oyster-gray flowers and was stuck

90

to her body from perspiration. John hollered, "Go ma, I'll bring your stuff in."

Her priest in Mikova once told everyone in church that it was possible to lead a cow upstairs but not downstairs. In Mikova she doubted that she would ever have to put this piece of information to use, but when she climbed down the flight of steps to the basement apartment, she spoke in a loud voice: "Now I'm a cow that does the impossible."

Her voice pierced the dirty, paisley-papered walls. Her youngest son heard it, opened his door, glad she had come. He was thin and his face was broken out. His colorless hair had thinned. She was relieved to see that the cross she and his father had given him when he had his first communion still hung around his neck. Before she could embrace him, a Siamese cat stepped up and smelled her feet. She shoved it with the side of her shoe and walked inside the apartment, put the cookie jar on the narrow kitchen counter, bent and picked up a red and white striped boat-neck shirt crumpled on the kitchen chair, smelled it, made a show of holding her nose.

Her shoes stuck to the greenish-yellow linoleum floor. The garbage can cover did not fit and deposit bottles were lined up on the floor against the wall. John set the heavy pot on the stove and lit the gas with his metal Zippo. Julia told her youngest son, "You need looking after. First we eat."

New York, 1959

Julia wore her coat during Mass. The heavy brown pocketbook hung on the crook of her arm. After Mass she put a dime into the slot at the top of the money box, pulled a long match from the holder along with a handful of slim, handmade candles. She found a space among the many dripping orange beeswax tapers topped with dancing flames, placed hers into the sand and struck the match, whispering, "Andrej, I old. I'm glad you no see me this way."

She lit a second candle for her dead daughter, Justina, another for Matsuka, one for Nonya, one each for her many dead brothers and sisters. Of the 15 her mother had borne only six lived. She crossed herself after saying each name. When she was ready to go, she took the handbag off her arm and held it in her fist in case anyone tried to grab it. The priest, Father Kusakova at St. Mary's Church of the Byzantine Rite on 15th and Second Avenue, knew her. She never missed 10:30 Mass. He was aware that she lit many candles but only made one donation. Inside the dimly lit church were icons and candles and incense, like in every church she had known. Outside, it was not at all like the church in Pittsburgh or in Mikova because the architecture was white cement, unadorned, modern, like an office or a bank.

On the 15th Street side was a small fenced park. Sitting on a lone forest-green wooden bench, with wild green and brown hair pinned to the top of her head, was the same woman she had seen on many sunny days who usually was thumbing through a newspaper or applying nail polish to her nails. The woman had painted black cat eyes, wore harem pants in a bright coral crocodile pattern, a polka-dotted blouse, a sweater over the blouse and Chinese slippers. From the deteriorating condition and odor of her clothes it was obvious to anyone who came close that they had not been cleaned in a long time. At the woman's feet were two heavy brown paper shopping bags brimming with things. Today she said something to Julia when she came down the steps past the park. Julia did not understand, because of the woman's accent. Hoping if she shouted, she would be understood, Julia shouted, "Say again."

The woman pointed to her ear, made a gesture that said, 'I can not hear you.' She got up, came out of the park, disturbing the migrant bird that was beating its wings in the puddle of water at the bottom of the stone fountain. She handed Julia a key ring with a plastic goat dangling from its chain, said, "Maybe your son need a model? My husband moved away to Maine and doesn't send much money to me anymore. You told me your son does drawings for magazines…"

"Maybe," Julia replied, "we see."

*

Julia and her son had recently moved from their basement apartment to a fourth-floor walk-up above a bar on Lexington Avenue. Though the living area was larger, the bedroom was again small, with just enough room for two mattresses on the floor, hers under the window, his against the wall. The kitchen-living room had a big table for work and eating with four straight-backed chairs piled with papers, bills, mail, Czech newspapers, drawing supplies, an envelope that held cancelled stamps from Mikova, another with American stamps. The chairs were so full, there was nowhere to sit. This wasn't a problem, since things could easily be taken from one chair and loaded onto another.

Her son was a commercial artist. When he worked, she worked with him. Underfoot were kittens who did not always make it to the litter box. A bucket filled with a mix of water and bleach and a mop stood ever-ready against the wall. She was sitting with her son at the table, helping him do his work, finishing drawings, coloring and signing his name. She stood up, lifted the lid on the big pot, let a cloud of steam escape.

"Don't cook, Ma, I'll take you out."

"Plenty kapushta, fat, meaty short ribs, sweet cabbage."

"I'm sick of it, Ma. I want to go out."

He wanted to go to the Bellmore Cafeteria. She preferred to eat at home but, if he insisted, she liked the counter at Woolworth's. Because it was hot, he wore nothing but white under-shorts that had red pinstripes, also a dingy white T-shirt. As usual in summer, she was wearing the shabby purple print housedress with short sleeves. He finished the drawing he was working on and she finished the one she was coloring. The drawings were cartoonish renderings of women's high heels for I. Miller. For several years now he had been drawing shoes. The pay had become substantial. She looked at him with tears in her eyes, said, "I happy. This most happy time of my life."

The shoes he drew made her laugh.

"You draw good, I taught you good. But who walk in those shoes? Those shoes make feet crippled for life. No feet so narrow."

He said nothing, got up from the chair, stood behind her and examined the sketch she had colored.

"I draw better than you, Andek. Only thing you draw better is men's erections. I don't want to know who modeled for you. If I see these drawings I turn face down."

"Oh, Ma."

"Why you no paint ladies like real artists do? There's a lady at church who was model for big artists."

"Like who?"

"The biggest ... a name like a mattress ... a famous one. I no remember who else. Her name is Claws, like a bad cat use to scratch. She needs a job. Her mind is away."

"Bring her to lunch. If her feet are okay, I'll use her."

She poked him, "When you last take bath? Look. A ring of dirt around your neck. Your fingernails black, too. You think the lady like a smelly boy?"

"Leave me alone or I'll send you back to Pittsburgh."

She picked out a blue and a dark green pencil from the box of Venus Pencils and began filling in the drawing he had just completed with color, then signed his name at the bottom with another pencil, this one cinnamon-red. A shopping list was pinned onto her apron with a safety pin. On the list: Pickles. Band-Aids for corns. Straight pins. Coffee cake.

Cimiez, 1940

He knew perfectly well that a glass of water with a flower was different from a glass of water with a lemon. He knew what made color scream. He knew and had always known that a drawing should have the decisiveness of a good slap, but the letter he received in the morning mail from his wife of 41 years was another kind of slap and made him grind his teeth:

... I am leaving for the reason you know of. I, too, hope that we shall find the calm that we need and that you will be able to pursue your work in peace and quiet.

Her insolent tone had exacerbated the indigestion, curdling the contents of his stomach. Of course it was generally believed that he had been unfaithful to her with Lydia. The accusation made him, a lapsed Catholic, a mostly imperturbable man, ashamed. But, as a not-very-well man of 70, it was a source of pride that there was still grist about his carnal life being chewed on. The matter of fidelity bothered him less than the matter of ... of what? The division of property? The effect on his daily structure? The effect on their children? The letting out of air from some kind of sealed chamber?

Overall, it was the stiffness in his neck and the tireless, pincer's grip of indigestion that he minded the most. The intrusion of physical matters on his work was the only thing, at this point in his life, that might break him. There was, of course, the disturbing matter of the call-up for soldiers to put on metal helmets, bring oiled blankets with fresh underclothes and socks to mobilize at rail stations. Because he was a man with sons of conscription age, the call-up was menacing. But if he could do his work, he could endure anything.

His cane had a gold pommel. His trousers were flannel. There were four of the five allowable cigars in the pocket of his tweed jacket. He passed

Bermond Park, passed the Russian Cathedral with its five golden domes that evoked Lydia. A seller was hawking peanuts. Nothing relieved the knots, the churning, the putrid reflux. He no longer cantered vigorously on his horse and had, for many, many years, stopped the invigorating afternoon visits to brothels. He was on his way to a gallery that was exhibiting his paintings. Afterwards, he planned to return home to review the day's work.

An orange cat was eating a fish head as he approached the gallery. Not being the only bearded man of a certain age wearing spectacles in Nice, he hoped he could remain unrecognized. Inside the gallery, he skirted a group of convent girls wearing matching blue jumpers and thick barley-brown wool sweaters. The girls were standing in an orderly double line viewing his work. A nun in black habit with pleated cornette encircling her face and coif headpiece, stood at the rear of the line. He overheard a girlish voice: *"Hideaux! Hideaux!"* The words splashed icily against his ears.

A girl at the back of the line spoke boldly, "Are you the painter Henri Matisse?"

He took a cigar from his pocket.

"No."

He left the gallery, had to shake out the handkerchief kept in the lapel pocket and take hold of his nostrils and tilt his head because a nosebleed was beginning. The softness of the air, the clearness, cleanness of the blue sky was why he had been coming south for almost 40 years. When it seemed as if the impending nosebleed had been stanched, he examined the splash of red on the cloth, then refolded it, pushed it back into the pocket as the lines of schoolgirls marched onto the sidewalk. They stopped while the nun counted heads. With the discretion that had given him the reputation as a polite but basically cold man, he drew the nun aside, said, "Sister, I am indeed the painter Henri Matisse but I should never have dared admit it to children who judged my painting so severely. Forgive me my fib."

He walked in the direction of the tram that would take him uphill to Cimiez, glad for the cane. He lit the cigar. Cook had promised a hot onion tart. The tram laboriously passed lemon groves, fig trees, climbed the hill above Nice, unpleasantly grinding gears.

*

Although he had given in, sent Lydia to live elsewhere, Amélie had given him an ultimatum to get rid of her entirely. Even though she had once been as fond of Lydia as he had, Amélie had done an about-face. For reasons he could not fathom, she did not even want Lydia to arrive in the morning as his studio assistant. When, for the good of his work, their work, he ignored the ultimatum, his wife left.

What more could he have done? He wrote to their son:

> *Your mother knows that without Madam Lydia here I would never have painted the Rockefeller over-mantel. I need her to set up the studio, to keep it clean, and to be ready with the colors that I require, hour by hour. I count on you to back me up in that, and I only hope that your mother will be conciliatory.*

Knowing his son's understanding of art, he added:

> *... given the poetical nature of my work, Lydia is essential to me.*

And, knowing his son's squeamishness, he also wrote –

> *My doctors are very much disturbed at the state of cerebral tension that I had got into. They told me that I might have had a stroke.*

For 41 years work had come first with Amélie. It was unforgivable that she had put ... put what? – female vanity? ... jealousy? ... tyrannical control? ... her own nervous system? – ahead of his work. That he no longer sat across from his wife in comforting silence at meals was sad. That his wife wished him calm in such a cold tone was having the opposite effect. Affixed to the wall of the Régina was a poster – *Appel Immédiat.* Approaching his apartment door, he could hear the caw of his birds. Once inside, he took off his pistachio-colored twill jacket, went from plant to plant, pushing an index finger into the paprika-red earth. Flagging, he stretched out on the bed. So many things in the rooms evoked Amélie and their long life together. He picked up pen and paper and began writing to his son Pierre:

Plan for Marguerite to make an inventory and work out the division of things. Every painting and drawing will be entered in ...

but stopped and dropped it into a trash bin. He decided to inventory his birds – the cardinals, the nightingales, his favorites, the white pigeons and doves that flew freely through the apartment so that daily life was punctuated by streaks of color passing through various kinds of light, by the shushing sound of wings against air, by occasional splats of unwelcome green slime landing where it did not belong. The white of the white birds was various – powdery, icy, feathery, snowy, blinding, wedding-white. He lost count, called, "Lydia!"

Large windows looked over the rooftops of Nice as far as the Bay of Angels. He had first come to the Mediterranean in 1898, in the month of February. He and Amélie were on their honeymoon. Now he sent her 7,000 francs a month. Since 1898 he had never once tired of drinking in this landscape of Le Midi from one vantage or other. The transaction had been completed the previous week and, late in the afternoon, the buyer of 30 of his birds arrived with empty cages, departed with full cages. The birds could be heard shrieking long after the door shut behind them. It was chilly and smoke was rising among the groves below. He said to Lydia when she joined him, "If I were religious I would beg God for an extension of my life. I need time. I need years. My work is not finished."

He walked onto the balcony and looked down at the eucalyptus tree below that stood among various plants – queen palms, shrubs, plantings – on the grounds of the convent in which he had so often strolled, on less chilly days, among silent nuns dressed in black. He spent the morning painting oysters, then he and Lydia lunched. After lunch he took a nap. When he woke, he paced up and down the vast glass-enclosed hallways for 40 minutes. His goal was to walk 3,300 meters. Instead of counting steps, he ticked off various colors as he walked: rose pink, ultramarine, black, ivory black, viridian, cadmium yellow, cobalt blue, yellow ochre, pure black, gray ...

Through the afternoon he again painted oysters, then returned to the hallways to walk some more. He ticked off: cadmium red, cobalt violet, ultramarine, silver, white, black. Up and back, up and back.   Two thousand   meters completed, he joined Lydia for tea among his many plants.   As he sipped, his eyes wandered up the wall toward works he owned and loved by Cézanne and Courbet.   He could no longer imagine his life without Lydia.   She poured more tea into the half-empty cup.

*

They   wandered   through   a   mildewy secondhand shop.   Nothing much caught his eye.   He spied a puppet made in New Guinea carved out of hardwood; yellow and white feathers were attached to its wooden head the size of a grown child.   Its legs and arms were fastened to the body with coarse rope, had been painted bright shades of blue, yellow, black, red, green. The proprietor wrung his dry hands.   Of course he knew who the buyer was, had heard about the woman with him, the Russian mistress who had caused the breakup of his marriage.   Getting a close look at her, he saw she was blond with the face of a Renaissance Madonna, not pretty in any appealing way.   It was only as the shop door closed behind the painter and his émigré mistress, that the proprietor realized the puppet must be worth more than he had charged.   He regretted that awe had made him stupid.

The puppet was folded over Matisse's arm. He and Lydia walked to the movie theater that was showing Jean Renoir's *The Rules of the Game*.   Lydia's light eyes were hooded with anxiety. Because she had experienced starvation in her youth in Siberia, she was braced for, and predicted, the worst if Poland split open like an eggshell. Not a fatalist, he held out – not hope, but a belief that it was possible for something ecstatic to override her worst fears.

Paris, 1940

When the dreaded war was declared, he traveled with Lydia to Paris. In spite of the panic of war, he tried to see to his work, keep to his usual schedule, but he was unable to paint. While Lydia laid out the Patience cards again and again, he drew repetitively. Sheets of drawing paper piled up. Most of the sheets contained variations on the same subject, the magnolia that was in the painting *Still Life with a Magnolia*. Every night he and Lydia sat in darkened movie houses that were full of Parisians who were hiding in the dark for the same reason. Since coming to Paris, they had seen every movie in town. He had once been strong and healthy, was a long-distance walker, a horseman, a vigorous rower. He did not understand why his strength, like cream that should rise to the top of fresh milk, was not seeing him though to the end.

He regretted that, indispensable or not, he would have to leave Lydia in Europe. A few days ago he had guiltily booked a single steamship ticket

104

to Brazil on a ship that would leave Le Havre. His work had to come first. It was the exotic in Brazil that he hoped would shock him into – into what? Renewal? Virility? Regardless, the ticket would take him away from frothing Europe. Of course Lydia would understand and forgive him. Much was indisputable: That the German army had crossed the Meuse at Sedan, that Amélie and Marguerite were in his vault on rue de Rivoli, at the Banque de France every day inventorying, dividing, valuing his life's work, that he was fighting off a strong urge to go to rue de Rivoli, into the vault, to close his old circle around him once more and have his wife lock him with those ironclad eyes of hers, have his daughter Marguerite provide their marriage with ballast.

A week after booking the precious ticket he returned to the office of the steamship line. It was jammed with desperate people. As the hour passed, the crowd gave off a smell much like fermenting beets. The air-raid siren wailed, but no one left the line. When he finally reached the ticket window, the news that the old man with the white beard was not buying but was cashing in a ticket to Brazil caused ripples. A leathery foreigner asked in pidgin French, "Are you mad, Monsieur?"

He did not reply. There was no need to inform the gentleman that he had not been mad for a single moment of his long life. By the time he left the steamship office, he was not feeling well. He walked back toward the Lutétia. If he stayed in Europe, it would surely be wise to get out of Paris. And soon. And, if he was able to continue working as he hoped, he needed Lydia. But, how to arrange transportation when the entire population wanted the same thing? He stopped at his tailor to cancel the order he had given for four white linen suits for Brazil.

Back in his hotel room, he wrote to his son Pierre:

Had I gone to Brazil I would have felt like a deserter.

Irrespective of the strings he tried to pull in the coming days, it was not possible to arrange transportation south. Roads were packed with cars despite the difficulty of obtaining petrol. Mattresses were tied to the roofs of these cars in case the Germans began to dive-bomb the roads. The Louvre was shut down. Its great treasures had been transported to safer places. Trains were not running properly but he acquired train tickets through a contact and, carrying as little as possible, he and Lydia went by train to le Gironde where his dealer lived. When they arrived, he changed his mind, decided that it was better to keep going, and so they continued southwest to Ciboure where he rented rooms. From the rooms was a view of boats, the sound of gulls. A fishy smell hung over the harbor. He was exhausted and ill. Lydia feared the worst. They ate local *ardi gazna* cheese made from sheep milk that seemed to have the effect of steadying his nerves.

Pittsburgh, Pennsylvania, 1921

It would take 14 hours in Mikova for Julia's husband to earn what he earned in one hour in Pittsburgh. Andrej had left Mikova for Pennsylvania before World War I. Julia had waited nine years for him to send money to her so she could join him, and when he finally did, her only child, a daughter, was dead, and so were her parents. She bragged to Eva and Ella, the young sisters she had protected after her mother died, that she would soon bring them to America to join her.

Once she arrived in America by ship and went by train to Pittsburgh, she made Andrej's small apartment into a home for a married man instead of for a tidy bachelor. She wrote to Eva and Ella to tell them to the penny exactly how much money he handed her in his pay envelope that first week. She also wrote:

The copper on the church's dome looks like gold when the sun's rays hit it, like real gold.

She folded one dollar into the envelope and licked it shut.

In a later letter she told Eva and Ella about the shooting flames she saw all night and all day at the steel mill:

It's like a dragon shooting fire. I keep strong coffee in a big percolator on the stove all day. No vermin. No howling wolves in Ruska Dolina neighborhood where we and all like us live.

Like the church in Mikova, inside St. John Chrysostom was a field of burning candles made of yellow wax. Every morning before Mass Julia lit one for Justina, the dead daughter never far from her thoughts. She filled a cardboard box with various colored scraps of cloth – jelly purple, paprika color, red and white like a barber pole – for dresses, also packages of sugar. When the box was full she posted it by sea mail to Mikova. Every week she put a few quarters from her house money into the cookie jar toward steamship tickets for Ella and Eve.

Her first son, John, was robust. Just when it seemed as if there was almost enough in the cookie jar for tickets to send for her sisters, many of the men in the neighborhood were laid off. Nine months after John, Paul, even heartier, was born. To help bring in money, Julia cut open used tin cans with the razor-sharp can opener. She pounded the tin on the kitchen table, cut the flattened tin into flower shapes, painted them blue, red, green, then took her handmade decorations door-to-door in the better neighborhoods, selling one for 25 cents, two for 40 cents. With her earnings she bought seeds for vegetables and planted carrots and cabbage in the backyard. Beets grew nice and big – dark maroon – but did not taste like beets grown in Mikova. When they did not have enough to get by she began cleaning houses for one dollar a day. Because there was still no work, Andrej traveled by bus to the coal mines of West Virginia. He sent money but hardly a note. When she gave Andrej a third son, she wrote to Mikova:

One more son, God be praised. We name him Andek. Andrej say, You must fatten him up. My runt is fussy, he got colic from the bottle but not from my milk.

A few years later John passed down his comic books to this sickly scarecrow of a brother, who was as colorless as an albino. The doctor told John to tell his mother that the little one must stay inside in bed for four months because he had St. Vitus Dance. With the long shears that had a broken tip beside him on a chair next to his bed, Julia and skinny Andek cut pictures out of comic books and magazines; they cut and pasted onto colored paper. She taught him to draw. Because the sick boy did not like to be alone, she sat with him while he slept, stood beside him when he shat. Julia was fearful that he would die like Justina had. She squeezed oranges for juice as quickly as she could in order to return to his bedside. When it was time to go into the kitchen to prepare food, she carried him in and sat him on a kitchen chair with a red and green handmade afghan around his pointed shoulders.

Julia wrote:

Finally Andrej come home. Finally the doctor say the little one can go back to school. I pick nice clothes for him. I say, Here, put on. He like what I pick. I say, Go show Nonya how handsome his baby son. He go and show. He cannot go to school unless I find his shoes, find his tie, find his homework for him. He say he want to be a tap dancer when he grows up.

Pittsburgh, 1942

Andrej's heart stopped. Julia leaned over, smelled sardines. She held a feather under his nose. When it did not move, she twisted one of the yellow doilies from the arm of the couch until the priest came. Andrej's sister Mary and the church ladies laid him out, washed and dressed him in his Sunday suit in the bed in which he died. Paul went to pick a casket from the mortuary and Julia lowed like a calf. When the coffin was delivered, John and Paul lifted Nonya into it. Julia and her big sons sat on kitchen chairs beside the casket that was surrounded with dancing candles all day. The little one would not come out from under his bed and no one forced him out.

With no stern husband to stop her, Julia painted designs on all their kitchen chairs, on the wooden spoon she used for stirring stew, as she had in Mokova. She taught Andek how to help her. She packed a big box with Andrej's suits and shoes and shirts folded inside, also the jacket with the fur collar he had given her when she got off the boat. The dream of tickets for Ella and Eva had dried up. She found additional houses to clean, got more empty tin cans – from stewed tomato and cling peaches – from every neighbor. She soaked off the labels and cut and hammered flower sculptures from the tin, decorated, made them quaint.

*

She wrote:

I do as doctor say but don't feel good. I don't cook. I don't clean. I lie down. I can't do cleaning jobs so Mary do them for me. John makes me go to the doctor and tomorrow we go back again.

After an hour's wait in the doctor's office, the nurse called them into the office. The doctor told John, "She has colon cancer."

John told Julia in Ponasemu, "You have colon cancer."

111

Julia said to John in English, "I no know this sickness. You talk to doctor please."

The doctor told John, "She must have a colostomy," and told Julia, "You can live a normal life with a colostomy bag."

They waited for the doctor to explain more but he did not, he only said, "The nurse will set up a date for the surgery."

Waiting for the nurse, Julia whispered to John, "Maybe Mary knows this sickness?"

The nurse overheard, promised, "I will tell you more when the time comes."

Pittsburgh, 1948

Julia begged, "No go."

As Andek pulled away from her grasping hands, she got down on her knees, put her arms around his calves.

"Ma, stop it."

Again she tried to grip him, but he wriggled away even when she warned, "You'll end up dead in the gutter. Don't go."

He left to buy his bus ticket, so she lay on the couch. She was wearing her apron spotted with spaghetti sauce. It began to rain so hard that rainwater leaked under the front door. When Andek walked in wearing a new corduroy cream-colored suit, she turned to look, shouted, "What kind of man's suit is that?"

"I got my bus ticket."

She turned her face toward the moss floral wallpaper. That night, when he fell asleep, she sat on a kitchen chair beside his bed all night watching him sleep. In the morning, as usual, he knelt beside her under the crucifix to pray. Seeing his luggage piled at the doorway, she got the cookie jar from the kitchen shelf, reached inside, extracted the bills and a fist full of coins which she put into a paper bag, folding it at the top. Then she wrapped a thick rubber band around. She put the bag into a second bag that held a stack of bologna and mayonnaise – his favorite – sandwiches. She added an orange wrapped in wax paper that was cut into sections so it would not drip on the box of Malamar cookies. John took hold of her shoulders, insisted, "Go to church."

She took off the apron, put on the well-worn fudge-brown wool coat, the new Christmas head scarf that was green and had blue with yellow-blue decorations, then bent to pull shiny black rubbers over her shoes. She walked to church along an unevenly paved sidewalk. After Mass she told the priest that this was God's punishment for failing to send tickets to her sisters in Mikova for all these many years. Now she was the one who was left behind.

New York, 1959

Julia was tired because they had moved once again. In the morning after Mass at St. Mary's, she saw Claws in the park, sat next to her on the bench.

"My son want you to come to our place. He like famous people."

"I'm not famous."

"But you say you was a model for famous persons so you famous, too. You look like you don't eat right. I want make you and Andek a famous lunch. You have time?"

Claude was about to go home to sleep for an hour before foraging through the trash baskets up and down First Avenue. She had not eaten in two days.

"I have time."

She followed Julia to the bus stop. Julia paid two fares. During the bus ride and the stop at the A & P, Julia hugged the brown pocketbook against her chest while Claude looked jealously at so much food.

Just inside the house's entrance was a couch covered with a hair-coated sheet that was meant to protect it from greasy cat hair shed by the many Siamese cats. In the room were piled paint cans, paint mixers coated with paint; various large canvases were stacked against the wall. There were colored blotches on the floor that looked like Roy's paintings.

Julia led her down a flight of steps into the kitchen and cleared a section of the large table for the grocery bag by pushing a pile of laundry, magazines, mail, bills, books of S & H green stamps, glasses and plates – some washed, some not – into a clump on the sticky tablecloth. She took junk from one chair and added it to the junk on another chair. Said, "Sit!"

All morning the pain in the heels of Julia's feet had been wicked and her ankles were swollen again. She took off her shoes and put on well-worn gold and mustard-colored fuzzy house slippers. As soon as the percolator on the stove began to bubble, she poured a cup of very black coffee for her guest and finished counting out the green stamps given with the purchases. She licked line by line, glued each line inside the half-filled book, making sure she has not been cheated by having a second look at the receipt.

In the paper shopping bag was piled a pound chunk of unsliced bologna, yellow cabbage, milk, bottles of 7 Up, a loaf of bread, Malomar cookies. She sliced the bologna with a sharp breadknife. Piling a stack of sliced bread on a large plate that she pulled from under a pile of magazines, she smeared mayonnaise and bologna on every slice then cut the stack in half as Claude's stomach rumbled. Layers of newspaper were scattered over the Granny-Smith-green kitchen linoleum that crinkled when Julia walked to the kitchen counter to drop the change from the shopping into the cornflower-blue cookie jar. Finally, she put the plate piled with sandwiches on the table, and Claude took one. Julia sighed, "I send to my sisters in Mikova. They waited 30 years for tickets to America, but stop waiting."

Claude held out her cup so that Julia could fill it again. Since the move, she and her son no longer had to sleep side by side on the floor. Her son had gone to Bloomingdale's, had bought two new beds. When they were delivered, he put the four-poster into the large bedroom on the second floor for himself, the three-quarter bed with enamel headboard went into the small bedroom in the basement behind the kitchen for Julia. In the past few years, beside earning money for commercial art, he was doing other kinds of messy, unconventional things he called art in the parlor they had passed through. A kitchen towel that had red and green designs covered a bird cage in which a grape-green parrot perched. When Julia removed the towel from the cage, the bird ignored her as it did all day even though she sang and talked to it. The parrot's long nails curled around the wooden, shit-covered perch.

"The parrot shows off for my boy. Shuns me. He shriek like a lover for my boy." She asked the parrot, "Deya Andek?" told Claude, "I've been up since six."

One of the cats must have shat or pissed under something because the smell was rank. Julia filled the bucket with hot water and a quarter of a bottle of Mr. Clean, mopped into the corners of the kitchen behind a radiator.

"We laugh about the ka-ka because instead of the fresh cat ka-ka, maybe I find old cat ka-ka. One way or other, I find."

Julia noticed that the stack of sandwiches on the plate had vanished, said, "I make more."

"Yes, please. Where is your son?"

"We wait."

*

At noon Julia mixed the contents of a can of frozen orange juice with three cans of tap water in a jar and stirred the orange slush with a spoon. On the long kitchen counter was an electric mixer squeezed beside several half-full red bags of Eight O'clock coffee and a full black bag of Bokar coffee. Also on it, a tea pot, receipts clipped together with a wooden clothespin, more mail, envelopes stuffed with cancelled stamps, more magazines, bills, a snow globe of the Empire State Building, a tin of Johnson & Johnson's Band-Aids. Julia filled a large and a small drinking glass with pulp-free juice. She complained, "Maybe it time to tell Andek to pull the plug and let the dye go down the drain of the bathtub? I no wash my hair in a long time. My scalp start to itch."

So the soup did not boil over, she kept a piece of glass from Mikova at the bottom of the saucepan while it simmered. The smell of soup mixed with the smell of cat leavings. She handed a drinking glass of juice to Claude.

"Stay. I go wake my baby."

*

A few minutes before, he had risen to a sitting position in his four-poster bed. Barely had he opened his eyes, when his mother was bending over him pushing the glass of orange juice into his hand. Suffering Christ carved in hard, dark wood writhed against the antique crucifix nailed to the wall above his bed. He was accustomed to the monologue that would not end until he left the house to go out for the evening and perhaps not even then. Impatiently she demanded, "Get dressed quick. The lady is here."

He swallowed an Obetrol pill with the juice. It left a bitter taste but would quickly clarify everything. He was a man of monosyllables, a man who never interrupted, who never minded his mother's talk. He handed back the half-empty glass so that she would leave. Her voice was audible from everywhere in the house including the bathroom.

In a while he came downstairs into the parlor work space. He sifted through a pile of records, chose a 45 and slid a yellow plastic centerpiece down the metal spike, dropped the record onto the spike. He pulled back the arm mechanism so that the record would repeat and let the needle drop onto Dan Hicks and the Hot Licks doing "How Can I Miss You When You Won't Go Away?" The TV against the wall was on with no sound. He fiddled with the radio until he found a station playing Tosca. His tight jeans were covered with chartreuse and egg-yolk-yellow paint. He had doused himself with his only luxury – Chanel. Walking down the stairway, he heard his mother was saying, " ... I walked barefoot in the snow ... "

He looked at the lady.

"Hi."

"She was model for famous artists."

Claude looked up from her sandwich, saw that Julia's son was a sheepish ghostly man with pimples on his nose.

"My mother told me you modeled for the artist Henry Mattress?" he flatly stated.

His voice was so quiet that she was not sure she had heard him right. She was taken aback, then realized he was joking, while Julia looked from one to the other. He earnestly confessed, "I want to be Matisse."

"*Pas possible.*"

He studied her while he ate Cheerios and milk from a bowl. When the bowl was empty, he sorted through various sheets of drawing paper until he found the one that had not satisfied him and held it up to his mother, who scrutinized it.

"Is okay. Okay, trust me, I know."

119

Julia told Claude, "A boy in my village swallowed a puppy that lived ... yes ... lived ... inside his stomach. It make yelps, barking noises. Hard to believe but true, I swear on my daughter's head."

He and his mother got down on their knees beneath the crucifix and said morning prayers while the tenor on the upstairs radio warbled the aria "Recondita Armonia." Julia was about to grab hold of the oven handle to pull herself up but saw that the laces of his sneakers were trailing.

"Tie your laces ... you trip on yourself, God forbid, break your neck."

He did nothing, so she blocked his path, went back down onto one knee and tied them for him.

"Stay still. Claws is the age your sister Justina would be if she not die. Same age. Different everything. One dark one light."

Greedy to look at the many new magazines she'd seen on the kitchen counter, Claude picked up *Art in America*.

"I've got to go to work. I can't hire you to model because your feet are flat. If I get a job illustrating hats, I will because your head is made to wear a hat."

"Anything would be fine. I need money to live."

New York, 1963

Upstairs, his new assistant let himself into the new house. He waited in the lightless, wood-paneled room that had a Victorian flavor, in which they would work. The windows were covered. Andek, called Andy by everyone except his mother, had added a cigar-store Indian and a pink carousel horse to the room's furnishings. Everything, including the prized white wicker couch that had replaced the chunky upholstered couch, was covered in cat hair and splashed with ink and paint. A roll of fresh canvas was propped against the carousel. Half a dozen silk screens depicting Puss'n Boots cat food tins were piled against the wall. The pay for the assistant's job was $1.25 an hour. Andy sat on the couch, pulled his knobby legs up under him. His eyes pinned the assistant, Gerard, like sharp nails, while Gerard described what he had eaten for breakfast homemade sausage and toast, what everyone on the subway was wearing – raincoats, rain hats. Work began. Julia clumped into the room, Claude following her.

"I invited Claws back after Mass like you tell me."

Andy turned to look. He had not seen her again in several years, not since his astonishing success. Though her carriage was still regal, her shoulders sloped. It did not seem as if she had washed her clothes since he had seen her last, and her makeup and lipstick had gone wild. She sat on the couch, looked at what he was making. Wrapped in Julia's old pink mohair shawl because he was cold, he watched the assistant lay the framed screen on top of a canvas then waited for him to pick the color for the printed drawing of the Puss 'n Boots tin to be made. Andy decided on cerise, watched while Gerard mixed it to suit him.

An hour later, silkscreen in hand, Gerard placed the frame on a fresh canvas, then sat down. Julia had been asked by Andy to draw tuna tins with a fat pencil when Andy had gone off to talk on the telephone. The day's news blared from the TV.

Julia finished what she was drawing and went downstairs. In 20 minutes she returned carrying food and drink on a tray.

"I no make potato salad. In America have no taste. No taste good. Taste like nothing. In Mikova a potato was a meal ... a boiled potato ... boiled until very soft ... with a little oil if we have ... butter once in a blue moon ... a little salt ... can't be described."

Claude, who had been sitting on the couch looking through a pile of magazines, took a sandwich from the pile; when she heard the word "butter" she asked, "Is there butter?"

Julia set the tray down on the couch, turned, clumped back downstairs to quickly return with a stick of butter in an orange ceramic butter dish. While Gerard drank a can of 7 Up, Andy sipped from a glass of milk and walked while he chewed off the thick coating of peach-colored nail polish from his thumbnail. He took a detour around Julia, put the milk glass back on the tray and took half a bologna sandwich.

" ... so delicious. Two ... three ... four potatoes ... not big ... medium size ... for each. I pine ... dream for potatoes ... "

Andy took a bite and put the half sandwich back on the plate. He wiped his hands on the leg of his pants. On the radio the opera *Mignon* was being introduced by an announcer with a silky voice. The music began to play while Andy bent and carefully mixed a bright apple-green color. Between them, Gerard and Claude consumed the remaining sandwiches. When he was satisfied with the brightness of the green, he took a Hydrox cookie from a pile of cookies overflowing a pink and brown polka-dotted cookie plate. Julia described the plot of the latest episode of *I Love Lucy*:

"Ricky can't find his drumsticks. By mistake Lucy put them in the refrigerator."

In the background, a mezzo-soprano was singing the aria "Connais-tu le Pays?" Pointing at the completed silk screens – many rows of Puss 'n Boots tins repeated on a background of silver gray – Julia commanded:

"No more cat food. I bring the lady home so you do portrait. You pay her please. Do a real lady not cat food or boy's pee-pees ... You say you want to be Matisse ... so be."

123

Claude bit into bread and bologna to which she had added butter. Andy told Claude, "I want to do your portrait."

He handed her one of the silkscreens that had gotten messed up, "A gift."

Her mouth was full of bologna, gummy white bread, pale butter, but she said, "Thank you."

Carefully she examined the gift. Finally she spoke up: "I like this better than the others. You may do my portrait."

New York, 1964

Julia stood alone on the sidewalk until the taxi carrying Andy and Claude turned the corner. She walked to the butcher on Second Avenue and bought stewing meat. At Gristedes, around the block, she picked out the ripest tomato from a pile of tomatoes, then selected onions, brown pepper, garlic. Walking around to the next aisle, she added a large bottle of Heinz ketchup to the cart. Although she thought there must be something else she needed, she was feeling queasy so she looked for the check-out counter.

On the way home she stopped at the liquor store on Lexington Avenue to get a bottle of Dewar's for Andy who now had so many friends he no longer drank spirits with her. Her brown pocketbook was stuffed full of money. Andy gave her $500 a week, every week, and she could not spend it all. She counted out the money for the bottles, returned the wad to her pocketbook, then pressed the silver clasp as hard as she could. On the Third Avenue bus, she unscrewed the top of the whiskey bottle, smelled it.

Relieved to be back in the basement, she sat on a kitchen chair, pulled off her shoes and slipped on the new fluffy shrimp-pink house slippers one of Andy's helpers had given her. She glanced at the game show on the television screen while rubbing her swollen ankles. Before *One Life to Live* began, she went into the bathroom beside the kitchen to check on whether she needed to change the colostomy bag. She did not. She put on her apron, poured and drank a vodka mixed with coke. With one eye on her knife, she chopped brown peppers while watching the soap opera with the other eye.

Once all the vegetables were chopped, she turned the gas on under the saucepan filled with water, added what she had chopped, spoke to the cats:

"I come with food, Sam. I coming, Sam. Will Andek come home later? Maybe bring Claws home for hot soup? Maybe Andek can marry this famous lady? My Paul has seven children, John has three, even if Andek have only one puny one, I die happy. Maybe he take her to big studio? I no like new studio. Why get? Why pay? No necessary. He work good at home, I can help him."

She lowered the gas. Something smelled bad. The odor was coming from under the stove, or from somewhere else. She looked and sniffed but could not find the source of the smell. A framed photograph of the face of President John F. Kennedy was hanging on the wall beside an illustration of a bleeding Jesus Christ wearing the crown of blue thorns, also framed. The president was smiling at her, listening, interested in what she had to say. Christ was suffering, listening, too.

"He work too much. My boy work like I work in Mikova. I paint and make decorations in Mikova. He do like me. I teach him everything. He make things because I show him. But I tend goats and chickens, too. He no do labor work. He no strong like me."

She poured a half glass of Popov and topped it off with what was left in the Coke bottle that she had to yank off the counter because it was stuck to the Formica. On the floor was a big cardboard box of foodstuffs, cloth, new towels. Beside it was a Maxwell House coffee tin she had stuffed with bills and change left from the month.

She looked everywhere and finally found the sheaf of drawings under the telephone book and sat down with his colored pencils. One by one she finished them off as she had promised, signed his name to each.

*

126

The taxi drove along Lexington Avenue to 42nd Street. His mother had always spoken about Justina as an angel. No photo of Justina survived. No photo of anything, even his mother and father's wedding, had survived World War I. Julia's descriptions of Justina had varied so much during the years that he could not help but wonder if Claude was like Justina in some way. There was no other way to explain his mother's attachment since Julia had not made one other friend since coming to live with him, had no desire for friends.

When the taxi stopped, they crossed 42nd Street, stepped over spilled fruit and went inside a penny arcade that was noisy with the sound of electric pinball machines. They passed a row of pokino machines, a line of Skee-Ball machines, walked to a counter at which a ruby-haired woman wearing a white captain's hat with a shiny black brim was redeeming coupons won playing Skee-Ball. She was upset, kept pointing up at a cream and red alarm clock, her skin bright fuchsia.

"I want the alarm clock."

The attendant behind the counter was breaking down rolls of quarters. He did not look up.

"You don't have enough coupons for the clock."

"I do."

The attendant pointed to a lower shelf that contained large foam dice in several colors – blue, pink, yellow, green – also green plastic backscratchers, tiny brown monkeys at the end of key chains.

"This is your shelf, miss."

The highest shelf that displayed alarm clocks also held piggy banks, various stuffed animals – stuffed sheep with curly coats of black fur, a row of large silky black and white stuffed panda bears. The attendant took three twenty-dollar bills from Andy and handed back a cardboard bucket filled with quarters. Andy went over to the photo booth. Spinning the hard, round, plastic seat counterclockwise to raise it, he instructed Claude.

"Sit on the seat."

Since her hair was dark with streaks of gray threading through the brown mixed with strands of hunter green, he chose dark on light and pulled back the azure curtain, revealed the white wall.

"Sit inside."

She did, straightened her back.

"Look at the small glass window. Hold a pose when the green light goes on. Change it after it turns to red."

Quarters clanged as they dropped into the machine. A little green light lit, flashed. He spoke in a flat voice.

"Don't blink!"

"Turn to the right."

"Look up."

"Make a face."

"Make another face."

128

He was not sure if she understood English. When she did everything he asked, he gathered that she did and, as his mother had told him, had followed an artist's orders before. After the light had flashed four times, he stuck his head inside.

"Wait. It'll go again."

He was surprised that a heavy sexual atmosphere was now surrounding her.

"Fabulous."

At the sound of more coins, she opened her eyes wide and the light flashed red, each flash an ember of fire. She changed positions before each flash, sniffed, tossed her head like a ram. Not only had she followed directions, she had obviously done quick poses, too.

"Don't blink."

When the light stopped flashing, he reached his long white hand inside and pulled the curtain behind her head to give an azure background.

"Great."

Quarters dropped into the machine.

"Great."

The lights went on and off and on four times, four times, four times, four times. Finally he stepped back.

"That's it."

Claude mumbled a prayer of petition, stepped out of the booth. She drifted toward the counter, looking up at the stuffed animals, while Andy leaned against the photo machine. He followed her with his eyes, chewed his thumbnail as she looked longingly at the stuffed animals. In 10 minutes, black-and-white photos, four to a strip, began to drop out of the machine one after the other. Because they were still wet, he gripped their edges, lined them up along the glass top of a horseracing machine to dry. Images appeared.

"Gosh!"

Claude came to look at the strips. Each contained four images of a face that did not always seem like the face of the same person. Once dried, he dropped the strips one by one into a paper bag.

"May I look?"

He handed the bag to her and walked away. She pulled out the strips, looked at her many faces. None of these faces belonged to a nun. He returned and put a black stuffed sheep into her arms. She wrapped her arms around the sheep's belly and followed him into the street. While he hailed a checker cab, she rubbed the sheep's fur.

"Where can I drop you?"

"At St. Patrick's church."

He sat on the jump seat, stared at her face. She could pass for Jeanne Moreau's older sister.

"If you pay me in cash it would be better. I worked one hour."

"Let's make it a half day – four hours. I pay $1.25 an hour."

He handed her five dollars. She looked distastefully at his jacket, his dark glasses; his tight black trousers were like a Nazi SS. He had once seemed such an effete boy, but now he was dressed like a Nazi.

"Here, please."

The taxi stopped, and she got out at the statue of Atlas holding up the world. The taxi drove on. Before returning to the house to change his clothes, he had the taxi driver stop twice – once for pastries and once to pick up the Czech newspaper for his mother.

New York, 1965

Julia sat on the chair in his bedroom beside the antique crucifix, watching her son sleeping in his four-poster canopied bed. She looked up, saw that Jesus was looking at her with tears in his eyes. Two cats sat like sphinxes at her feet. A brown leather jacket, black jeans, black T-shirt, a pair of sheer pantyhose were crumpled on the floor on top of shiny, black, pointed high-heeled boots. In a few hours he would go away again and, except for Claws who was not a regular at the park anymore, church, *I Love Lucy*, cooking, shopping and writing letters to Pittsburgh and Mikova, she would be alone with the cigar-store Indian, the wooden carousel horse and shitting cats.

What had he done with the parrot? It was gone, but not its cage. As much as the bird bullied

131

her, she missed it. Even before he went to work, while he slept, she missed him. The boys and girls who answered his office phone were nice, but were obstacles. She mooed to the cats.

"Why he no get engaged?"

They were not listening, so she mooed. "Why not marry?"

Asleep, his face was alabaster. His face was her face without glasses.

"Why you need all those wigs in green boxes?"

A cat began to meow. She picked it up.

"I feed. I feed. Shusssss. Go."

She made the sign of the cross over him.

"If he would marry one of the boys or one of the girls, they could make little Andeks. One. Two. Ten…. I care for all little Andeks. Even ugly, hairless ones with pimples."

The cats followed in her tracks, got under her feet, almost tripping her as she climbed down the steps to the basement, banging her rump against the railing as she went. The priest had been wrong all these years. A cow could climb down as well as up stairs. Neither was natural, but both were possible when need be. The cats meowed urgently. She bent down and picked up three cans from a cardboard case of Puss 'n Boots cat food. It was a strain to open them because the old metal can opener was gummed up. She emptied a mound of silvery-gray cat food onto dried food stuck to a red paper plate on the floor beside the stove.   Ants had gotten into the leftover food again.

"So what if you eat a few ants. Good protein, haha. Perhaps I die in a room with many cats?"

It was time for *One Life to Live*. She watched while chopping carrots. She chopped potatoes. She chopped up cloves of garlic. She chopped an onion and began to cry. She took a slice of white Wonder Bread from its sack, put it between the upper and lower bridge of teeth and bit down. Soon the tears stopped.

*

She poured two fingers of Popov into a Sau-Sea Shrimp Cocktail glass and drank it down, then buttoned her woolen coat over her apron and hung the big black pocketbook over her arm.

"Where is it?"

She went through one pile of papers on the kitchen counter, then another, but could not find what she wanted. Finally, she found the catalogue she was searching for on top of the refrigerator. Earlier she had wrapped a sandwich in wax paper and jammed it into her pocketbook. A bottle of pickles came crashing down when she pulled it out from under. She threw up her hands and walked upstairs through the living room. The walls were newly painted with cream and gold-colored paint. She stopped to catch her breath, held onto the Mobil

Gas winged horse to balance. She closed the door without locking it and took the bus downtown.

She was in luck, she found Claude slouched on her bench in the strong sun with two brown bags at her feet. She was wearing a halter top, pedal pushers decorated with black and orange spots, Chinese slippers. Her eyes were encircled by black eyeliner. Julie beckoned.

"Come. Come to Mass."

When Claude hesitated, Julia said reassuringly, "Bring. Bring the bags into church. God no mind if you're a Roman Catholic. No one take."

Julia reached out to take hold of one to help, and Claude let her. Once inside the church Julia squeezed into a pew; Claude followed. Julia waved the catalogue that had written on the spine, *Ileana Sonnebend*.

"See. Look."

The silkscreen on the cover made from 16 little photos of Claude was titled *My Sister Justina Sixteen Times*.

"Antek go to Germany. They buy all. Pay much.

Julia sang a few words of a sad song in Ponasemu.

"I had headache but I fix my head like we do in Mikova. I fill handkerchief with salt. I make sack. I make hot in the oven, put it across my eyes. I have headache when I remember the grave of my little daughter."

She sniffled.

"Everything Andek wears is black or brown. Only come home for breakfast and to sleep. No need me no more. Good people no like Andek. Bad people love. I tell him, pay better. He no pay workers good. Why? I no cheap. Maybe Andrej taught him to be cheap."

Julia took a coffee can from her shopping bag.

"There's $7,000 inside. I save. I give you. I never will see Mikova again."

She pushed it into Claude's brown bag, sniffled.

"Bad things happen."

From her bag she took the sandwich. She took off the wax paper, handed a bologna sandwich smeared with butter on one side and mayonnaise on the other to Claude. She lowed, "Andek work all day. A girl who wear white gloves come with gun. Shoot gun holes through big paintings. Paintings of green money. Green stamp. Some green like grass. Some green like jungle. Sammy come with gun, too. Make my Andek get on his knees. Give chills to my soul. Why?"

Seeing the priest on the alter, Claude leaned toward her.

"You must tell the priest? He will milk you, Mrs. Warhol. Go, *chérie*."

Garonne Valley, 1940–1

In the beginning of summer, the Germans advanced. Lydia and Matisse packed and traveled again, went east, inland, into the hilly Garonne Valley where fruit had ripened on the trees. He set his heart on painting peaches. For lunch at the local bistro, Lydia ate the *cassoulet*. He did, too, but it caused reflux. After lunch, Roquefort, more wine. The burning intestinal pain was no worse or, for that matter, better for it. It seemed like enteritis was flaring up again. In his room was a basket of downy peaches. He drew peaches. When he lay down to nap, the pain worsened. The window was wide open; breezes blew the yellow-ochre curtain into, then out of, his room. Lydia massaged the calves of his legs, hoping he would sleep for even half an hour.

"We've outrun the advancing German army."

"For now."

Her strong fingers kneaded out the leg cramps. He dozed but awoke abruptly to the craven blast of an air raid siren. Never used to the siren, she reached into a bowl of mixed nuts and cracked open a walnut with an antique implement. He propped himself up on an elbow, cracked open a nut as she had, admired the Cézanne he carried with him everywhere. He could put it off no longer, he needed to tell her that he had been diagnosed with cancer of the duodenal. How to say it? How to say that his

136

work life was ending though he was far from finished? Would that the words be put into his mouth along with this walnut.

He dozed again. The sound of a siren woke him. He was alone and the room was dark. Mingling with the shrill siren wail was the engine noise of a low-flying aircraft. He raised himself to a sitting position. Hair askew, Lydia appeared at the doorway. All color had drained from his face.

In a panic he told her, "It can't end now. I need five more years. My work isn't finished."

Lyon, 1941

While he was in Lyon in the hospital having surgery, his paintings were declared "decadent" by the Germans. Those that remained in museums were removed. In January he underwent a long complex surgery, reacting strongly to the anesthetic. The morphine had circulated through a mask that had covered his nose and mouth. Morphine hallucinations brought back Belle-Île-en-Mer. When he could talk again, he dictated what he hallucinated to Lydia because later he would want to be reminded of the journey on which his psyche had led him.

"I saw myself, Camille, our baby, Marguerite, along with a group of artists, wives, mistresses, children, all grouped together on a paddle steamer. Under one arm, I was carrying a study that copied

137

the oysters and dead fish in Chardin's *The Skate*. With my free hand, I steadied a wheelchair in which Renoir sat. Renoir's eyes and hands were wrapped with bandages. He was very old. It was a struggle to hold the wheelchair and not let the wind take the copy of *The Skate*. Amazing, eh?"

When she had written what he told her, he described another hallucination:

"The steamer veering when the first sight of Belle-Île-en-Mer came into view. The children clamored. Renoir demanded, 'Describe it to me, I can't see. Be precise.' I described it this way: 'I see ... dark jagged rocks fringed by foam, appearing like ... teeth starting from the deep to devour any hapless ship that may come within reach.' There was panic in Renoir's voice: 'Where will we stay? Damp affects my rheumatism. I'm old. I'm in pain. You must find us a warm place so that I can get back to painting. I can't hold a paintbrush if the air is cold.' All my resistance failed. I let myself be pulled down into the monochrome blue sea. It was bracing, salty. Because I was then strong, I could swim even in a wild sea, but, not for long, because I was pulled down into undulating blond foam."

He stopped speaking until she had written everything. Then continued.

"There came a new scene: I was walking in a high wind on a high cliff. I approached a bonfire, my friends were roasting sardines caught by local fisherman. I asked Camille, 'Where's Renoir?' just as

138

her hat blew off in the wind. I turned my head and saw him in the wheelchair. I walked over. He was clutching a jar of brushes that were soaking in turpentine, though he was asleep. The smell was ghastly. At that moment, I wanted nothing more from life than to paint Camille. Imagine that, Camille from over 40 years ago."

He dictated the next hallucinations more slowly, so that she could keep up with him:

"I believed I was in the half-room, half-barn we had rented from a peasant farmer. The air was so warm that the doors were wide open. I removed my collar and cuffs. Our baby sat spay-legged in the dirt drinking buttermilk. Renoir's wheelchair was turned away from the sea and a hot wind blew so hard that Camille's skirt billowed up above her ankles. The heat became oppressive so I stripped down to my underwear. I ate a sardine and though I felt thirsty, I went back to the painting of Camille. She was trying to maintain a pose though the baby was pulling at her ankles. I called out to Renoir, 'Shall I turn your chair toward the sea?' 'Don't bother,' Renoir called back, 'The heat is breaking. We're in for or another storm. Move me inside, please. Why do you paint when you can't?' As Renoir spoke, the sky went black. I pushed the chair inside the half-house-half-barn past chickens and a cow just as the storm broke. In very close quarters were me, Camille, the baby, the cow, the chickens, Renoir's large wood wheelchair. I would never have guessed that it would be Amélie

139

and not Camille with whom I would spend the next 40 years."

Although he survived the surgery, one January day after his 72nd birthday, the night nurse, Sister Annemarie, was at his bedside when he was stricken with a pulmonary embolism. It was doubtful that he would live out the night. She prayed for him through the night. He hung on through the following night, the following week, the following month.

Two months later, on March 3rd, Sister Annemarie was also tending him when he had another embolism. This one was so severe that even a man in his prime could not have survived it. Once more Sister prayed. Days and weeks passed and he remained in the semi-comatose state, but breathing, his hands by his sides under the sheets, his face as colorless as his beard.

*

In Spring, despite terrible pain, he was able to sit halfway up. He asked for pen and paper and made a drawing. Sister Annemarie shook her finger at him.

"Never disparage the power of prayer, see ... God has brought you back from the dead."

He sank back onto the pillow, awash in pain but uplifted. When the pain had subsided enough for him to be able to speak, he said, "I'm not a believer, so please give thanks for me in your prayers."

In her prayers she gave thanks to God in his stead. He was fitted for a corset that enabled him to stand upright for short periods of time. When there was an air raid, he was unable to go the distance to the shelter. He asked Lydia to bring his copy of Henri Bergson so that he could read while others went down into the shelter. In May, though pessimistic about his chances of recovery, his doctor gave in and released him. His intention was to use the time remaining to work. In the taxi on the way to the train, driving through streets destroyed by bombardments, he begged the driver to make a stop in the business center of Lyon. The driver did as asked. He begged Lydia to go into a small factory and buy a roll of woven silk, the kind that could only be found in Lyon.

"What a fool I'd be to go home without silk from Lyon."

Outside the building sandbags were piled. A German convoy passed. Not a meter from the car window was a green wood cage in which two yellow canaries perched silently side by side on a rung. Just as Lydia emerged from the shop with a rolled piece of oyster-gray silk, the air raid siren sounded. Matisse gripped Henri Bergson and bit through his lower lip to stanch the pain as Lydia and the driver helped him down the steps into the shelter. They left him there, returned to the street to help an old

141

woman with her grandchild in its pram down into the shelter.

Through the many hours below ground, the taxi driver flirted with a teenage girl who had diamond-bright eyes; Matisse sucked at his bitten lip and read; Lydia laid out her Patience cards on the ground and wept.

"IN PARADISUM"

New York, 1964

The girl's bell-bottom trousers were peacock blue, the boy's were mandarin orange. Peter Yakatori compared them – alike but different – through the glass storefront on East 10th Street that was melting in the hot morning sun. Leaning closer for a better look, he was able to reach right through it, since it was not glass at all, merely the sheen that had settled over everything now that the pill he had just taken – Placidyl – was taking effect. Inside the store was a hand-lettered sign – FREE STEW AND COFFEE DIGGERS FREE STORE. The boy and girl who had first caught his eye were serving coffee and bowls of beef stew to two customers. One was a small man wearing a black shirt with a Nehru collar whose head was shaved. He reminded Peter, whose real name was Junichiro, of his father in Tokyo. He could easily imagine this man or his hairless father as a hairless gorilla. Another was a sleepy woman wearing mismatched clothes – a silky shrimp-pink peasant blouse, tight toreador pants the color of candied violets cinched by a buttercream plastic belt – who was as juicy as an overripe peach. She was about 50, made his penis stiffen.

Peter went inside, sat across the table from where the woman was eating a second bowl of free stew. He accepted a bowl of his own and a glass of tap water in a mug from the waiter. When the sexy woman finished her second bowl, rust-red juice had dribbled onto her blouse. She picked up a brown shopping bag stuffed with magazines and balls of aluminum foil. He followed after her, watching her without her knowing. She stopped often to reach down into garbage cans to retrieve various objects. He kept 10 feet away, his left hand inside his yellow raincoat pressing his genitals as she wandered across town to Second Avenue, turned up Second.

While walking, she filled her bag with various discards that caught her eye – two shoes and shoelaces from a wire trash basket, a handful of discarded magazines and newspapers bundled beside a secondhand bookshop on Second Avenue, held together with twine. She reached First and 11th, leaned over to sift through an almost empty trash basket while he stood with his back against a brick wall, rubbing and kneading his erection. When she went into a building, it became lax. He swallowed a green and pink capsule and took out a cigarette. His hand was shaking when he lit the match.

She came back out holding a buttered roll and his hard-on stiffened once more. He followed until she was about to enter a building, then politely went up to her and spoke in correct but accented English.

"Forgive the rudeness of speaking to you. I am an exchange student from Japan. I am here in New York studying art and have been searching for a subject. I think you could be that subject. Is there a chance you would allow me to use you as a model?"

She brightened.

"It happens to be the work I once did."

"I would pay you by the hour."

"I would say yes."

"May I telephone you?"

"I have no telephone but if you tell me when and where, I will go. I need the work. My husband moved to Maine, stopped sending money. I'm stranded here."

"I'm living with a fellow student from Tokyo in a tiny room at the Broadway Central Hotel. Perhaps you can suggest a place where we can work?"

She told him to come to her apartment, which happened to be on the third floor of the building in front of them. She told him when.

Since arriving in New York in October, Peter had been gluttonizing on the city. Neither he nor the city slept. He walked every day, all day, every night, all night, helped by various pills. He was partial to this Lower East Side neighborhood, admired the freshly baked breads through the window of Lanza's and Veniero's Italian bakery. At night he danced at the Dom on St. Mark's Place. He read signs tacked to electric poles promoting free poetry readings, attended those on Monday nights at Le Metro on Second Avenue. He had visited every avant-garde art gallery on the Lower East Side, in the Village, every established gallery on the Upper East Side and on 57th Street.

On his way to the appointment with the object of his inspiration, he stopped at a bookshop and bought her a copy of a popular poetry book – *A Coney Island of the Mind* – as a gift. He took a shortcut across Tompkins Square Park that had the four-story-high mural of Isaac Hayes and a monument that depicted two children staring up at an ocean liner. The plaque explained that liner sank in 1904, took down more than a thousand, mostly German, people from the neighborhood. The monument made him cry, not because he cared about a tragedy so long ago but because the pill he had swallowed had kicked in.

Inside her apartment, he was upset by the unmade bed and dishes crusted with old food. He asked her to undress, watched her do so. When she was unclothed, he instructed her to stand at the small window, her back toward him. After two hours he said that the session was finished. She put on a caramel and beige robe and indigo slippers. He gave her a twenty-dollar bill. He had done more than 60 drawings. She said to him, "You're fast as a rabbit."

"This is New York. If I don't hurry I'll be stepped on."

*

He had promised to take her to the school at which he studied art because they employed live models, so he picked her up in the morning in a taxi. The school was the Art Students League on West

148

57th Street, where he guided her to the administrator's office, presented her with a flourish. She impressed the administrator with her credentials, was hired to pose for two life drawing classes. After she left the building, Peter signed up for both.

In her first class, Peter relished the salmon-pink lipstick coating her inviting lips and the tomato-red nail polish on her fingers and toes. He gazed with appetite at her neck and inner arms. These were two of the places on a woman's body that excited him. He could not see as much as he wanted because the instructor had seated her on a three-legged wooden stool and draped a plaid twill throw across her lap. He leaned toward Impero, the man who shared his hotel room.

"If I could rest my head against her, I would be happy to ejaculate into the palm of my own hand and could without doubt draw a masterpiece."

Impero did not see what he saw, merely warned, "Don't get deported."

Peter's glassy black hair was combed back, giving him the look of a swain from the 1920s. His throat and underarms were soaked with Paco Rabanne scent. After class he saw her eating scrambled eggs in the cafeteria.

"May I sit with you?"

"Yes."

"May I sketch you while you eat?"

"Yes. I need money."

While she ate, he made a dozen quick sketches of her face. She had applied a new shade of lipstick, lobster red, exaggerating the outline of her lips. He chose red charcoal to use to make his sketches. When she stood up to empty her tray, he gave her $20. He did five more drawings as she walked away.

New York, 1965

He wanted to sketch her as she went about her life in her apartment, told her to pretend he was not there. He stood against the wall preparing himself mentally, studying her as she removed the slipper-shoes, saw dirty feet with puffy toes. She picked up a newly retrieved magazine and sank into the corner of the soiled sheet on the mattress of the convertible couch. She shut her eyes for a few minutes, then opened her eyes and glanced again at the magazine. He made a few lines on a page of his sketchbook and quickly turned to the next page. One of the magazines was fat and swollen, the pages curling at the corner. He saw tiny squirming white worms between the pages of the magazine.

She pushed the worms aside, took up a scissors that was beside her and cut out an article that told about a Matisse exhibition, a retrospective show that had opened in Washington. The article mentioned that Matisse had died on November 3rd,

150

1954, at age 85 and that the finale of Bach's *The St John Passion – In Paradisum* by Gabriel Fauré – had been played at his funeral. Matisse had been buried at Cimiez.

She counted how many years it had been since he died. When had she stopped praying for his longevity? Why had she not known about his death? She tried to clear her mind. She must have been in Florida where Roy never took the newspapers. She read:

... Matisse was on his way to the last sacrifice when he built the chapel in Vence and dedicated it to Notre Dame du Rosaire. Its walled garden, the windows letting in the crystal light through the colors of his magic palette, and his Stations of the Cross. That is how he did end on an organ note.

Reading this gave her a sharp stab of regret. Why had she not returned to convent? She had always imagined she would walk in the walled garden in her older years and that Matisse or his spirit would look down and see her as she once was.

She took a half sandwich wrapped in silver foil from her bag, ate and slowly read:

... Russian emigrée Lydia Delectorkaya, born in Siberia in 1910, schooled in Harbin, Manchuria, married briefly to a Russian whose identity is unknown, was penniless when she left the U.S.S.R. and friendless when

she arrived in Nice, speaking no French. Among various jobs, she worked part-time as a nurse caring for Madame Matisse in 1933. After six months she became a studio assistant to Monsieur Matisse, remaining with him as his companion until his death. One writer on Matisse has said of her – 'Lydia arrived with nothing in 1933, walked out with nothing in November 1954. She gave everything that was given to her by Matisse to Russian museums. When Madame Matisse complained about Lydia Delectorkaya, Matisse wrote to his son Pierre – 'Perhaps even your mother will admit that the wildly acclaimed high quality of my recent painting owes something to Lydia's services. At my age, inspiration is fragile.' Lydia Delectorkaya was not invited to the funeral of Monsieur Henri Matisse. Though she lives in obscurity, she recently published a book on her years with Matisse.

She was glad to know about Lydia's past. All her impressions had been that Lydia had no life except serving Matisse. She had never heard Lydia speak about herself, had never indicated one way or other if she and Matisse shared intimacy of an erotic kind. Neither had he. Her suspicion, unlike almost everyone else that knew them, was that they had not. She glued the accompanying poem, "*Luxe, calme et volupté*" by Baudelaire to a sheet of black construction paper:

> *La tout n'est qu'ordre et beauté*
> *Luxe, calme et volupté*

(There all is order and beauty
Luxuriant, voluptuous and calm)

She glued the poem beside the clipping, cut
two rectangles from a sheet of brown construction
paper and glued them together in the shape of a
cross. She stood up and glued the assemblage to the
front of the refrigerator door that no longer opened
properly. Peter put down his sketchbook and chalk.
He had filled every page. He said he was hungry
and invited her to go with him for a meal. She told
him he could get good delicatessen sandwiches on
Second Avenue, to bring one for her, told him what
she wanted, then added, "Matisse died, you know."

*

When he was gone, she sat with her hands in
her lap. The door was cracked an inch so when he
returned, she would see him before he saw her.
Shortly, she saw him approach the door and reenter
her apartment. Before he did anything else, he
scrubbed some dishes with a new plastic bottle of
liquid soap which he had picked up at a bodega on
the corner. When there were clean plates, he
unwrapped and laid out sandwiches – pastrami on
rye, brisket on a roll, also sour pickles with black
peppercorns clinging to their skin and a cardboard
carton containing warm kasha varnishkas. She
asked, "Do you like strong mustard?"

"If you do."

She mixed a few spoonfuls of Coleman's dried mustard with water and lobbed mustard onto the meat. From a paper bag squeezed among rolls of yellowing newspaper under the bed, she took a bottle of red table wine a student at the League had given her. Peter uncorked it with a rusty corkscrew she gave him. He popped a pill into his mouth. Seeing him crumple up the pager bag in which the food came, she pulled it from his hand and smoothed it out.

"Never waste."

She greedily ate while he turned the sketchpad upside down and, using pieces of pastel chalk, made a few quick close-up studies of the fat sandwich, the hand, the mouth full of yellow mustard and brown meat. He drew her tongue licking the knife blade. When she finished eating, smears of mustard were left on either side of her mouth. Soon the pill took effect, and the slovenly aspects of her room and her person no longer bothered him. He went down onto his knees and kissed the tips of her thick toenails. He cradled her crusted heels in the palms of his hands, kissed his way up her legs. When he got to her mouth, the pill had burst open even more and her passive lips became fat, dancing, living things.

On his next visit, he took a pill on arrival and gave one to Claude to swallow with a glass of red wine. As soon as she fell into a coma-like sleep, he got on his knees and put his head in her lap and wrapped his arms around her legs. He stroked his penis for a while, undid her clothes, then made love to her. Afterwards, while she continued sleeping, he covered her with a piece of fine red silk, cleaned up the apartment as much as he could. He swept the dirt-encrusted rug, poured strong blue fluid into the toilet. When she opened her eyes, he was naked, standing against the window, making a drawing of her in a large sketchbook. A pinching pain in her neck had traveled down to the right side of her buttocks and she smelled ammonia.

While he drew with red chalk, she took the mirror from her shopping bag and put on fresh makeup – cat eyes outlined in green, red lipstick on her puckered lips. She fluffed up her hair, searched for vertical lip lines and eye crinkles. After putting the mirror back into the bag, she curled up on the bed-couch. He continued working while she cut things from magazines, glued cut-outs onto colored paper. She cut out a photo of a giraffe and glued it onto a photograph of the New York skyline. She glued both against a Moroccan design. She wrote with black Sharpie:

A giraffe visits New York.

"Roy took the sketchbook Matisse gave me as a gift for my marriage."

She had become a limp rag, clutching his wrist.

"Please find it for me, *chéri*. I'll let you do any intimate thing to me you want if you do."

Portland, Maine, 1966

The overnight bus left from the Port Authority. The trip to Maine took all day. There was a rest stop in Boston South Station at two in the morning. It was dawn when the bus pulled into the Portland terminal. Peter had a terrible headache, took two Darvon and took a taxi to the address on the envelope Claude had given him. The taxi drove around a group of boxy sky-blue cottages and stopped. He told the driver to wait, got out and knocked at a cottage door. A small woman wearying black opened it.

"I'm looking for Roy Foot."

She had beguiling dark eyes.

"Roy Foot died."

"Did you know him?"

"I'm Rosemary Foot, his widow.

"Did your husband know the French artist Henri Matisse?"

"Did he! He was his protégé. Mr. Matisse raved about his work, wrote a glowing recommendation for him. The letter was his proudest possession."

"Did he ever mention a sketchbook of Matisse drawings?"

156

"A sketchbook?

"Perhaps he might have mentioned taking the sketchbook away from his wife?"

"I'm his wife"

"I mean his first wife."

"I'm his first wife."

"I mean his French wife?"

Peter heard a tea kettle begin to whistle from inside the cottage.

"If you mean the mental case who followed him to New York from Florida, then go ask her."

There was nothing else he could think of to say.

Fernandina, Florida, 1963

Thirty-seven hours later, Peter's taxi drove past Victorian-style houses to the Harbor Marina in Florida. He told the driver to wait while he got out at a restaurant and asked the bartender for something cold and wet. After a few minutes of mixing, he was handed a tall, pink, frosted glass.

"It's made with Russian vodka, Grand Marnier, cranberry, lime and pineapple juice."

He drank it. By the time he entered the coffee shop of the Howard Johnson's motor lodge in Fernandina an hour later, he was woozy. The strong drink started to interact with the Placidyl pill he had swallowed on the bus. He saw a single man in late

157

middle age sitting in a booth eating a pile of lemon-ochre pancakes encircled by crimson rings, like rings of Saturn. The man shaded his eyes.

"Have a seat."

Peter did. The gentleman spoke with a southern intonation.

"Banana pancakes are first-rate here. If you want lunch, the gumbo's primo. I'm Roy's brother, Sam."

Peter ordered a glass of orange juice and drank it, red rings and all. He ordered the pancakes but could not eat them when they were brought, covered as they were with whipped cream and strawberries.

"What happened to the house Roy and his wife built when they left Florida?"

"You mean abandoned, because that's what Roy did. He walked away. So did the woman he brought from France ... but later ... way after Roy left. Our mother gave her money and she went to find him in New York City and she never came back. When we heard that Roy had remarried, we hoped the French lady had gone back to France."

"She didn't."

"The house was empty for a while, then our sister and her husband moved in, bringing his mother with them. After a couple of years my sister died in a road accident and her husband stayed on with his mother."

Peter ordered another glass of juice.

"My brother-in-law remarried and went to Atlanta but left his mother in the house. Very quickly she stopped paying taxes ... she said she didn't believe in taxes. She became demented ... was probably demented all along but you couldn't tell from meeting her because when anyone met her she just sat and knitted sweaters, balls of all colors of wool rolling around at her feet."

"Did Roy and his wife leave anything in the house?"

"They left everything. I know because my sister could move right in. Roy's wife collected all manner of junk that she kept in the house. Only junk seemed to make her happy. My sister put everything into cardboard boxes for Roy, for when he came to get his things."

Peter's eyes were burning because the auras were undulating.

"Of course, Roy never did come back. He died. He and my sister both died the same way, in car wrecks."

"Your brother's French widow claims she left important papers in the house when she left."

"No doubt she did. I tell you, the place was filled with all manner of papers and books, art things and ... well ... junk."

"She has sent me to retrieve her things. I'd like to send a moving van to collect her possessions."

"I'd like you to, son, but ... my sister's mother-in-law who stayed on burned large piles of

159

stuff from the house in the yard before they took her away and locked her up."

He pushed an envelope toward Peter. Inside was a check for $30,000.

"We'll pay her $36,000 to settle the case, but we took out $6,000 to pay the lawyer and back taxes."

Peter took the envelope, canary yellow, amber, salmon rings encircling it.

New York, 1966

Claude was curled up when he arrived at her apartment. He told her, "I feel a pain in the right side of my buttocks after so many hours on the bus."

She grabbed at his hand.

"My *cadeau de mariage* ... *chéri*, did you get it back for me?"

"I tried."

Her face fell.

"*Voleur*! Roy stole it from me. *Ça ne fait rien*! Never mind. All my gifts are gone ... *Peut-etre John Kennedy Jr. pourrait me trouver mon carnet ...* "

Peter held out a white jewelers' box. Inside, two amber and pearl earrings set in gold pressed into a piece of milk-blue velvet. He put them into her hand. She reached for a jar of apple-cider vinegar in which, for safekeeping, she kept the string of pearls she had received from Roy, and dropped in the earrings. Peter was startled.

"Don't worry. I, too, thought that pearls would melt in vinegar, but they don't. No thief would ever think of looking for valuables in such a hiding place."

"No thief could find anything here."

"You're right, *chéri*. I am not very orderly. You see, until I met Roy I lived in a cubical in a convent with a narrow bed. I had nothing except one change of underwear, a breviary, a crucifix and beads. I had not ever seen my face in a mirror except in a shop window *en passant*. I've never had to ... control more than that. I know how to scrub floors but nothing else. No one showed me how to clean a rug."

"You can't live like this."

"Why? I know where everything is. Clutter suits me. Matisse liked clutter, too."

*

When Peter received a birthday check from his father, he took her by taxi to the Stork Club on 54th Street for a lunch of oysters and champagne. Afterwards, tipsy, they walked around the corner to the Museum of Modern Art. Peter led her to Picasso's *Guernica*, his favorite work. He became emotional, moved on to the next artwork, pulled her with him.

"You're impatient."

They came to a painting by Matisse called *Le Bateau*. Several visitors were looking at it, so Claude and Peter stood aside, waited until the visitors moved on, then went closer.

"It's wrong."

"Wrong ... how can it be wrong, it's done by Henri Matisse."

"It's hung upside-down."

"I doubt it."

"I'm not going to argue. I sat for Monsieur Matisse."

"No disrespect but ... this is the Museum of Modern Art! I've read a biography of your Holy Matisse. He used everyone around him. Just like Picasso did. He used you, too."

She walked pridefully toward the next painting. He followed. She turned and hissed.

"The Museum of Upside-Down Art."

They sat in the sculpture garden near to his favorite Picasso sculpture, *The Goat*. She was hungry, so he got her a frankfurter from the café. While she ate, he crouched near *The Goat* and got out a drawing pad. Using a fresh piece of red chalk, he roughed out a drawing of her naked, with *The Goat* superimposed. She looked at the drawing and saw an obscene woman. He angrily told her, "Matisse was a Mama's boy. He only painted because his mother wanted to keep him busy since he spent months in bed."

"What was wrong with him?"

"Imagined bowel disorders. He was a hypochondriac, you know?"

"I can attest to the fact that what he suffered was real."

"He was a coward, too."

"Prove it."

"I read that he went with his cousin to the opera. Their seats were in the very highest stalls. As soon as the opera began there was a fire ... the stage had ignited."

"I've seen fire, too ... licks in peach, black and yellow. These licks spread into flames."

"Matisse thought nothing about helping his cousin. He saved himself. His uncle later said to him, 'You think only of yourself?' It was true. He was selfish and mentally unstable."

"Unstable?"

"Yes, he was subject to hallucinations."

"Hallucinations?"

"He saw things. He was schizoid."

"When?"

"In Collioure in 1906. The book I read told how he practiced the violin in the seaside boardinghouse when his children and wife had gone to the beach. Afterwards, he put it back into its case that was padded with blue velvet. He was dizzy. The room began to swell, so he lay down on the bed used by his children. The walls sweated, the floor breathed, when stripes of blond sunlight came through the spaces between the shutter slats he hallucinated tiger stripes and began to scream."

"Why do you hate Matisse so much? I'm going home. But first the money you owe me for the drawings you made of me. Now."

*

When next he saw her at the Art Students League, he asked her to come to the cafeteria with him. She followed him. He sat when she sat.

"Forgive me, please."

When he began to sketch her face, she laid her hand on his, stopped him from continuing.

"God forgive me. I do respond to you, Peter, but I do not respond to your art. To do what you do you do not need a model. You should go back to Japan and study erotic printmaking."

She got up because she was due to pose at a life drawing class. Since he was in the class, he followed her to the studio.

"If I was George Grosz, would you speak to me the way you just did?"

The instructor told her to undress and sit on a straight-backed wood chair, told the class that they were to do fast drawings. Peter began a drawing that looked like Claude as a goat with teats hanging down. The teacher instructed Claude to change to another position. Peter drew horns on the goat's head, also a gaping vagina-like opening on its underside.

She skipped her next class, went home. She cut squares of red out of magazines, also cut up a piece of white striped cotton cloth found in a trash bin on Houston Street. She sewed small hankies from it. When she did not show up for the next classes at which she was booked, the administration did not know whether or not to fire her. But after they received an unsigned letter suggesting that the school should be aware that the older model, Claude Foot, was sexually harassing male students, following them into the men's room then grabbing their private parts as they urinated at the urinal, they had their answer.

*

The administrator was wearing a very short skirt.

"We can no longer employ you as a life model."

Claude was looking at the skirt, said nothing in her defense.

"Aren't you going to ask why?"

"No. Others will employ me. There are artists ... important ones ... who want what I have."

She stood up. "*Au revoir.*"

She walked purposefully from the administration office but soon slowed her step and sat down on the bench in the lobby near to the bronze Pegasus given to the school by Andrew Carnegie. Inside her Klein's shopping bag, in a bag of its own, was the caramel and beige robe, also the indigo slippers she put on during the five-minute breaks between poses. She took this second bag out and put it in her lap. Soon she dozed off, remained so for the rest of the day. At six o'clock she took the subway home to the Lower East Side.

The next morning she waited at Julia's church for 10:30 Mass to end. She had not been going there for very long while. When she saw seven or eight old ladies leaving the church, she knew Mass was finished. She waited, but no Julia. She took the bus up Lexington Avenue. At Julia's corner was a phone booth. Bringing her shopping bag inside, she pulled the door shut. Reaching deep into a bag, she brought out a little yellow phone book, found the number, found a coin, dialed EL 5-9941. The phone was busy, so she gathered her things and walked to the house.

After pushing the bell three or four times, she applied a thick smear of Turkey red lipstick to her lips. Andy came to the door wearing a starched shirt and tie. On his head, a coral-colored wig. She entered the foyer in which there were a dozen silkscreens of cows propped along a wall. The cows were pink, on yellow backgrounds. A crushed automobile fender painted green and yellow stood at the stairwell that led to Julia's kitchen.

"Ma's not here."

"I was looking for you, not her. I lost my job."

A young woman wearing a transparent plastic dress with a zipper down the back came up behind Andy. She was naked under the dress, a skinny, doughy body, whiskey-colored nipples but no breasts. There were long strips of Scotch tape holding parts of the dress together. Her coral wig was the same as his.

"You can use her in the movie," she told Andy who looked carefully at Claude.

"Would you be in my new movie?"

"If you pay me."

The woman laughed. Andy was cross.

"She needs money, Edie, you don't. She's my mother's only friend."

Edie wrapped a white mink coat around her shoulders.

Edie went ahead and hailed a taxi. Andy and Claude got in and Edie told the driver the address. When the taxi stopped, it had gotten windy. The streets were hectic with rush-hour traffic. Claude followed the twin wigs into an elevator that led into a room decorated with aluminum foil. There were balloons that looked like silver clouds. Everywhere were silkscreens of pink cows in many rows, like wallpaper. One entire wall was filled with Polaroid photographs held up with push pins, each Polaroid of a different penis. A denim-blue bird, alone in a large antique cage, chirped without pause.

167

A very young man with pine-green eyes carried over a table loaded with makeup. He coated her lips with frosted white lipstick, outlined her eyes in jade. Edie touched her hand.

"Strip."

When Claude had dropped her clothes onto a couch, Edie opened a tin of Johnson & Johnson's Band-Aids and covered each of Claude's nipples with a white one. A boy wearing a leopard-skin cape told her to sit on an easy chair that had been upholstered with indigo felt. Andy had been standing behind a camera that was a few feet away. He gave no instructions. A red light on the side of the camera was on, which meant that it was already filming. Soon a naked black man whose penis had shrunk into his scrotum carried over a pan of soapy water, knelt at her feet and began to scrub, heel to toe. Andy watched, said, "No. No. That's not how you wash someone's feet."

He bent down and, using a cloth instead of a sponge, washed her feet.

"See how?"

The naked black man did as Andy had. Claude closed her eyes while her feet were being washed. At one point she opened her eyes and saw, though the camera was still filming, that Andy had wandered away.

When he was finished with her, his assistant gave her $25. Andy returned to stand behind the camera when Claude's co-star began washing a man's bottom using the same soapy water. The assistant smiled at Claude.

"Come and join us for a meal at Max's. Andy picks up the tab."

"I would rather have money and get my own meal."

The assistant gave her another five dollars. Someone was laying on top of her clothes on the couch. She asked the person – not sure if it was him or her – to get up. She got dressed. Someone called out, "Andy, your mother's doctor is calling from the hospital."

Andy said, "You talk to him," and went back to the camera, gazed into the viewfinder.

Claude asked the assistant, "Is his mother sick?"

"Yes. She's in the hospital."

"What's wrong?"

"Yesterday she and Andy were eating ham and cheese sandwiches. Andy went upstairs to make a phone call and heard her screaming, 'I'm going to die. I'm going to die.' He ran downstairs and blood was pouring from her nose. He's not good with blood. He phoned me and I was there in 20 minutes. I called an ambulance that took her to the hospital. They think she had a stroke. Andy's brother is coming from Pittsburgh because Andy can't stand going to the hospital."

"What hospital?"

"St. Vincent's."

*

St. Vincent's Hospital was not far from Union Square. She took the crosstown bus on 14th Street, got off at Seventh Avenue. There was some kind of parade blocking the bus. Marching in it were men dressed in women's clothes, looking like Marilyn Monroe; a few women were dressed in suits and ties, looked like Cary Grant and Paul Newman. She got off the bus, could not get across the street until a dozen black motorcycles ridden by large women wearing black leather jackets and black leather caps had passed.

In the lobby of the hospital was a white marble statue of the Virgin Mary. A wooden cross the size of a human being was hanging beside the elevator on the wall of the cardiac floor. It was a Catholic hospital, like others she had known. Inside Julia's room, a smaller crucifix was on the wall behind the bed; a nun wearing a short black and white habit, a small white headpiece instead of the traditional coif, was tending Julia, whose cheek bones protruded from thin, greenish skin. On the table beside the bed in a metal pan, a scissors, gauze coated with yellow salve. Claude stood at the door; Julia gestured to her to come into the room.

The room's walls were painted pale pink. Julia was hooked up to an IV attached to various machines. Her usually hidden flesh-pink colostomy

170

bag was clipped to the metallic bed frame, its lavender hose disappearing under the blanket. Beside it, also attached to the bed frame, a clear plastic deflated balloon into which bright yellow urine was dripping through a narrow clear plastic hose. Claude asked the nun, "Sister, do you speak French?"

"No."

The nun pinched Julia's hand, told her, "I'll be back with the chocolates your son sent, dearie." She turned to Claude, asked, "Please see to it that she doesn't talk. She's quite a talker and it isn't good for her heart."

The nursing nun left the room. At the foot of the bed was a tripod with a movie camera aimed at Julia. The red light on top was lit. Julia was giddy, her straw-like hair askew.

"Sit, Claws."

Claude sat in the chair that was upholstered with mint-green leather. The hue of Julia's skin was mustard-green, seeing Claude was making her even more giddy, also agitated.

"You know what the priest say at midnight on Easter? He say, 'Risen from the dead, trampling death by dying ... '"

As the nun had pinched hers, she pinched Claude's hand.

"Me die. My heart pop like pop art. Poor Andek. He think I dead. Help me, Claws, I want to go home. He think he no need me but he no know what he need. He need. He need."

"You're ill, Madam Warhol."

"Don't boss me. I'm strong. In Mikova I carry logs, sacks of potatoes, onions. Make me strong for life."

"Then you want to leave?"

Julia nodded, so Claude pulled the needle attached to the IV out of her colorless, thin-skinned arm. A trail of blood trickled from the puncture. Claude pressed the wound with used gauze she took from the metal pan. Reaching under the blanket, she removed the catheter tube.

"You hurt me."

"I'm sorry. I was once a nurse, I must have lost my skill."

Claude also pulled off the heart monitor that was attached to her chest with tape. Claude reached out her hand, Julie grasped it, was pulled her out of bed.

"My things are there."

She pointed to a metal locker that Claude opened, removed her coat, shoes, stockings, dress, scarf, pocketbook. While Julia held onto her colostomy bag, Claude helped her dress. She held Julia's arm and helped her to the elevator bank at which three nuns stood. When the elevator door opened, two policemen got off. After them, she could hardly believe her eyes, Dr. Antoine Robaud got off, bringing back the shock of Lyon. Claude snatched at the sleeve of his white coat.

"*Monsieur. C'est vous?*"

"*Oui.*"

The elevator door closed, with Julia and the three nuns inside.

*

On the way home she stopped at Lamston's 5 & 10 and bought some colored paper, also various eyeliners, rouges, lipsticks, an array of little bottles that contained bright magenta-colored nail polish. Peter was waiting when she turned the corner of her street. He followed her into her building and up the stairways. She let him into her apartment. He sat at the foot of her bed, gave her a package wrapped in a pale yellow silk scarf. He asked her not to open it until after he had gone.

"It's me the artist ... poor as he is ... who is aroused by you. Not me the man. You were right, I am jealous of Matisse, that you posed for him before you posed for me."

He sat beside her and rested his head in her lap. She picked up her sewing. As she stitched, she used his head as an arm rest. Her arm went numb, so she shook him and asked him to please go. He put three bills on her sink. She got up and counted how much money it was – three twenty-dollar bills.

"Perhaps you could leave a little more. I don't know what to do now. Everything my husband gave me has run out."

He left three more twenties, kissed her lips so hard that, when he left, Turkey red lipstick was smeared across his face. So much ice had formed in the freezer compartment of her refrigerator that the plastic door had broken. The ice block had grown so large that not even the cord she used would keep the door closed. She crouched down and unplugged the refrigerator.

She opened the package. Wrapped in the silk scarf, a small framed print of the very last painting Matisse did during his lifetime – *Woman in Blue Gandurah*. It was under glass, framed with white metal. There was also a framed drawing Peter had done with red chalk while she was asleep, entitled: *My Last Drawing*.

Vence, 1943

From the window in Vence could be seen red tiled roofs and the Dominican-run home for disabled little girls. By coincidence, he was always in view of Catholic nuns, touchstones of sorts, more of a comfort even while the war dragged on and on. The villa was set among orange and lemon trees, olive groves and sprawling Dianthus-pink carnation fields. Despite the many shortages because of the never-ending war, the orange and lemon trees leant the landscape a false opulence. He was surrounded by large drawing boards for JAZZ, had been working on a gouache cut-out. Suddenly he laid down the scissors because his fingers had become stiff.

He no longer asked Lydia to pose for him, and she was glad. She assisted while he worked, painted the sheets of paper with gouache in colors he described, erased for him, discussed color with him, organized materials, logged the day's work in a notebook, took dictation. She did not care whether she was happy or not since being a catalyst to greatness took preference over everything else; it had become her calling. She sat down on a chair and wrote with her notebook on her lap:

Today he composed a gouache cutout which he entitled Le Destin. *In it one finds, in the section with blue, yellow and a calm red, a small white couple on their knees, the woman apprehensively pressed close to the man, while, on the opposite page, there rises, dominating them, a figure in black and red with a violent expression ...*

She stopped and smoked three cigarettes in a row, then logged a handful of old sketchbooks that had not yet been catalogued. They contained rough sketches he had dashed off of those who had nursed him during his illness – Sister Annemarie, Sister Paule, Monique Bourgeois, Sister Lameijer.

175

Vence, 1944

On an August afternoon in Vence, during a day of bombings, a piece of flying shrapnel split open an ancient olive tree and sent a twisted twig flying into his open window. The twig landed on his bed sheets. Tears flowed. He was sure he had received a sign that war's end was imminent.

He was right.

While the Allies fought on toward Berlin, France was liberated.

He could not get back to where he was before the war, could not shake the dirt off his roots. He did not want to return to Cimiez, to his view of the sea. Perhaps because his wife had never lived with him in this inland ocher villa, he stayed on in Vence. It had been four years since the magnificent reprieve, four years since Sister Annemarie, Sister Paule, all the others, had asked God to give him more time. Then, he thought four would be enough, but it had not been enough. "I need four more years," he told anyone who would listen.

He'd been restless all day. He spun his wheelchair, rolling backward to take the china cup of tea that Cook handed him. He studied the pineapple listing on the table. Though he admired it, he doubted he would do drawings of it today. No matter. He picked up his cat by the scruff of its neck, dropped it onto his lap and wheeled himself over to the trash bin to scavenge. Since the reprieve, there was a sense of raw nerve about every day. Nonetheless, as contented as he had been in Vence, as ambivalent as he was about Cimiez, he could not stand the heat. Time to go back to Paris?

After the war years without information, he finally received news of the members of his family. While he was safe in Vence, his son Jean had worked with the Resistance, had escaped capture. His other son Pierre had remained safely in New York. He collapsed when he learned that, although they were alive, his wife and daughter had spent months in a Gestapo prison, could not get over the news that Marguerite had been tortured. To add to the news, shortly someone told him that, after so many years an invalid, his wife no longer was. Amélie had resumed normal life. He could hardly believe the irony of it. Now it was he who was an invalid.

Anger and shame aside, stomach pain and neck pain aside, work came first. All day he kept the shutters closed against the burning sun. Though he wore a pair of cool mint-green linen slacks under the lightweight smock, the clothing seemed heavy as rock. He decided for Lydia's sake to wait until her Orthodox Holy Week – fasting, et cetera – was finished, to tell her that they were going to Paris so she could begin the disagreeable process of organizing, packing for travel.

Paris, 1945

The wartime gloom in Paris had not lifted. Many of his paintings had gone missing during the war, could not be traced. It was fitting that the exhibition at the Galerie Maeght took place in the gloomiest month – December – and that it was titled *Black Is a Color*. Whether or not his wife or daughter saw it, he could not find out because, knowing it was an awkward subject, people no longer spoke to him about them. Though he stood off to the side, the gallery owner asked him his thoughts on the color black.

"I use black as a color in the same way as the other colors – yellow, blue or red. This is not a new thing."

He gave as an example of black used well, a velvet jacket done in Manet's painting, *Luncheon in the Studio*, 1868. He described it as " ... blunt and lucid black. Before, when I didn't know what color to put down, I put down black. Black is a force: I used black as a ballast to simplify the construction."

He named another Manet, *Portrait of Zacharie Astruc*, 1866, another velvet jacket, its " ... blunt luminous black."

He thought, mulled, then continued: "Like all evolution, that of black in painting has been in jumps and starts. But since the Impressionists, it seems to have made continuous progress, taking a more and more important part in color orchestration, comparable to that of the double bass as a solo instrument. Renoir complimented me on my 'deft handling' of black."

Later he asked Lydia, "What more could I say about black?

"Perhaps more about what Renoir said."

"I didn't care to explain how much Renoir disliked my work ... that he told me he thought I was a very bad painter, that the only thing that redeemed me was, when I used black, I didn't, like so many other painters, make a 'hole in the canvas.'"

His eyes were stinging, he had begun to crave the visceral penetration that only a model gave him.

"Find me a model."

On the way to the model's cafe, Lydia had a sudden longing to speak Russian. She detoured to a tailor shop run by Russian émigrés. The owner, a former aristocrat, wanted to speak about Stalin, curse him as usual. Lydia enjoyed the sound of the Russian language, let the anti-Soviet rant wash over her. An adolescent girl with round raspberry cheeks, green eyes, reddish hair was mending frayed sleeves of men's shirts. She asked the shopkeeper about the girl.

"She's my daughter."

"Perhaps she would like to earn some money?"

"How?"

"Merely modeling for an artist."

"What artist?"

"Monsieur Henri Matisse, a reputable man."

"Dressed or undressed?"

"Dressed."

"Her name is Doucia. Please pay us, not her, when he has finished using her as a model."

Vence, 1947

Why had he not died in Lyon? He was in bed drawing the window and curtain opposite the bed.

" ... sometimes there is a real split in me: I no longer know what I'm doing, I identify with my model."

He and a visitor were speaking about drawing.

"A voice opens, and from then on I'm only a spectator watching what I do."

He was tense. Lydia asked why he was upset.

"I'm not upset. I'm scared."

He smoked a cigarette to calm himself, then put down the drawing pad, got up and began applying color to the canvas he had been preparing. He told Lydia he would need flake white, cadmium yellow light no. 2, then ivory black, for the body, cobalt violet for the couch, cadmium medium. Also, generally, cadmium red light, strontium yellow, more pure ivory black.

Paris, 1950

His bed, from where he sometimes worked, was surrounded by the usual clutter of china crockery, bolts of colored cloth, some rolled, others half unrolled. There were scraps and curls of colored paper at this feet: azure, chestnut, indigo, amber. An opulent fur-lined pink silk Chinese robe with a high collar made of white fur lay across a chair. He called to Lydia, asked who was booked to sit that morning. The housekeeper answered.

"Madam Lydia is out, Monsieur."

He splashed a few drops of eau de cologne on his neck. His cat leapt up onto his lap and he stroked its thick coat.

The work in progress hung opposite his bed so that he could meditate on it during bouts with insomnia. The background of the painting was not yet right – strontium yellow and cadmium yellow middle no. 3. He had said to Lydia when he backed away to study what he was doing: "A little yellow must more skillfully be incorporated into colors of the body. More yellow on the left buttock until there's a hint of greenish-gray. Remind me of this tomorrow after my model leaves and I'll work some more."

He heard the front door open and close.
"Who's booked this morning!"
Lydia's voice answered.
"A new one."

"Where did you get her?"

"Pablo recommended her."

"Why isn't he using her?"

"She's not his type."

"*Eh bien.*"

Though he had mixed feelings about Pablo, he trusted his judgment on models. He liked and did not like the man. He liked him enough to give him a brace of white pigeons, but had heard the gossip that, while having soup with Mademoiselle Françoise, on seeing a hair floating on the surface of the soup, Pablo had commented, "It looks like a line drawing by Henri." It was ridiculous that such coarseness, such petty jealousy, could rankle him, but the tiny Spaniard was skilled with his little peccadilloes.

He heard the sounds of the arrival of his model and, as it had for his entire working life, a flush of blood coursed through his arteries. Once more there was the possibility of a *coup de foudre*, a thunderclap. He strained to stand in order to properly greet the woman with the small body and deep black eyes whom Lydia showed into the room, but could not garner the strength, so he greeted her from the wheelchair. He gathered materials while the model went behind the Chinese screen to undress. When she emerged, he looked, thought, looked. He abandoned the idea of the Chinese robe. He took in the mismatched, small breasts, the bony hips, the glistening lick of pubic hair.

182

He told Lydia to drape a Turkish fabric across her thighs. Behind her he wanted the great standby, the azure and white-dotted vase. There was something about this model's dour but sweet face that reminded him of Camille. After an initial ripple of pleasure at the reminder of Camille, an ache of remorse bit him. Poor Camille. What a disaster. He would not let the remembrance upset him. What a sad life she had had. The doves cooed. Lydia brought materials, moved into and out of the room. Time had not diluted his gratitude for Lydia's efficiency, indispensability. Not once had he looked at Lydia with complacency.

He wondered if he should rearrange the girl's pose from sitting to laying on a perch of cloth? He craved a cigar. He called Lydia.

"Please remove the vase of flowers, it has lost its freshness."

He instructed the model to lie on her side, hip arched, to curl her arm over the protruding hipbone so that her hand limply hung down. She obeyed his instructions. Her weak, bony hand dangled, the fingertips touched a curled pubic hair. Again, he was not sure about whether to keep or change the pose. He asked Lydia for the Congolese tapestry that never tired him as a backdrop, then turned the page of his drawing book and started a fresh drawing. Despite swollen feet and the reminder of Camille, if this was the last day of his life, it was a fine one. His fingertips were young when he held the chalk; the awaited penetration came.

After an hour he noticed that the model had goosebumps. Discarding the nub of chalk, he called Lydia.

"Please light the stove."

Because he was no longer allowed to drink coffee, he called for the cook to bring tea and, while they waited, the model covered herself. Thoroughly pregnant with inspiration, impatient to begin again, he rolled the wheelchair over to the window to admire the view, not bothered that the birds were cooing loudly. Again he craved a good cigar. When the model had gone, he told Lydia not to hire her again. One Camille was enough for a lifetime.

HOUSE DUST COMES FROM DEAD SKIN

New York, 1970

On the way to his first day in art school, he passed the Russian Tea Room and Carnegie Hall. He discovered a bar on Seventh Avenue that smelled of beer and went in. It had an antique urinal. On its brown papered walls were glossy photographs of opera singers. With a smooth, chrome-colored face, a puzzled expression on it, from upstate New York, still green around the gills though it had been two years since returning from the Vietnam War, John Lightfoot, in his late 20s, drank the cool glass of beer in one go. The bartender, Yvette, was wearing a loose-fitting morning-glory-blue T-shirt over a white vinyl skirt. John's exotic good looks took her breath away; she gave him a second glass of beer on the house, wondering if he was hetero or homo.

He was nervous because he, a Lightfoot, who had never seen a piece of art until a few years ago, was about to study art. He paused on the steps of the Art Students League on West 57th Street, to gaze up at the opulent façade. Just inside, his eye was drawn to a piece of stained glass made of shapes like teardrops done with green, yellow and blue glass. He jumped at the sight of a woman sitting on a bench. Her makeup was cheap, had been applied with a heavy, theatrical hand. Around her eyes were Egyptian cat eyes outlined in black. She was sitting vividly on the end of a mahogany bench in the entrance foyer across from a large statue of Pegasus.

187

The exaggerated makeup was thick, had been applied in layers, like pigment. Her cheeks were rouged; full lips were coated with bright pink lipstick. She was half reading a copy of *Art in America*, half dozing. Several well-worn shopping bags were clustered around her white slingback shoes.

He had seen bums and lunatics and derelicts before but had never seen a mature woman in such a state of exotic disarray. The sight was enticing rather than repugnant. Outlandish as she was, her comportment had not lost dignity; her neck was regal. She had defined cheekbones and alluring wet, gray and cocoa-brown eyes. If he ever was asked to make a human portrait, he would begin with this woman's lips.

Students came and went through the lobby. Female as well as male students did not miss this new student's good looks and more than one set of eyes gave him the once-over. He noticed that, when a student greeted the strange woman in passing, she did not react to greetings. Either she was deaf or aloof. A woman wearing a green hat greeted her. To this one she responded with a few words spoken with a heavy accent. In general, she snubbed people outright, majestically turning her shoulders away with a sleepy look that said she stored grudges like a squirrel does acorns. She seemed to be in her own world, did not have a full grip.

John's classes included watercolor, oil painting, art history, life drawing. The first model on the podium in front of his first class, named Mimi, was in her early 90s and blind. The teacher explained linear perspective, shade, contour, light, proportion, to meld observation and imagination. Mimi took a different pose every 15 minutes. To John, inexperienced at this, drawing a live model was as daunting as solving a mathematical problem. He wished he had had another beer or two to loosen up.

At the break someone told him that Mimi was once a dancer. Despite her advanced age, she could hold any, even an uncomfortable, pose as long as necessary. After a while, she fell fast asleep. John made a few hesitant starts on paper, studied her supine aged form with puzzlement, too inhibited to move his pencil very much.

The teacher of his artistic anatomy class was a tall, patrician man with a wry sense of humor, wearing a gray flannel suit, named Robert Beverly Hale. Hale held two long sticks. One stick had a chamois cloth at the end for cleaning, and the second had a charcoal attached. He explained facial muscles.

"There is a muscle of irony and there is a muscle of anger. There is a muscle of sneering and a muscle of grief. There are expressions of sneering and of grief, and in New York, they are often the same expressions."

189

Through the day he passed the odd woman who had either curled up on her bench in the lobby or was picking at food on a tray at a particular table in the corner of the cafeteria. At both of her stations the battered brown shopping bags brimming with magazines, newspapers and what looked like packages wrapped with plastic or silver foil, encircled by rubber bands or tan twine, were at her feet.

*

This odd woman walked up to John's table and tried to clear away his dirty tray. When he told her, "I don't want any help," she shrugged and turned away, cleared someone else's tray. His drawing book lay in front of him on the cafeteria table. As he should have done but was too uptight to do in his life drawing class, he began a drawing of her upper body using his ballpoint pen. When he put down the pen, she came back to his table.

"May I look?"

"I'm a rank amateur."

She picked up the book, turned the pages slowly.

"Don't be afraid. Your teachers will help you."

*

Late in September, on a day of soaking rain, students clustered in the lobby. Black raincoat dripping and thick blue-black hair glistening, John joined the onlookers who watched as the clownish woman was pulled to her feet by two policemen in midnight-blue uniforms. She was a garish sight, had on pantaloon-like green trousers, a white and green checked jacket draped with a dark blue, mauve and black scarf in flowered patterns and Chinese slippers. Everything she was wearing was wet from the rain. Her hands clenched the unwieldy brown bags. Her overgrown fingernails were painted metallic brown. The woman who worked in the administration office giggled, "Poor dear ... our sphinx without a riddle."

A student who came from Frankfurt added, "I heard that her bags are full of money. Is that so?"

John hurried upstairs because he liked to get to Mr. Hale's class early in order to get a front seat. Once there, he sat beside a white-bearded man who had been in the lobby earlier.

"Sad, sad woman."

"Who is she?"

"She's not friendly. She's been nodding off in the lobby with those unsanitary bags for years now. The joke is that she lives in a penthouse on Park Avenue, gets picked up and dropped off by a chauffeured limousine. "

"Really?"

"I'm joking. Actually, I think she once worked here as a life model but got into a fight with

191

the administration because ... I'm not kidding, this is what the gossip is ... she sexually harassed a student from an influential family. Also she stole sandwiches from the cafeteria. After she was fired, she continued coming to school almost every day, began sitting in the lobby. No one has had the heart to throw her out until now. I heard she modeled for all the artists in Paris in the 50s. Her name is Claude Foot. Funny name for a French person."

The classroom filled up. Mr. Hale entered. He pointed his long stick at the dangling skeleton, then touched the bones of the foot with it.

"Matisse understood the human foot. He said that the foot is a bridge."

Hale moved his pointer up to the skeleton's hip bone.

"The pelvis fits into the thighs to form an amphora."

*

The disco known as Blow-Up was on 49th Street, down the street from the United Nations. John drank half a pint of Jameson whiskey for courage while he paced back and forth in the snowy street watching pretty people arrive. Finally he put up the collar of his indigo peacoat and went inside. He had heard that Blow-Up attracted heterosexuals as well as homosexuals of both sexes. The diminutive writer Truman Capote was dancing with boys and girls in a tangled mix on the cramped, oval dance floor. Blacklight flickered, capped teeth looked bone-white in it. A strobe flashed on and off, making it seem as if bodies had frozen.

A woman with light brown hair cut in a pageboy pressed against him, cupped his buttocks with authoritative hands. John turned around to look, saw smooth-skinned arms wearing a sleeveless burgundy cashmere vest. Emboldened by alcohol, he overcame his shyness and reached his hand inside the armhole of the vest, cupped her warm bra-less breast in the palm of his hand. She uttered, "Stick with me."

She pulled him toward a table covered with empty glasses and an overflowing ashtray, pushed him into a chair next to a man with short salt-and-paprika-colored hair who had a ramrod-straight back, wore rimless eye glasses. Two blond women entwined in each other's thick hair shared the table. She shouted over the loud noise of music, "This is Ben Goldwyn. I'm Alice, his wife. They're Pat Hemingway and Rita von Hoff. Rita is German. Pat is a legend in her own time."

Pat emptied her glass. The man named Ben called the waiter.

"Vodka Negronis all around."

Ben took a long look at John, told his wife, "Let's try to keep this one away from Andy and the vultures."

When icy glasses filled with dark red Campari were brought to the table, John pushed his away, called the waiter back.

"Bring me a beer."

While he waited for the beer, he was curious and tasted the bitter sweetness of Campari and bitters set before him. The taste was wonderful; he drank it down. After four beers and four Negronis he went into a blackout. When he came out of it, he was in a large bed shaped like a Santa's sleigh coated with Mandarin orange shellac in a room painted pale pink and pale orange on alternating walls. In bed with him were Ben as well as Alice.

Alice kissed him and Ben took his penis in his mouth. Beneath them, a peach and willow-green Veronese silk bedspread. Until then John had not known that it was possible for three people to have sex together. This was as close to heaven as he had ever been. The bliss was short-lived because he blacked out again.

When he came to, he was lying on the thin yellow mattress in his tiny, Upper West Side rent-controlled walk-up. Sun leaked through the window, making leopard stripes across the worn wood floor. He had no idea how he had gotten home. In his pocket, a silky business card: *Benjamin Goldwyn*. Handwritten in ebony ink: *We'll see you at Blow-Up on Wednesday. Alice.*

He took a cold shower, soaped the strawberry-colored scratches that had been made across his shoulders. When he looked in the mirror afterwards he found a metallic scab had formed above his lip. He got dressed, drank a quart of orange juice from a cardboard container and walked to the subway downtown. He stopped at the White Rose Bar and ordered a double boilermaker from Yvette, then rushed to class.

Inside the lobby, Claude had reoccupied her bench. When he saw her, the boilermaker was spreading across his insides. He pushed a five-dollar bill into her shopping bag. This was food money for the week, but so what. Without looking up from the *Architectural Digest* she was reading, she chirped, "*Merci, chéri.*"

In life drawing class, a model named Tina was posing. She was exotic, dark, had flat breasts like envelope flaps. The students thought she was from India. The gossip about Tina was that she was once a maid who put the family cat into a clothes dryer and got fired. John was dehydrated and thirsty, more interested in when he would be able to have a cold beer and how he could stand waiting until the night he would see Ben and Alice again, than in studying Tina's breasts, profile, feet, torso.

*

It was late November when John slid one dollar into Claude's shopping bag. She handed him a "gift" tied with ribbon. He slipped off the ribbon

195

and she held out her hand until he handed the ribbon back to her. The "gift" was an ad for Marlboro cigarettes, rolled up. John looked at her closely, saw thick hair, Egyptian cat eyes, bright violet lipstick. She was wearing a marble-patterned halter top, orange and black polka-dotted pedal pushers, white plastic high heels.

Thanksgiving was a few days away. Impulsively he asked, "Would you like to join me for Thanksgiving dinner?

"I might be busy."

"Just come if you're in the mood. Meet me at two on Thursday at the Flame Coffee Shop near Ninth Avenue. You see I have no one ... nowhere to go. Maybe you don't either?"

"I have a friend but I never see her anymore."

He was now spending most nights with Ben and Alice Goldwyn dancing at Cheetah or at The Church or Sanctuary or Blow-Up, afterwards orgasming in their sleigh bed. He didn't like that they would be spending Thanksgiving in Greenwich, Connecticut, with her parents and grown children. When he complained to Alice, she snapped back, "Exactly as I feel when you two are mauling each other and I'm left twiddling my thumbs."

On Thanksgiving Thursday the only thing open on Columbus Circle was a United Cigar Store. A police car was slowing cruising. Walking west from the subway, John saw Claude outside the Flame like a sad tree in the chill wind. Her shopping bags clustered around her legs that were encased in mauve and poison-green harem pants meant more for August than November. She followed him into the long, narrow, overheated coffee shop. She pointed to a revolving glass case stocked with grossly large cakes and pies. He sat her down at a table beside the case.

"What would you like?"

She pointed at the coconut cream cake. He laughed and ordered it, then ordered the traditional Thanksgiving fare. Quickly a small mountain of food was brought – roast turkey, dressing, cranberries, peas and carrots, potatoes. She took up her fork and knife. With care she separated the various foods. One by one she shoveled forkfuls into her mouth. When her plate was emptied, it was removed and a luscious slice of coconut cream cake was placed before her. She picked at it with her fork, then wrapped it along with the leftover bread, butter, sugar envelopes, Sweet'N Lows, paper napkins on the table in pieces of used aluminum foil. These she tucked into the side of a shopping bag. John had hardly eaten, took his leftovers with him in a foil-lined doggy bag.

On the street in front of the restaurant, chalky steam poured out of a grating. It was carried away by gusts of wind. Claude handed him a package. He tore off wrapping paper made with pages torn from *Variety* and *Downbeat* that were taped together. Folded inside was a white silk bathrobe. It was not new. The frayed sleeves and belt had been repaired with minute, almost invisible, identical white stitches. It smelled musty. Half in the chalky steam, he asked, "Do you know Utrillo?"

She nodded.

"Can I tell you a dream I had?"

She didn't say no.

"I dreamed that Utrillo appeared to Ben, a man I know, and insisted, 'Make sure that John paints. Make sure he paints flowers. He must paint three orange flowers, milkweed pods.'"

"I like still life."

"Do you think I should work in watercolor or oil?"

"I can't say. If you chase two rabbits you catch neither. *Je sais* ... you should try everything."

"Maybe I'm a fool. I can't tell Rembrandt from Reinhardt."

"You can tell a pencil from an apple, can't you, *chéri*?"

Paris, 1950

Matisse called out to Lydia to ask who the new model would be.

"I thought it best not to use the same girl as yesterday, the one who reminded you of Camille. Kiki found someone to replace her at Le Dôme."

"*Eh bien.*"

He gathered up pencils and charcoal, a fresh sketchpad. A few early morning sketches done with white pencil on black paper were already piled on the table. The model arrived, a familiar face.

"Have you sat for me before?"

A pale pine-green blush crossed her face. She said, "Perhaps you remember me? I stood in for your nurse after your surgery for a few days at the beginning of the war."

"*Ah oui*! Sister Paule!"

She gloated.

"Didn't I tell you then that you would not die? That I would pray for you."

"You did. I have had nine extra years. Thank you for those."

A rose tint spread across the part of his face visible above his white beard, behind his thick glasses.

"I see you left your order."

"Temporarily."

"You're planning to return?"

"Eventually."

"Will that be possible?"

"If God wills it."

He saw that she had undergone wear and tear. He looked across the room at Lydia, locked eyes with her, then turned back to Paule.

"You've changed your name."

"I'm Claude Boule now."

When she had removed her clothes he saw a body he wanted to draw. The pile of discarded clothes gave off a scent of mildew combined with a tinge of sage. She stood before him face-on, eyes averted. Her breasts were firm, her legs were stocky. She had a round, proud buttocks, squarish hips, a burst of tangled pubic hair, the wide, flat, pinched feet of someone who had never worn shoes that properly fit. Her head was unmistakably French, with a quantity of dark untamable hair. She had a tender, albeit leathery, neck.

*

There was one subject on which Matisse and Lydia always disagreed. His favorite songbird was the nightingale, and hers the starling. Hers, because it reminded her of Tomsk and the piquant sound made when the starlings swirled from the belfry into the sky when the church bell tolled. He liked it that humans had been unable to domesticate the nightingale. He had been working well from his bed against a pile of amber cushions, when he realized that Lydia had gone inside to tell the cook to bring morning coffee and something sweet, also sausage for the model. Claude had said nothing about a cramp in her calf from holding the same position but he had noticed there was a distant look in her eyes. He kept working while they waited for morning coffee.

He told Claude, "This just might be the last day of my life. Or maybe the last day I will be able to lift a stick and expect my arm to control its movement on paper. So be it. I've been given the gift of these extra years. I have you to thank."

To judge from the awful time he had had the night before, and how bloodless he looked, this might really be the last day of his life. He had said very little else that morning. Though people thought of him as unemotional, stiff, there was always a sensual connection between him and his model, like plasma, their milkiness circulated with his blood.

After coffee, he and Claude resumed work while Lydia laid out her cards, playing Patience. The first card she drew was the King of Hearts. She wondered out loud, "Why is the King of Hearts the only king without a mustache?"

New York, 1970

When the robe came from the dry cleaner, John tried it on. He felt like Louis Jourdan, the sexy French movie star. He left it at the Goldwyn's town house in half of a closet that Alice had cleared for him beside her unused fur coats. He was relieved to have completed the commission he had unexpectedly gotten, to paint a mural in a suite on an upper floor of the Sherry Netherland Hotel. He guessed that the commission had come his way through Ben, and

201

Alice. Who else would want to make him happy? He had painted 57 birds along one wall.

At Christmas, school was closed. Ben and Alice took him to the Garrick Theater on Bleecker Street to see Andy Warhol's new film, called *Trash*. A Warhol – *100 Dollar Bills* – hung in the guest bathroom. They and Warhol met often at various parties, traveled in many of the same circles. Many mornings, Alice gabbed to Andy on the telephone. They had just attended Andy's 42nd birthday party, but hadn't brought John with them. They preferred not to bring John anywhere near Warhol or any of his crowd. They had discovered John. He was theirs alone and they wanted to keep it that way.

In the dark movie house, Ben sat between Alice and John. His arm encircled Alice's shoulder, fingers stroked her silky hair. With his other hand, he felt John's crotch as an erection inflated inside his tight pants. Ben undid the gripper at John's waist, unzipped the fly, reached inside the jockey shorts and wound his fingers around it.

In the course of the film, the topless actress Geri Miller could not cause Joe Dallesandro, the dirty-looking, well-endowed star of the film, to get a hard on. She tried jerking him off, tried dancing for him. Nothing helped. She whined and complained that he used too many drugs, tried to convince him that sex was better than drugs. Just when Geri Miller said, "Isn't it great when you come?" and Joe

Dallesandro replied, "No. It's over," John groaned, semen seeped between Ben's fingers.

Later, in the big sleigh bed, Alice demanded that they make it up to her, so each in turn brought her to orgasm. Ben, orally, John, with considerate penetration. When Ben asked her, "Isn't it great when you come?" Alice replied, sourly, "No. It's over."

The day before Christmas, after the Goldwyns left for the Bahamas, John invited Claude to the Flame for Christmas lunch. It was a cold bright day; she was waiting inside the coffee shop when he arrived. He ordered two grapefruit juices. From the inside breast pocket of his peacoat, he removed a flat silver flask. He tipped the silver lip of the flask over his juice glass until blond vodka flowed. He swallowed half the liquid, then added more vodka. He ordered baked ham with pineapple slices for Claude, macaroni and cheese for himself. He laughed at the macaroni and cheese, told her, "In Troy, my mother made macaroni and cheese almost every day. We lived on it."

"Do you mean Troy in ... Turkey?"

John shook his head, topped off his glass with more vodka.

He picked at the food. She ate almost everything, also wrapped his leftovers, plus sugar, bread in pieces of aluminum foil that she stuffed into the shopping bag. From her shopping bag she pulled out a small, flat package wrapped in newspaper tied with purple silk ribbon. She slid it across the table toward him. The newspaper had been decorated with green crayon drawings of flowers and dogs. After removing the ribbon, he pulled out little squares of mustard-green silk fabric delicately sewn together to resemble a Christmas tree. Bells cut from cherry-red fabric had been sewn across the bottom. A little hook was stitched onto the back.

"For your door, *chéri*. *Chéri*, you are an American Utrillo."

He noticed her back teeth were missing. She pointed at a fluffy lemon meringue pie, said to the waiter, "Please?"

When the plate with the pie was deposited before her, there was ice cream on top. She scraped the ice cream off to the side, looked at him and explained, "I don't like to eat cold things. My teeth …"

His shyness had gone. He asked, "Are you from Paris?"

"I'm from Marseille."

"Your family?"

"I was brought to the convent orphanage after my mother died. There was no father. I became a nun to pay the sisters back for giving me a bed and feeding me. When I was a nun I took care of the sick and dying."

He was amazed.

"I nursed people, too. I was a medic in the Marines."

"Once I looked after the sick, now I dream of an angel who would look after me." She poured sugar from the sugar bowl into a plastic bag. "Terrible things happened in the war, things that should not happen to a nun, could not be told in confession. I was ashamed. People helped me, brought me to Paris, told me I could model for artists and earn money. Did you know that I modeled for the Polish painter Alice Hoska and for the French painter Henri Matisse?"

Splashes of ice-blue rose in her cheeks.

"I still haven't been to confession, but I must if I am ever to return to the sisters. You know I'm not a lesbian?"

He could not imagine what had made her say this.

Troy, New York, 1966

John Lightfoot secretly believed that house dust came from dead skin. He grew up in Troy, New York, an upstate town encircled by dark tree trunks in winter where once church bells were cast. Because of his theory, he grew up with an aversion to dust, fearing that if dust got inside him, through his nose or mouth, he would have imbibed human flesh, would be a cannibal. For 70 years it was a Lightfoot who rang the bells at St. Patrick's Church in Troy. He was the grandson of a Sioux Indian on his father's

205

side and a Scots Presbyterian on his mother's. His lamp-black hair was as thick as a broom, otherwise his body was almost hairless. His parents had delayed sending him to school, so he was always the oldest boy in his class.

Like everyone else in high school, he was fearful of the draft. He was the most handsome boy in school and yet he had never had a girlfriend, had not lost his virginity. He was accepted into an upstate community college but did not have the money to go. After graduation from high school, no one offered him a real job because his draft status was 1-A, so he began working as a house painter, working alone, which suited him.

Because his hours were inconsistent, and his white painter's overalls were usually splattered with wet paint, he stopped eating at the kitchen table with his parents and began living on canned spaghetti. He washed the spaghetti down with a quart of Budweiser beer. He slept late and worked late. One day he went into New York City. He wandered past the Museum of Modern Art. He had never been inside a museum. He had heard that paint splashed on plywood was considered art. As someone who had splashed plenty of paint, he was curious.

It took so long to look at each painting, he hardly got farther than the one room. He decided he would go back again soon, but before he could get back into the city, a draft notice arrived. The postman, of course, knew what was inside the envelope and, unasked, told John that the only way to have a say in what happened in the military was to enlist, so quickly he enlisted for a four-year stint as a non-combative medic. He was willing to do hospital work but unwilling to kill anyone in Vietnam or anywhere else. Immediately after induction his thick hair was shaved away.

South Carolina, 1967

He was placed in a field service medical school. Near to the training camp was a constructed village and swamp meant to simulate Vietnam. Training was an ordeal – climbing, shooting, crawling through stagnant swamp water on his belly while the trainer shouted, "Get the gook before he gets you!" When he informed his superior that he refused to bear arms, he was brought up on charges, a court-martial pending. He was confined to the base. While he waited, the rigid training schedule, at which he was mocked and menaced, continued. The drill sergeant liked to push his big red face into John's face, angrily hissing, "I'm putting you on a plane to Vietnam. That's Da Nang, Republic of Vietnam. You'll eat beans and motherfucking C-rations until your ass puckers. I promise you'll come back in a body bag, pretty boy."

A Unitarian minister wrote letters daily to say: *Prayers for you are being said.*

If he had been a Seventh Day Adventist, he could have said, "Killing is against my religion." But, he had no real religious leaning so did not know how to answer the questions. The beliefs he grew up with were visceral, not intellectual, not easily justified or explained. Because he was not someone who could express himself articulately, he stammered repeatedly, "I'm willing to go to Vietnam. I'm not willing to carry an M-16. I'm not willing to shoot a human being."

While he spoke, there was a scaly look in the officer's eyes. John feared that it was just a matter of time before he got orders to go to Vietnam.

St. Albans, New York, 1967

John was assigned work on the large ward at St. Albans Naval Hospital in upstate New York where he encountered injured men returning from Vietnam. Some of them wore necklaces of dried ears that had been chopped away from people they had killed. These necklaces hung over olive drab shirts. Some had returned from Southeast Asia with pseudomonas, a bacterium that caused suppurating infections that oozed bluish, greenish pus. After a short stint in the general ward, John was assigned work in the malaria ward, after a while he was moved to a cardiac ward. Soon he was moved again, this time to an intensive care ward. Often, in this large ward, he was alone with 40 patients who, along with various other needs, had ongoing blood/plasma transfusions and dextrose drips.

He gave shots through the night, brought and emptied bedpans, distributed medications. Snorts and curdled cries rang out up and down the ward. He was overwhelmed with so much responsibility. There were too many lives in his hands. He was 25 and wished he worked in the laundry sorting soiled linen. He was on duty for 12 days and had two days off. At one point on night duty he nursed a sailor from Oklahoma who had burns over his back, backside and thighs. The sailor's name was Hershel, a name he had never heard before. Aware of the acute pain of burn-blisters, he administered generous doses of morphine, rubbed egg-yolk-yellow salve ever so gently over these blisters. He craved a cold beer.

He was alone on the ward. The scales of life and death balanced and re-balanced all through the night. He noticed that Hershel's buttocks were shaped like a ripe apple and that the amber salve used to treat the burnt areas gave its contours the look of a sculpture he had seen in the museum in New York City.

His company was given notice that they were being sent to Vietnam. Just as he had dreaded. Someone told him that if someone dated a nurse with seniority, it might help. He invited a nurse named Virginia Nye for a beer. She was in her late 30s, had

Turkey red hair done in a blunt cut, was about as high up in rank as a woman could be. Her breasts pressed against her starched white uniform when she moved. Her eyes were the blue color of Windex glass cleaner.

He and Virginia drank all afternoon. He woke up on a narrow bed in her tiny private room. He remembered nothing except squeezing an empty beer bottle onto the night table that held a photograph of twin boys around five years old in a small chrome frame. He saw that his trousers and jockey shorts were turned inside out. She was holding a fresh, white uniform, white stockings, white shoes, a white cap. There were gobs of cum on her stomach and thighs. He was not sure if he was still a virgin or not. He remembered nothing

A week later when the date was fixed for his company to be sent overseas, he waited for Virginia after her day shift.

"Would you like to have a beer?"

"When?"

"Right now."

"I'm loaded for bear, gorgeous."

He had not had anything to drink all day, was afraid that he would not know what to do with her. When they got to her room, his balls were shriveled like small fists. She produced a bottle of rum. She took a sip and handed the bottle to him, then unbuttoned her blouse, pulling it back to expose her breasts.

He swallowed a quarter of the bottle before he handed it back. Her breasts rose up as she breathed, had fierce orange nipples. When she told him to taste them he had no trouble doing so. She smoked a cigarette while watching him remove his uniform. She found his shyness alluring. As he pulled off his shoes, then his trousers, she got undressed and leaned back on the bed, began touching herself in a way that frightened him. He drank more rum.

Entirely naked, he squeezed himself beside her on the coarse, green, Army-issue blanket, when she took charge. He realized that Virginia would do it all. When she began to roll like a rocking horse, he shut his eyes.

After that, whenever possible, Virginia and John went to her little oatmeal-colored room and drank themselves into nakedness on the green blanket. She taught him how to pleasure her by way of – as she explained – the "front door" and the "back door", too. She trained him in giving and receiving oral sex. When his squad left for Vietnam he was not with them.

New York, 1968

He took the train down into New York City. The day was his. He walked through the museum room by room, intrigued by everything he saw,

211

wondering how artists contrived to make such beguiling things. He sat in the museum garden wishing he was dead rather than back on the base. From the museum, he walked to Seventh Avenue and took the subway to Sheridan Square to find the neighborhood called Greenwich Village. At a newspaper stand he asked the agent, "How do I find a queer bar?"

The man pointed at a yellow street sign. John read: CHRISTOPHER STREET. His stomach was queasy so he entered a coffee shop and ordered orange juice, tipped rye whiskey into the juice from the flask Virginia had given him. The people sitting at the counter were watching a hanging television screen. On it, a flashing sign: BREAKING NEWS. On the screen were reporters, photographers, a crowd of people standing in front of the emergency room of a hospital. A reporter was shouting into her microphone, "... shot in the stomach ..." Another camera showed a taxi pulling up to the hospital. From it stepped a distraught old woman, her hair covered with a scarf, wearing crooked glasses, a coat with black and white cloud-like blotches. Helping her was someone who looked exactly like Elizabeth Taylor. A voice shouted out, "It's his mother." The camera followed the two into the waiting room.

John watched as he sipped the alcohol-laced orange juice. On the screen, the reporters followed behind the women past another set of doors, into a cubical. The old woman rushed toward a figure in

212

the bed that had been hooked up to flashing machines. The figure had tubes in his arms and tubes in his nose. The face and head were swollen like a round pumpkin.

John added more rye whiskey to his juice. The camera zoomed in on a chair on which were pointed black boots, a crumpled T-shirt stained bright red. The old woman sank onto her knees beside the bed, mooed like a sick animal. The old woman made the sign of the cross over the large head as the gurney was wheeled away. The old woman grabbed the T-shirt and boots from the chair and squeezed them against her bosom as the nurses pushed the camera and reporter out of the room.

Again, BREAKING NEWS flashed on the screen. An entirely different scene in which an anchorwoman stood with a mic in her hand, tall palm trees in the background. The scene showed a crowd outside a large California hotel. The strong sun whitened all the faces. The reporter said with a shaky voice, "Ten minutes ago in the Roosevelt Hotel in Hollywood ... Robert Kennedy was shot. We do not know the extent of his injuries yet ..."

Tears filled John's eyes. He left the coffee shop and walked along Christopher Street looking into the window of every bar he passed. Poor Robert Kennedy. In one window were young men around a pool table. He went in and stood at the bar, ordered rum with a side of Coke. On the barstool beside him sat a man wearing a white and green cowboy shirt with a green string tie. He tried but failed to engage John in conversation.

When the coppery eyes of a young sailor in tight white pants speared him, his groin uncoiled. Was this boy on his way to Vietnam? Was John? Now that Bobby Kennedy was shot, the war would probably never end. John knew what condition boys like that ended up in when they returned from Nam. He drank four shots of rum, made a beeline for the sailor.

The sailor's was named Leroy Waco. He brought John to a one-room apartment on lower Broadway someone had lent him. By the time the door shut, a crescendo of sexual anticipation had built up between then; Leroy pulled off his shoes and pants. When John took him by the shoulder and pulled him close in order to kiss him, Leroy ejaculated, spraying semen as far as the bedside lamp. He was ashamed.

"I couldn't wait one more second. You remind me of Monty Clift."

John did not believe him. He undressed while Leroy put a record on the phonograph – Ravel's *Boléro*. He sat on the bed, watching Leroy finish undressing. When naked, Leroy stood against the door, his erection bulked up again. John went to him and kissed his mouth that tasted like beer.

"You're fast like a rabbit."

He stepped away from Leroy and picked up a ballpoint pen along with a pad of yellow lined paper and drew a caricature of Leroy naked with rabbit ears. When he stopped drawing, Leroy looked at what he had drawn, asked, "Can I keep it? I wouldn't have guessed by the look of you that you were an artist."

"What do I look like?"

"Monty Clift, I told you."

"Seriously?"

"Tonto, the Lone Ranger's sidekick."

"And what does an artist look like?"

Leroy picked up the arm of the record player and set it back to the beginning of the record, replied, "A bad boy, someone with no inhibition, like this music ..."

John glimpsed himself in an oval mirror on the wall. He saw an uptight, red-skinned man. He picked up another sheet of scrap paper and did a quick drawing of Leroy's body, of himself in the mirror looking at himself in the mirror. Leroy was about to get up but John snapped, "Don't. I want to look at you."

Leroy did as he had been asked. John observed that Leroy's eyes were more cinnamon than copper-colored; the skin of his hands and feet were brownish-tan, like sagebrush, but his face and back were more like a mocha drink, more like his own face. He wished he had colored pencils instead of a ballpoint pen that wrote with blue ink.

Leroy rolled over onto his back. Was John seeing right? Leroy's penis was barley brown,

215

circumcised, encircled by maroon and blue veins. He decided that if he was not killed in Vietnam, perhaps there was a teacher back in Troy who could teach him how to really draw Leroy.

South Vietnam, 1968

Virginia arranged for him to receive training in respiratory therapy. She had a bag full of ripe cherries brought to his training session, embarrassing him. When he asked her why she wanted him to study such dull work, she told him, "You may not enjoy this work, but wherever you are in the world after you're discharged, you'll be able to earn a living."

Hoping it would excite her as it had him, he told her about his adventure in Greenwich Village with the sailor. It not only did not arouse her, it repelled her. A few nights later he saw her draped against a handsome soldier from Georgia. She looked at him as if she did not know him. He regretted telling her the truth because he still wanted her protection and liked their frank fucking.

Soon after he finished the course, he was transferred to South Vietnam where he was attached to a hospital used by a helicopter squadron. The heat was awful. Everywhere screamed fat mosquitoes. His squadron was being trained for combat. John was strapped into a fake airplane harness, was ordered, "Jump!"

Sure he would die, he jumped anyway. After more perilous jumps from airplanes and various other trainings, he was assigned to a medevac hospital in which he took X-rays, worked in a blood lab. He learned how to do a tracheotomy by opening up the patient's throat and easing in a rubber tube. He learned how to give heart massage to Code Blue, how to pick forgotten shrapnel out of unhealed wounds. Very often there was a shortage of personnel. One night after a motorcycle accident, he was the only one available, so he took the X-ray, read it, put a cast on the victim's broken bone, sewed up his shoulder.

After three months he was transferred to a small aircraft carrier and began to work on a helicopter that picked up men wounded in combat. He and two other medics triaged wounded until the helicopter was able to return to the hospital. The work was dangerous. It, and the confusing war, were like the hot air always blowing against his face. Because he could not stop scratching his many mosquito bites, some on his arms became infected and these infections would not heal because of the heat and humidity. All the while, he could not tell which Vietnamese were allies, which were enemies.

In bad weather the aircraft carrier that held his helicopter rose and fell. A helicopter could easily roll over and sink like a stone. On a night just before his 26th birthday, his helicopter was radioed to make a rescue. It landed, picked up the victim, a pink-skinned 19-year-old boy with crushed vertebrae who had internal bleeding. John and two other medics strapped the boy in and the helicopter lifted off into white flares and yellow tracers. The boy was wearing a flak jacket. Tight curls of rose-red hair stuck to his forehead.

Barely had John attached the IV when a storm came up, jostling the patient, straining the needle of the IV. The storm tossed the helicopter so violently that the pilot lost control and crash-landed on a beach. The boy died in John's arms. It was not the first death he witnessed but it was the first death he blamed on his ineptitude. Every night, in his dreams, he revisited the boy, trying, but always failing, to keep him alive.

New York, 1971

When John had three watercolors accepted into an exhibition at a gallery on Mott Street, Alice attended the opening wearing a silk Pucci dress that had evergreen and canary-yellow designs she had gotten for the occasion. Ben happened to be away on business, but sent a magnum of expensive champagne to the gallery. Alice kept their glasses full. A skinny man who had coral-colored hair and was wearing a black leather jacket and carried a miniature dachshund steered through the crowd, toward Alice.

"Hi, Alice."

"Hi, Andy. I heard about the shooting. I'm glad to see you alive."

John looked at Andy.

Andy laughed, "If I wasn't stuffed into a corset, my insides would leak out."

Warhol looked John up and down. He asked Alice, "Who is your friend?"

"He's a young painter. Those are his."

Andy aimed his Polaroid Big Shot camera at John. The powerful flash on the camera went off, photo paper rolled out of the bottom of the camera and hung there. Alice reached for it, but Andy got it first.

"Where's Big Ben?"

"Out of town on business."

"Are you sure?"

Alice's cheeks reddened. Andy turned his gaze on John, mumbled, "I've been collecting photos of cocks and balls for years. I even have Alice's husband's cock and balls. Would you take off your pants so I can photograph yours? We could match yours to his."

"Haven't you seen enough cocks and balls?" snapped Alice.

"There are never enough."

He hadn't stopped gazing at John, told him, "Do come up and see me, it's an open invitation ..."

"For once you might take a look at his paintings instead of his dick, Andy."

"I like his paintings. They're hot. He's hot."

John's glass was empty. Hot? Him? His paintings? Didn't they know he was a boy from Troy? He walked away in order to find something besides champagne to refill the plastic glass to calm his nerves. It made him unhappy that Ben was far away. As Warhol passed on, every wine-sipping guest followed him with his or her eyes. Once the excitement made by Warhol's presence had faded, John started looking for Alice. From across the room, he saw that she was in the corner, in conversation with the owner of the gallery.

He wanted a beer. He knew Warhol had flirted with him because of his slinky body, not his art. He said goodbye to Alice and went home, stopping for a six-pack of cold beer on the way. His throat hurt. He stripped off his clothes and started working on a new watercolor.

*

Alice surprised Ben and John with something called a waterbed. It seemed like it would be a perfect complement to their mini-orgies. But, rather than enjoying the sloshing and rolling, it made John's erection deflate. One night, during prolonged foreplay, John passed out from too much drink. In the morning while Alice showered, Ben told him, "Go see Dr. Fishman."

"Who's he?"

"She. A psychiatrist."

"You think there's something wrong with me?"

"Well ..."

"I know what's wrong with me. Frankly, I love both of you but I'm madly in love with you. That you and your wife sleep together, had children together, live together, have lived together for twenty-something years, is driving me mad"

Ben's mouth clamped down onto his. Ben's fat tongue reached as deeply as it would go. Later, he quietly pleaded with John, "Just give it a try. For me ... Fishman will send me the bills. It's Alice who thinks you're coming unwrapped. You can tell Fishman anything, everything ... about us ... don't worry."

Hungover on Tuesday, John stopped at a White Rose Bar on Columbus Avenue and had two beers, then walked over to Riverside Drive. He loaded his mouth with Sen-Sen. Dr. Ruth Fishman's office was on the ground floor in a large, pre-war high-rise. While he sat rigidly on an ocean-blue settee in the windowless waiting room, he heard the sound of a sneeze.

When she opened the door to her private office, John saw that Dr. Fishman had soft, jade eyes, must have recently lost weight because her clothes were too large and hung like clothes on a scarecrow. He entered and she closed the door, told him to sit down. Face to face he told her he was willing to speak about Ben, about Alice, but he was not willing to discuss Vietnam.

"Why is that?"

"No one except those of us who were there understand these things."

"Okay. Do you drink, Mr. Lightfoot?"

"Who doesn't?"

"How much?"

John popped a piece of Black Jack gum into his mouth, jiggled his leg and told her, "I've never counted."

"Why are you here, Mr. Lightfoot?"

"I have a feeling of impending doom."

"I'm told you're an artist."

He shrugged.

"What makes you think you're not a real artist?"

"My God. Just look at Vermeer. Look at Marc Rothko. Look at Warhol, even."

"Let's begin with that next time."

He hadn't remembered agreeing to return to see her again, but did as she suggested. By the third appointment, Fishman suggested he consider studying Sumi-e with a master brush painter at the School of Koho. He was offended: "I'm already going to school." But he was curious, asked, "What is it?"

"Sumi-e is the technique of painting bamboo that has been practiced in Japan for a thousand years. Something about you tells me you might like it."

"I'm not really the Zen type"

*

On the way to meet Ben at the Sherry-Netherland for drinks, John stopped at the Art Students League to see a former classmate's oil painting in a show in the school's gallery. Although he was still registered and had paid his fees, he had not made it to class in months. As soon as he closed the front door against the wind, he saw Claude, looking waxy but no older, staring down at the gray and green ceramic floor. Her dry gray-green-brown hair billowed like an unruly bird's nest. Her eyes were swollen, the cat's eye makeup looked as if it had been applied many days before. He would have liked to add a smudge of cadmium red across the flake white of her skin, touches of black and ultramarine along her neck. She was dressed in pink, leafy green and cornflower blue.

She grabbed his sleeve with claw-like nails, causing him to feel a little queasy being close to what smelled like mildew. She whispered, "*Chéri*, I didn't know how to find you. I'm being expelled from my apartment."

"What's the problem?"
She had not heard.

"What's the problem?"

"I did not pay my rent."

"How much are you behind?"

"Four years."

"My God ... they'll evict you!"

"No. I am an old lady. Why would they evict a poor old lady? Besides, I'm going back to France."

She pulled a legal paper from her shopping bag and stuck it under John's nose.

"Why didn't you telephone me. You're due in court tomorrow."

"I'm intimidated by the phone."

"Why?"

"Because of my accent."

She hung her head.

"I'm not good at taking care of the papers."

*

He left the taxi double-parked in front of the Art Students League while he loaded Claude, along with her shopping bags, inside. At the courthouse on Centre Street, they did not have to wait long to be called in front of a judge.

While John told the judge, "Mrs. Foot is not familiar with our language. She's from France," Claude unwrapped a series of white Kleenex tissues. Inside each, money folded like Japanese origami. John smoothed and counted while the judge pinned her with a grave look.

"You must pay every month ... "

She stood like a cold potato. The judge directed his comments to John.

" ... she must pay the landlord. It isn't that much; she's living in a rent-controlled apartment that costs $47 a month."

The judge let what he had said sink in.

"Do you realize that her apartment is a serious health hazard? Frankly, they'd like to evict her and institutionalize her ... "

Back in the taxi, needing a beer, John asked Claude where he could take her. She told the driver to take her to First Avenue and 12th Street. When the cab stopped and Claude got out, rather than directing the driver to a local bar, John got out after her. She walked away from him, stopped in front of a brick building on 11th Street. When he followed her, she poked his chest.

"Thank you, *chéri*. I must go now, I have much to do."

She walked inside an old tenement building. He grabbed the heavy door before it closed and followed her up three steep flights of steps. At the top of the third landing the door to apartment nine was open a crack.

"Let me see your apartment, Claude."

"Another day."

"I can't help you if you don't ..."

She crossed herself, moved aside. He pushed the door but it only moved a few inches so he pushed until it opened a foot and a half, enough for him to squeeze inside. His eyes needed a minute to adjust to the dimness. When they did, he saw things were piled around the door, which was why the door would not open more than a few inches. She squeezed in after him, stood so close her breasts touched his back. He could feel them tremulously rise and fall because she was breathing heavily.

It was a studio with a tiny kitchenette. Clutter was everywhere: full shopping bags, piles of newspaper, cardboard cartons, tangles of clothing and cloth. The decorative style might once have been Moorish but had decayed. There was a pathway through piles of newspaper and clumps of clothing that led to the place where she slept. When he crossed the room, whatever he was stepping on crunched. A brackish smell pervaded; he was nauseous, began to panic. The place was coated with heavy dust – a kind of bacteriological film. The only area where he was able to stand was near the bed. Newspapers were scattered on the floor and what had crunched was under them. Assorted bottle caps, loose change and clothespins had escaped from under the newspaper. The room looked and smelled like decomposed soil.

Where there were no newspapers, what once must have been a rug had deteriorated into sorrel-colored sand. The sleeping place was a fold-out couch. It was so worn in the center he could have put his hand right through the thin mattress. He could tell from the indentation in the mattress that she slept on the left side of the hole, curled around it. He made his way to the bathroom. She followed. The bathroom walls were painted black. He looked into the tub, saw it was awash in blackness, filled with oily sludge or water. Orange peels floated in the water.

"Orange peels give ... perfume ... ah ... fragrance," she mumbled.

A scattering of dead plants could be identified in the debris. A long dead tree leaned against a pile of something in a corner of the room. There were drapes covering the single window. They were made of a material that had rotted and disintegrated, had once been bolts of various fabrics. Almost everything in the room had turned chestnut brown. When he touched one of the bolts of fabric, it fell apart into dust mixed with thread. Panic and nausea were increasing. Chunks of ceiling had come down, plaster had broken away from the molding, was swollen and hanging. He backed toward the door, in a hurry to escape.

"What happened to the ceiling, Claude?"

"There was ... *une fuite*."

"Leak?"

"Yes. A leak."

"Didn't the landlord fix it?"

"Don't be silly, *chéri*. When *le propriétaire* ... the landlord tried to get in and repair it, I wouldn't let him in."

"When was this? "

"Five years ago."

Claude wrung her hands that were zinc yellow in the muted light.

"I made a life of my own. They want to take it away. Help me, John."

*

The next day, after John got over his hangover, he telephoned the city-run agency Protective Services that was meant to look after the elderly. He made no headway on the phone, so he went to the office. The receptionist sent him to a social worker, Miss Sheridan, who told him, "We have a big file on Mrs. Foot."

She went into the files and found a folder that was marked DIFFICULT. After she glanced at it, she handed it to him.

"It would help so much if you would act as an intermediary with this difficult woman since we've had disastrous dealings in the past. Would you?"

His silence meant no.

"I'll send a case worker. Could you at least be there when my worker arrives?"

"I'll do my best."

After he left, he walked aimlessly for a while, ended up on Fifth Avenue. He turned west on 14th Street, heard a blunt thump, realized that a crosstown bus had hit someone. He rushed over, pushed two people who had rushed to the scene aside, saw it was a gentleman, shouted, "Don't move him, don't touch him. His neck might be broken. I'm a medic. Call an ambulance."

He knelt and cradled the fallen man's head in the palms of his hands. The victim was about Ben's age, was wearing a butterscotch-colored cashmere coat showing flakes of dandruff on the shoulders. Colorless eyes looked up at him through gauzy film. Of course he must surely be in severe shock. John held his head until the man's eyes closed. Ten minutes later, the ambulance and the paramedics from St. Vincent's Hospital arrived and confirmed what John already knew.

*

In the morning *New York Times* there was an obituary for a music critic named Karl Castro who had been hit by a bus and killed on 14th Street. He must be the one. Noticing that a funeral Mass would be held at St. Paul the Apostle's Church on 59th and Ninth Avenue, John dressed and took a taxi there. The Mass in the ill-lit church was almost over when he entered, so he stood at the back of the church, frightened by the atmosphere in the massive space. He had never been to a Catholic Mass before. Once it ended, people milled. John asked the priest to point out the next-of-kin, who turned out to be a middle-

229

aged woman wearing topaz and silver earrings, very much like his own mother's earrings. The priest explained she was Castro's sister. When there was a pause between those wanting to offer condolences, John walked over to her.

"I was with your brother when he died," he whispered. "I came to reassure you that Karl Castro didn't suffer ... "

She twisted the silver ring on her finger, went ashen.

"To give you some comfort, be assured he died peacefully. I was holding his head when he went."

When he got home with a bottle of vodka, there was a message on his answering service to call the new gallery on Mott Street that was showing four of his new watercolors. He took a mouthful of vodka from the bottle, dialed the number, got the assistant to the owner on the phone, who said there had been a sale.

"Which one sold?"

"All of them."

"To whom?"

"The buyer wishes to remain anonymous but thinks you're a wonderful watercolorist, wants to see more of your work. My boss did want me to tell you, though, that your colors, sexy as they are, could be even sexier. Keep that in mind when you bring me more."

After hanging up he went to his refrigerator, grabbed a metallic ice tray from the freezer, banged it against the sink until ice cubes came loose. He filled a bowl with ice and turned to the first page of a new pad of good watercolor paper. Before he could put down his first touch of color, a call came from the agency that a social worker was on the way to Claude's address. He put his unused brush into a clear glass of water and left.

After grabbing a couple of drinks at a tiny Skid Row bar on First Street and First Avenue, he paced up and back in front of Claude's building, watched while two hot men moved a piano into a pickup truck. At two a heavyset woman with blond braids that were wrapped around her head stopped in front of the building. He told her who he was, and she told him that she was the visiting nurse appointed by the city.

He led her up the stairways and stood beside her when she knocked on Claude's door. There was no response. She was about to knock again when the door cracked open. Claude's freshly made-up face appeared in the crack, a too-sweet look on it.

"You can't come in."

John excused himself and squeezed into Claude's apartment. He held his hand across his mouth, did not want to breathe in the dead skin. He spoke through his fingers.

"I went to a lot of trouble to get her here."

"She looks like ... *une Nazie*. I'll never let her into my home."

The social worker craned her neck to look into the apartment. She did not look long.

"I'm afraid I must send for a truck and laborers to shovel all that stuff out. It's a danger to you and to everybody in the building, Mrs. Foot."

John watched as Claude's pink arrogance was washed away by an icy pistachio shadow.

"*C'est ma vie. My oeuvre.*" And she tried to shut the door in the nurse's face.

John felt nauseous. He observed the huge mound of junk, his eyes took in the pile of decaying brown bolts of fabric. Seeing how he was looking at her fabric, Claude spat at him.

"That fabric is still good. I can cut around the bad parts. You Americans think everything that's not new should be thrown into the garbage. If that's so, I should be thrown away and, in 20 years, you should throw yourself away."

The social worker tried to push the door in order to get inside, but Claude blocked her. Before Claude could shut it in her face, the nurse stretched both arms through the space in the door, took Claude's heavily made-up face in her hands, pushed her own face up almost touching it.

"Listen, Madam. If you don't cooperate, I can pick up the phone and have you taken to a city home right now. The place is a danger to you and to the other people in the building. You have to pay attention to what I'm saying. We're trying to help you."

Claude pulled her chin out of the nurse's hand and tried to push the door closed, but the nurse put her foot against it.

"Look at all the dead plants. You know what happens when the plants die? Who do you think dies next? Answer me ... "

Claude was stronger. She pushed the door shut in her face, trapping John in a tomb of dead skin until the sound of the nurse descending the stairway was no longer audible, then she opened it again enough for him to squeeze out.

*

An envelope decorated with a thick black border drawn with charcoal came in the mail. Inside was a note on lemon-colored paper:

> *Dear chéri,*
>
> *Why did you bring that person to my home? They want to take away my life. They want to upset my oeuvre. Like my husband, you look at something but do not see inside. You Americans wash and sanitize so much, you washed away your vital bacteria. Have you forgotten that I'm not an American? If I see you on the subway in the time before I go back to France I will throw a brick at your head.*
>
> *Claude Foot*

233

Cimiez, 1951

Finally, he finished a painting – *Woman in Blue Gandurah*. It was the first he had been able to take to completion since 1948. He was exhausted. To catch his breath he worked on cut-outs, sketched and did drawings, doubting if he would ever have the stamina to again complete a painting.   No one wanted to tell him what Jean Cocteau had said about him: "The sun-drenched Fauve has turned into a Bonnard kitten." But he found out anyway.

Eye spasms returned.   The pain was excruciating.   One of his models told him about an acupuncturist living in Paris, an Indonesian.   He was willing to try.   Needles were inserted between his big toe and smaller toes, into the webbing of his feet. They were wiggled and left for an hour and 10 minutes, then removed.   The acupuncturist with the shiny maroon face had brown rings around his black eyes.

"I need to open your liver channel.   The pain is connected to your liver."

When the doctor left, it was as if he had rowed a boat for an hour.   He sank into a dreamless sleep, the deepest he had experienced in 60 years. When he woke he called to Lydia.

"Bring my sheers, bring paper ... bring the sheets you painted with flat black paint, sheets painted plum red as well.   And ... all the blues you

234

have – powder blue, cornflower blue, robin's egg blue, azure ... "

The acupuncturist's promise was kept, the eye spasms abated. Matisse could work. He called the newest work – made from cut paper – *The Swimming Pool*. He tried to contain it but it ended up over 7 feet high and over 4 feet wide. Unfortunately, within a month, the eye spasms returned. So Lydia arranged for the acupuncturist to call again. This time, when he had gone, Matisse did not feel sleepy. He called for his shears, began work on *The Parakeet and the Mermaid*, which came to exceed *The Swimming Pool* in size. Eleven feet high, 25 feet wide. This time the eye spasms were worse than before. One moment he saw Lydia clearly and the next he could not see her at all.

She told him, "You are not the only one experiencing heavy weather. Pablo has pneumonia. Marc Chagall's wife has fallen in love with another man."

New York, 1971

Out of curiosity, John went to an introductory class at the School of Koho. Flute music played and tea was served. Colors were prepared out of ink sticks made from pressed pine. John was shown how. He ground the charcoal-type Sumi-e stick on stone and mixed it with water. He ground down

Alice, the faces of the soldier he had failed to keep alive from his lack of talent.

Invited into another group show in Greenwich Village, he gave the gallery two of his newest watercolors. They were erotic renderings of Ben and Alice. Both sold at higher prices than his previous work. When Ben begged him to drink less and paint more, John said nothing, just put his arms around Ben's neck and pulled him close, stroked his neck, told him he had he found a studio for himself on Canal Street, asked Ben to pay the rent.

The day he moved into his new studio, he quit therapy. When the new session at the Art Students League began he did not sign up because he was establishing a new routine – painting and drinking in his studio all evening, drinking and looking at art books, color charts, all night, sleeping all day. There didn't seem to be any time left for class.

Two times a week Ben visited at lunchtime for an hour of sex. Every Thursday John met Ben and Alice for dinner. Afterwards, he slept between them.

One afternoon – unexpectedly – Ben threw open the door to the studio and said he had taken the afternoon off. After making love – every orifice still singing – they walked toward the Lower East Side. The sky was the color of green marble. Ben wanted John to taste blintzes at the Second Avenue Deli. On 13th Street, John's eye was drawn toward someone coming toward him who was wearing singing colors – quinacridone magenta, cadmium lemon, cobalt, violet, deep crimson. When the blots of color were close enough, he saw it was Claude Foot. She was steadying an old lady with a black and puce scarf over her head and a shabby yellow and blue flowered housedress that was ripped under the arm.

The old lady beside Claude seemed either drunk or deranged. She wore glasses and all he saw of her face looked like an old, bleached pear. The old lady ranted and raved in a madly emotional voice. When they got close enough, he heard the old lady speak with a heavy accent, "I known to tame wild dogs that ran through my village from out of the forest. My technique ... show no fear, make no quick movement, let it smell me as long as it liked. If the wild dogs ran in packs, that another story. Once a pack came to my village ... terrible ... until live chickens thrown among them. Chickens ripped into pieces by teeth like razors. Only then did the men in the village shoot dead every wolf in the pack."

The old woman stopped and looked at Claude.

"Are you listening, Eva?"

"*Oui. Oui.*"

"I never forgot that day because it was the day Nono gave me a big drink of spirits. After, I curled up against the oven like a dog and slept. My back burned so bad the skin peeled away in a sheet like the skin of an onion ... "

Claude steered her companion west onto 15th Street, then up the steps of St. Mary's Byzantine Church. Ben steered John south where they passed five- and six-story brick buildings with fire escapes, vacant lots, Polish and Jewish delis. Ben's long fingers inched down the back of John's jeans.

"You take my breath away. I hardly know my own thoughts when I'm with you."

At Lanza's and Veniero's old Italian bakery, Ben bought a loaf of fresh cornbread to bring home to Alice. He ate a slice and gave John one. The bread was warm and delicious. He had never tasted cornbread. John caressed Ben's belly suggestively; John said, "Let's go back to the studio."

"I've got a better idea. Let's hop a cab uptown and surprise Alice with warm bread and warm men. She was in the mood for some action this morning when I left for the office and I promised she would get her rocks off before the sun went down. I'm a little early, the moon hasn't yet come up."

John put his hands in his pockets.

"I'm having enough trouble with her scorekeeping. Oh, Johnny, please don't you give me a hard time, too."

*

On the first cold night, John joined the Goldwyns for dinner at the trendy Upper East Side

238

restaurant Laurent. Ben asked him, "What are you working on?"

"With cobalt yellow. Black with gold, Egyptian violet."

"I didn't mean with, I meant on."

"I'm doing small watercolors. Sexier than ones I did in the past. A dealer told me that my work could be sexier."

Alice said, "I wish you'd work larger rather than smaller."

Ben had his eye on the young waiter while coffee and stingers were served. Alice called for the check, told John, "We've got to get back up to Connecticut. My mother has had a stroke."

It had snowed, there were blue reflections in the snow, emerald-green illuminations as the lights of cars and busses went by. Ben pushed a fifty-dollar bill into John's hand.

"Go out. Have fun."

John turned away, didn't say goodbye. He hailed a cab, told the driver, "The Volney Hotel."

He walked through the stuffy, old lobby of the Volney, a mostly residential hotel in the east 70s, into a small club called Chez Pat. At the black polished piano bar, he sat next to a white-haired queen who had mustard-colored eyes. The man was drinking a Sidecar, said to the pianist, "Play 'Dancing on the Ceiling'."

The pianist played. The gent sang along:

"I love my ceiling more, when it is a dancing floor ... "

When the song ended, he asked for "Satin Doll".

The pianist complained, "How old do you think I am? I'll play 'Suzanne' ... the one about the bread and oranges that came all the way from China ... "

But seeing the sour look on the old man's face, he switched to the show-stopper from *Gypsy*. The old man's drinking partner was named Paul van Katz. When John and he were sufficiently drunk, John put his arm around Paul's shoulder. They staggered out into the snow and got a taxi. John told the driver, "33 Union Square West."

The driver could barely see because the snow was so thick. Finding Union Square, they got out. They were on the wrong side of the square, so they crossed the park through fresh snow. At number 33 they took the freight elevator to the sixth floor, where a life-sized, stuffed Great Dane greeted them. A party was in progress between piles of cardboard cartons, each labeled in black marker with a date and its contents. An assortment of drugged and drunk people gathered around the television waiting for what had been promised – a moonwalk. John did not have to look for Andy because Andy found him. He was wearing a navy blue plaid shirt, carried a can of Pepsi

"Are you ready for your close-up?" he asked John.

John laughed. Hoping this meant yes, Andy said, "Let me get my Polaroid."

It meant yes. Paul sat down on a white couch and watched as John removed his pants, and underwear. He left on his black T-shirt and leather jacket with the off-white lambswool collar that Ben and Alice had given him for his birthday. Andy handed the dachshund to Paul, told him, "Hold, Archie," and began shooting photos of John.

"That leather jacket with the wooly collar and no pants is fabulous. Hot. If you feel like jerking off, do it. But do it so that I can smell your crotch."

John asked, "What would you want me to do to you?"

"Nothing at all. I'll take care of myself like I always do. I don't really like being touched."

John gestured toward Paul, who had sunk into the soft couch clutching the dog. He told Andy, "I've got a date ... a date for supper ... maybe my last supper."

Andy took Archie back. While John dressed, Andy looked at the photos, put them into a paper bag. When someone shouted "Moonwalk," Andy said, "Come back tomorrow, Red Cloud," and wandered away.

Outside, it had stopped snowing. Paul steered them to a room at the Albert Hotel in the Village. He laid a fifty-dollar bill beside the bed.

While John used the toilet, he took off his clothes, slid the blanket up to his neck. John asked, "What do you like?"

"Let me explain. I live with my mother. Years go by between these urges like tonight. Usually I'm seen with ... high-profile women like Faye Dunaway. The actress. Gloria Vanderbilt ... the ... I don't know what she does really except that she's a Vanderbilt."

"I mean what do you like ... sex-wise?"

"Nothing cruel."

*

A large, baby-blue box was delivered to John's studio from Bonwit Teller. Inside, an opulent, white terrycloth bathrobe sent to him by Paul van Katz. After his shower, he wore the bathrobe and sketched on watercolor paper with a pale pencil. The first sketch was of John penetrating Ben as Ben dragged his tongue across Alice's neck. The next, John kissing Alice as Ben leaned his face against John's ass. What colors to use? Ben was ebony, caramel, spruce, tan, merlot, white chalk for hair, soft and melting. Alice was oatmeal, buttercream, amethyst, mocha. He saw himself done in sagebrush, clay, primrose, teal blue. Once finished, these watercolors sold at an even higher price. Again, the buyer asked to remain anonymous.

John took to holing up in his studio with a case of Popov, painting, brooding, waiting for Ben. The morning that Ben had a bunch of lilacs delivered, John was so hungover, the flowers wilted in the sink because he forgot to put them into water. The next week, Ben called to tell him that Alice's mother had died. After the funeral they were going to Connecticut.

John asked, "Are you two going to fuck without me?"

When Ben snorted, John snapped, "I take that to mean yes."

"Johnny ... we're married. We're going to a funeral."

"Then you won't mind if I go out to the trucks?"

"Naturally *we'll* mind."

"We'll! Can't you speak for yourself?"

"I ... will mind ... but things being what they are, I can't ask you not to."

The sound of an ambulance made it impossible to hear. After the sound died away, he heard Ben say, " ... we'll be back on Thursday, would you meet us for dinner at the Laurent? Come home with us afterwards?"

"What time?"

"Nine. And ... it would be nice if you shampooed your hair."

John laughed. He stroked his long greasy hair. Ben said, "I love you, Geronimo. I gotta go. By the way, Alice's mother didn't suffer. She died in her sleep. Thanks for your sympathy."

John unplugged the phone, drank all day. Around midnight he walked west toward the docks, went into the Eagle's Nest. He drank straight vodka and watched a naked man who was wearing a brimmed cap climb into a metal bathtub-like trough. One by one, leather-clad men walked over to the trough and urinated on this man. John finished his vodka, pissed a long stream of urine into the naked man's face and left. Close to the desolate pier he found a parked tractor-trailer, barely discernible in the scanty light, in which 20 men were in various permutations of sexual contact. Someone whose voice sounded familiar, like someone from Andy's factory, offered him a new drug.

"It's pink, it's psilocybin."

He swallowed what was handed to him. His penis was sucked into an anonymous mouth. At the same time, the man attached to the mouth was being sucked by someone else. Simultaneously John stretched out his other hand, felt a strong hand directing his fingers into a hot, wet ass. Quickly his fingers were suckled deeper. When one of the men began fist-fucking him, he let out a cry of pain.

At dawn, like a tired swimmer who was being dragged by the tide, he washed up onto the deserted platform of the subway at the Christopher Street station. He watched as a train burst out of the tunnel. The brake noise sounded like a scream. He looked at his watch. The watch face was breathing, was the face of a squirrel; the hands were whiskers. He watched three trains enter and leave the station, timed them. He figured how long he needed to have the timing right so that his body, not his legs, would be severed when he let himself fall onto the tracks. He smoked a joint and sat down on a bench. He wrote Ben's name and address on the small pad he kept in his back pocket. He began a sketch of Ben, but turned into a jellyfish before he could finish and the notebook slipped behind the bench. Soon a train stopped in the station. Two drunks got off and stole his wallet, his shoes, his belt with silver studs, his brown leather jacket. His jellied insides jiggling, gurgling all the while.

LAST SUPPER

At sea, 1980

His hair had grown down to his shoulders. It glistened with oil. The cargo ship on which he was traveling went through the Suez Canal. It crossed the Indian Ocean. It rounded Cape York. He had not had a drink since he boarded in Brooklyn – dead drunk. It docked for a two-day layover in Jeddah on the Red Sea but no one was allowed ashore. It remained at sea for 49 days. He painted the same spray of dead blossom and the same stalk of bamboo on a rice paper scroll over and over. On deck he sketched the Yugoslav sailors and Filipino deckhands as they worked.

One evening, a small honey-colored deckhand remained after the others went below. While John sketched him, the boy reached his brown hand inside his pants and began to masturbate. John reached inside his own pants and did the same. The boy satisfied himself with barely a ripple of expression and immediately ran down the steep ladder.

Every night after that, until the ship reached Australia, the two met on deck and slipped inside the canvas-covered lifeboat. When John disembarked, the deckhand gave him a medal with the pinkish face of St. Christopher on it.

Paris, 1980

From Sydney John flew to Tokyo and then to Paris where he stood in front of Monet's *Water Lilies*. He walked in the Tuileries. Hidden among locust trees stood a bronze statue of a man with lowered eyes. His sword was broken in two. Despite a steady drizzle that began falling, he walked over to a gallery that was having an Andy Warhol show – "Portraits in Blackface and Piss Paintings". The canvasses were blotched gold, citrus yellow, green because urine oxidized on contact with copper or gessoed paint. They looked like Rorschach tests but were beautiful, too. Not able to keep his unruly, thick hair out of his face and food, he had begun to braid it. In keeping with this look, he wore a turquoise-beaded headband traded with a hippie for a drink, Indian-style.

When he'd had enough of Warhol's work, he went to a bistro, sat at a corner table. He pulled out his tattered sketchbook and looked at the many drawings he had made. Among the stalks of bamboo and drawings of his deckhand, were drawings of Ben, of Ben and Alice, of himself, Ben and Alice in various stages of copulation. He began a drawing of Ben kneeling over Alice, when the waiter asked, "*Monsieur?*"

"*Café au lait et pâté.*"

The waiter grimaced. "*C'est pas possible ...* "

A woman at the next table overheard and laughed. She was fair-haired, pale, was washed in mocha in the bad light. She looked German or Dutch or Scandinavian rather than French. She spoke to him in Spanish. He shook his head. She spoke to him in German. He shook his head.

"Are you English?"

She spoke with a sexy accent.

"No."

"No? But you've just answered me in English."

"I'm an American ... one of their downtrodden Indians. My grandparents were Sioux."

She laughed. "Big Horn, then. The waiter thinks you're crazy."

"Oh?"

"You can't drink coffee with pâté. It's un-French. He wants to bring you wine or beer."

"I'm on the wagon."

The answer did not satisfy her.

"I'm drying out. I haven't had a drink in three months."

She called over the waiter, spoke rapidly to him, then got up and sat in the empty chair at John's table. The waiter returned with two glasses, a bottle of Badoit and a bottle of red table wine.

"It's what children drink with meals from age zero."

The waiter brought a plate on which was a hunk of pâté, also a basket of yellow bread.

"There's barely any alcohol in regular table wine, not enough to intoxicate a gnat."

John picked up the glass and smelled its sourness. This was how Alice Goldwyn smelled most mornings.

"If you're worried about drinking too much, I'll mind you."

She picked up his sketchbook. "May I look at your sketchbook?"

He didn't say yes, didn't say no. She raised her glass. "*Prost!*"

He watched while she examined his work. Her wool scarf was English green. Her eyes were cinnamon-colored with glints of magenta and citron. That she was looking at his work made him tense. When she finished turning all the pages of the sketchbook and put it down, she raised her glass to him in a salute and pressed her knee against his under the table. She was wearing a string of poppy-red glass beads. The wine reminded him of Alice and when he thought of Alice he thought of Ben. How could one sip of wine hurt?

New York, 1986

While he lived with Maria, the Swiss woman, in her small apartment in Paris, it seemed like he was able to control his drinking if he stuck with wine. She was rarely home because she had to travel often

252

to Geneva. She called him "Wounded Knee" and made sure he had everything he needed. It made her happy that he was such a homebody. At night she would close the shutters that were blue with time. He held onto her at night while he slept, like she was a life-preserver and he was in deep water. She kept him in big, coffee table art books and free passes to the Louvre. He filled piles of sketchbooks, liked to look down at the violet headlights of automobiles at night.

When his mother died, she bought him an air ticket to New York. Once back in New York, though he tried, he could not stick to his wine regime and went back to vodka, could not stop drinking. The first thing he did when he came to in the middle of the day was to pour himself a drink. The last thing he did before he passed out – usually at dawn – was to refill the glass. His face remained russet. He trimmed his hair using a small nail scissors. He was desperate for cash and cast his eye around the studio for something to sell. He remembered the pile of drawing books and framed watercolors covered with a paint-splattered drop cloth. He went through the books, wondering if he had anything that he could sell. He remembered that Warhol liked his erotic watercolors, so he picked out two, wrapped a pillowcase around them. He put on a pair of tight black chinos, a tight black T-shirt, knocked back the quarter bottle of vodka and took a taxi to Warhol's house on the Upper East Side.

Warhol's Asian maid opened the door, asked his name and told him to wait in the living room. He suddenly had an awful headache. He stood among dozens of shopping bags that filled the entire room. There were also marble statues, busts – Napoleon, Ben Franklin – a painted carousel horse, cookie jars, piles of familiar file boxes numbered and dated with black marker, crates, Navajo blankets, a pinball machine, birdcages, a carved and painted Indian, the kind that stood in front of the cigar store in Troy to whom he had been likened to. Across one entire wall John noticed a huge painting of *The Last Supper*, a kitsch copy of Leonardo's. It was made up of panels. It struck him that if he did not get back to work soon, all his ideas, like the Last Supper idea that he'd mentioned to Andy at the gallery opening years before, would be appropriated by other artists.

Looking ill, his face a mix of flour and water, Andy came down the stairs. He wore an oyster-gray wig, was glad to see him.

"Hi."

John unwrapped the two paintings.

"You once said you liked my watercolors. I'm broke. If you feel like buying them, I wouldn't say no."

Andy looked at them.

"Sure."

From the bluish cast to Andy's face, the tension in it, he realized that Andy was suffering. As a former medic, John guessed it was a gallbladder or stomach problems, or perhaps after-effects from his shooting. He pitied him. Would Andy let himself be taken to see a doctor by him? Probably not. He seemed so stoic. If John had morphine and a syringe he could easily take away his pain.

Andy reached into his pocket, handed John five twenty-dollar bills.

"Will this help?"

John took the money.

"You look like my cigar-store Indian. You make me want to do a series of paintings of cowboys and Indians. When I'm feeling better, I will."

He handed John another $20.

"Thanks for the idea."

John pointed to *The Last Supper*. "How about that idea?"

Andy smiled, peeled off two more twenties.

"Oh. Thanks," added, "I gotta lie down."

On the way back to the studio John picked up a bottle of Popov vodka and settled in for the day. The studio – its smells, canvases, brushes, oils, turps – was getting on his nerves. As if something had erupted inside him, he could not stand not seeing Ben for another minute. He got his wallet and raced out into the street. Grabbing a taxi, he gave the address to Ben and Alice's townhouse, his heart thumping the whole way.

He pushed the bell in the way he had in the past, two short rings, two long. Wearing a long silky bathrobe, Alice opened the door. Ben stood in the kitchen doorway wearing his tartan plaid robe. Ben asked, "Would you like a mimosa? Or would you like some toast? And? Or?"

"What's a mimosa?"

"Champagne and orange juice."

"And not or. But could you make it vodka and orange juice?"

Ben's skin looked unhealthy. He had grown a closely trimmed moustache. Alice must have had her eyes done because the usual pouches under them were gone. By the third mimosa, Alice gave the maid the day off. Both John and Ben had rock-hard erections. Fumbling their way to the bedroom, they revisited their sexual past.

Alice went to the telephone to order Chinese food, while the men were showering. As he soaped Ben, John felt swelling glands in his groin, also under his arms and behind his ears. After showering, they went back into the bedroom, towels around their waists. When the food was delivered Alice squeezed everything on a big tray and carried it into the bedroom.

"He has a yeast infection," Alice told John when she got up to bring more napkins.

As if it had never paused, the affair resumed, only to grind to a halt when Ben came down with a high fever that raged for weeks. Alongside the fever, he had an infection, called pneumocystis. John realized he could easily pass away, so he went home, packed a suitcase and moved into their guest bedroom.

After two weeks hovering between life and death, Ben suddenly snapped back almost to normal so John moved back into their bedroom. But, before another week had passed, Ben stopped shaving, let white stubble coarsen his cheeks once again, and within a month he was diagnosed with shingles. He started having night sweats, strange fevers, more infections, another bout of thrush. Then a yeast infection left patches of chalky white inside his mouth.

He told John he was seeing a light turning from green to red. Did John see it, too? He did not. The doctor diagnosed a newly named illness – ARC – an early stage of something the press was calling "Gay Plague." Alice sent John back to the guest room, bought throwaway plastic glasses and cutlery. Had she or John contracted something, too? Alice timidly suggested John get tested. He refused.

"Why?"

"Because I don't want to know."

"Why?"

"The terror of not knowing is less than the terror of knowing. What about you?"

"I've already been tested."

*

257

On a Sunday morning Ben woke with his body covered in deep purple, medallion-shaped violaceous lesions – Kaposi's sarcoma. His lips had turned a cyanotic shade at the same time. His doctor had no idea how to treat these lesions. Someone they knew told Alice about an unorthodox treatment that had helped a few men with ARC whose CD-4 cells were dropping. Why not give it a try? Ashamed of the lesions covering his face, Alice found an old cowboy hat that Ben had once worn to a Halloween party. She had John bundle Ben in a charcoal-gray cashmere scarf which he wrapped around the neck of his smart caramel-colored cashmere coat.

John and the driver helped Ben into the taxi. Alice gave the driver instructions on how to find the Yin and Yang Healing Arts Center in Chinatown. When the car pulled up at the curb, Alice went to the drugstore to fill a prescription and John walked Ben into the building and into the windowless waiting room. Ben looked as if he would faint. Decorating the walls were framed photos of Vietnam – rice paddies, banyan trees, rice fields, small straw houses, a water buffalo and someone in a coolie hat pulling a plow. The photos showed a poetic, dreamlike place, not the Vietnam John remembered.

When the door of the examining room opened and Andy Warhol walked out, there was nowhere to hide. Andy was wearing a long black leather coat. Seeing John, he said, "I thought this place was my little secret?"

Andy looked terrible.   Again John had the medic's urge to do something to help. Ben stood up.

"Hi, Andy."

Andy looked blank. Alice walked into the waiting room with the pharmacy bag.

"Hi, Andy."

Seeing Alice, he looked at Ben again.

"Gee. Ben Goldwyn. I didn't recognize you. That hat! Alice and Ben, Ben and Alice."

"Thanks. I hate to think I look that bad."

Ben took off his hat. Seeing the lesions on Ben's face, Andy recoiled. As someone who had suffered all his life from skin eruptions, he bent and put his hand on Ben's shoulder for a better look.

"Gosh.   Your face is worse than mine ever was."

He looked from Ben to John and back to Ben, then, in a bitchy tone, said to Alice, "Lucky you. If I ever have a show where I match up sets of cock and ball photos, I'll think of the two of you."

Sick as he was, Ben cattily muttered, "Don't hold your breath. Geronimo paints loins, doesn't bare them."

Alice took Ben's arm. Wanting to neutralize the tension, she laughingly added, "How about a show of all the dicks you've drooled and jerked off over through the years, Andy? You'd need a gallery as big as the Met to fit them all in."

Rather than being offended by her words, Andy was proud. The receptionist told Ben that the doctor was ready to see him. Leaving his coat, hat and scarf on the couch, Alice helped him into the treatment room.

Conspiratorially, Andy whispered to John, "I take it he doesn't know I have Polaroids of your cock."

"No."

"I didn't know that Ben had skin problems."

"He doesn't. He has ARC ... "

"You mean Gay Plague?"

"Yes."

"All I have is a bad gallbladder. Oh shit, I touched him. Now I'll get it."

In a panic, he snapped at the receptionist, "I need disinfectant soap. I need to scrub my hands."

John urged, "Andy ... take care of your gallbladder. It can kill you if you don't."

"Don't be a drama queen."

"I was once a medic. I heard you were afraid of hospitals."

"I hate hospitals."

"Don't be stupid, you must get it removed. You really must ...."

John reached out and touched his bony shoulder. Andy recoiled.

"Fuck you, too, then." He shrugged and walked into the examining room where Ben was stretched out naked on the paper-covered examining table.

Wearing a bleached white coat, a beautiful Vietnamese doctor stood beside him. She had ivory black hair, black eyes, was holding a chunk of glinting crystal over Ben's face. John looked hard at the healer. Here was a Vietnamese who had survived the war. Which side had she been on? If she knew that John had been an American Marine during the Vietnam War, what would she want to do to him? Ashamed, John turned away and studied the chart showing root herbs.

She held the glinting crystal above the lesions, moved it from purple lesion to lesion, from his face to his chest to his hips, thighs, groin, legs, feet. She told him to turn over and repeated what she had done on his back side.

Ben told them, "When she's finished with me, she'll do you, Alice, and when she's finished with Alice, I want her to do you, Johnny. Pray God whatever it is isn't contagious."

*

His symptoms diminished. John moved back into the king-size bed. But, after the New Year, Ben's CD-4 cells dropped to less than 200 and he needed round-the-clock morphine shots. John administered these shots. He realized that he could not drink and care for Ben at the same time, so he tapered off the booze and began injecting himself with Ben's morphine. He would give Ben a shot, then give one to himself because the doctor had given Ben more than an ample supply.

The purple KS lesions appeared again, covered Ben from head to foot. Mycobacterium avium-intracellulare – MAI – and pneumocystic, as well as other rampant infections, fevers, deliriums – followed. Ben's lawyer spent hours in the library whispering to Alice while John stood in the doorway of the bedroom high on morphine, watching Ben through what seemed like mustard-colored gauze, wondering all the while what he should do because Ben had begged to be put out of his misery.

Though Alice suggested hiring certified nurses, Ben did not want strangers around him. It was decided that John was qualified to nurse him, so, in the course of the next weeks, John changed set after set of sweat-drenched sheets by himself.

One day when Alice was out, he administered a lethal shot of morphine to Ben while he slept.

New York, 1987

The telephone rarely rang. On a dark winter day John was passed out, tangled up with that night's rough trade on the fold-out bed, when it did. The shades were tightly drawn, heat rose from a space heater on the floor. It could be night as easily as day. Because he had used up the residue of Ben's morphine that he had stolen after Ben was gone, and was afraid of heroin, he had gone back to drinking large quantities of vodka, was still drunk from the night before. He heard a soft male voice say, "I'm a social worker at the Florence Gold Nursing Home on 96th Street. There's a patient here who has requested we contact you."

John's voice was thick, "What's his name?"

"Her. It's a lady, a relative perhaps."

"Oh?"

"Could you just come down?"

The trick beside him in bed was a man with henna-streaked hair, strontium-yellow teeth, shaved chest. He had been wearing black leather chaps and a motorcycle jacket at the waterfront bar the night before. John did not remember his name, just that he was in New York on business from Rotterdam. Once roused, the trick daubed himself with water, put a hundred-dollar bill under the hash pipe. When he leaned toward John to kiss him goodbye, John averted his lips.

John dressed and took a taxi to 96th Street. He walked until he found a bar on Third Avenue. He had two shots of whiskey to steady himself, tried to think of the names of relatives he had lost touch with. The nursing home did not look too bad from the outside. A tired guard directed him to the office of the social worker, who was a blond young man, Mr. Walter, dripping with sensitivity and concern.

"She was malnourished, confused, when she was brought in. She had a bladder infection. We did a urine test, found E. coli. Her hygiene's pretty awful ... She says she's a nun, Sister Paule."

"I know a drag queen who calls himself Mother Superior."

"The ambulance attendant said she must have fallen into debris in her apartment. She couldn't get up. The only reason anyone found her was because she kept tapping on the floor with a scissors until a neighbor came up to check. Because the door wasn't locked the neighbor was able to get into the apartment. She's had the hip operated on, she'd fractured it. It's healing, though we can't get her to do exercise. She's quite lazy. Naturally we can't allow her to go back to her apartment as it is. It's a health hazard. A fire hazard. She's European."

Of course! Who else could it be? He didn't know what to say.

"Unless someone from the Catholic church takes her, we're looking for a residential nursing home for her. Or else ... unless a relative or close friend shows up who's willing to take responsibility for her."

"If it's who I think it is, she hasn't any family in this country ... or anywhere else."

"You're the only person she seems to know. You and someone called the Church Lady ... But God knows who the Church Lady might be and what church. You were easy to find, you're in the book."

"Why can't she just go home?"

"She can't take care of herself anymore. She will probably be made a ward of the state and put somewhere. Unless someone can be found who is willing to take responsibility for her, we can't legally let her go back there."

The social worker pinned him with bright blue eyes. "How about you? Would you be willing to become her primary caregiver?"

John stared back. "Quite frankly, I have a drinking problem, and can't count on myself for anything."

"I'd noticed the tremors in your hands. But, aren't you a friend?"

"Friend? Am I? She hasn't spoken to me in 10 years."

*

John stopped in the rest room because he was nauseous. He could only retch, not vomit. Afterwards, he washed his face with cold water, swished soap and water around in his mouth. The four-bed room was inhabited by three old ladies. And Claude. Claude's bed was beside a window. She had been scrubbed and combed, was wearing no makeup. Other than fingering a string of sap-green pop-it beads, she was docile, old, still not ordinary. Oyster-gray flesh against the zinc buff of the pillow and sheet and the unbleached cool silver white of the wall. When John loomed at her bedside, he pulled up a chair, sat beside the bed and touched her hand. Her fingers tensed, but she did not pull it away. Her eyes were bright, as if they were lit from behind.

"I want to go home. I tried to find my friend but I couldn't reach her. Will you help me go home? Take me *à ma maison*. Please take me home."

When John did not reply, pinkish anger bleached her face.

"Why won't you help me?"

"I'm messed up at the moment. Why did you say you were still a nun?"

"Maybe the people pray for a sister. Maybe I will be admitted to the convent Corpus Christi in the Bronx ... pray all day. Who will miss me if I am in perpetual adoration, if I return to a cloistered life?"

A tremor passed through his hands and she withdrew her fingers.

"*Chéri.*"

He acquiesced.

"Give me the key. I'll take a look."

"*Quel* key?"

*

John stopped for another drink, then took a bus downtown to Claude's apartment building on First Avenue. He was winded by the time he climbed the three flights. The door was pulled shut but unlocked. He pushed until he could squeeze inside. It was much worse than he remembered.

Debris now almost reached the ceiling. His skin began to recoil at the film of dust on everything – dead skin. There was a path through the debris that led to the worn-out nest that showed the imprint of her head on a filthy pillow. It smelled to high heaven.

He took Antabuse and shook for three days. When the shaking stopped, he took the emergency money that he kept hidden in a book of Turner sea paintings, put on old clothes and went to the Greek coffee shop on First Avenue for coffee. He saw someone ghostly and familiar walking by the window, saw it was Andy Warhol looking sicker than ever. He jumped up, ran outside, saw him getting into a taxi. He forgot to go back to the coffee shop to pay for breakfast.

When he got to Claude's apartment, he had rolls of large black garbage bags under his arm. He quelled the nausea and shakes as best he could. Dead skin in the form of sandy bits of sorrel-colored plaster soundlessly floated down from the side of the ceiling that was hanging at least four feet. Dead skin landed on his head. He wanted to tear his hair out. It was as if he was standing in a bizarre snow globe of skin flakes that were slowly tilting. Piled against the bed were folded clothes wrapped in plastic with big rubber bands around the plastic. He reached under the stiff rubber band holding the first pile together, and it disintegrated.

He examined what was inside the plastic. He guessed it was a moldy auburn coat with a moth-eaten fur collar and a missing sleeve. He checked its pockets, pulled out a handful of dollar bills. Putting the bills aside on her bed, he stuffed the coat into a black plastic garbage bag. He discovered money in almost every pocket of every article of clothing. He put aside a few articles of clothing that seemed intact, the rest he stuffed into the black bag for disposal. When the first plastic garbage bag was full, he reached for another.

Before the week was out, the store of industrial-size black garbage bags was depleted. He brought more. Because he had taken to wearing a gauze mask, he was less frightened of the dead skin. The found money added up to around $1,000, all wadded bills. Many articles of clothing were rotting, so out they went. He felt sick.

He found and hired a Ukrainian plasterer from the neighborhood who took one look at the ceiling and warned, "The ceiling is going to collapse at any moment. It will bury us both."

As predicted, while the plasterer was carefully tapping away decaying parts of the wall, half the ceiling dropped in a single sheet, just missing them both, bringing down a shelf that held an entire set of dishes that had been hidden by the debris. The plasterer became sick. A second plasterer did, too. A third wore a face mask and was able to work.

He remembered that Alice Goldwyn knew everything there was to know about clothing, so he called her and asked if she would help him go through Claude's remaining clothes. When she agreed, it was all he could do to not run to the bar downstairs and order a whiskey. When he saw her face for the first time in so long, his head began to throb. He told her what he was doing and she got right into sorting clothing. She found a Chanel dress, told him of her find.

"What should I do with it? Is it worth anything?"

"Dump it."

She told him what to throw away, what to keep. He began sorting what was packed under the bed. He found more money. Alice could not resist foraging around. She noticed a dirty silkscreen that could pass for a good imitation of a Warhol. She told John she liked "campy" knock-offs. Could she take it as a keepsake?

"Why not."

While he was elsewhere in the apartment, she put a few things she scavenged from the piles into her carry-all rather than into one of a black garbage bags. After a few hours she put on her coat.

"I've got to go ... I'm nauseous."

He preferred working alone anyway. Under one pile of clothes, he found batches of books. Under the books, a small television set that had rotten electric wires. He found a broken radio. There were

269

shopping bags filled with unopened Social Security checks. One whole Klein's shopping bag was stuffed with empty red and white packets of Lucky Strike cigarettes with the green circle. He left the radio and TV where they were. He found a scissors, knew she would want it, put it aside.

He had not thought about a drink all week. It seemed as if he could go it alone, so he stopped taking Antabuse. Perhaps he was okay? He was eating and had acquired a voracious appetite. He was less jumpy, hoped – like the years in Paris – that he was back in control.

*

At the Florence Gold Home, John waited for Mr. Walter to get off the phone.

"I hope you'll throw a wrench into the search for a nursing home for Miss Foot. I've been working on her apartment."

Mr. Walter narrowed his eyes, commented dryly, "Friend?"

When John's cheeks turned orange, the social worker gave him a smile that showed good straight teeth but the smile fell away quickly as Walter remembered what he needed to say, " ... the doctor discovered a lump in her breast. They did a biopsy ... the news isn't good."

When John got to the ward, Claude looked at him anxiously.

270

"Please let me come home."

"You can't, it's under construction."

"I can sleep in the corner."

By the time he left, she was sulking. In the afternoon, when he was back to work, Alice came by to see how he was doing, brought a small quantity of cocaine with her, hoping it might help him through his daunting task. How could he refuse? As soon as he had taken two snorts, he took her into his arms and deeply kissed her open mouth. She broke a popper, squeezed it into a Benzedrex inhaler and poked it into her own nose. After she took a long sniff on it, she turned into a ravenous, predatory monkey, so hungry for his body that saliva was leaking from the sides of her mouth. He did not mind because he was ravenous, too. He took a deep pull from the inhaler that smelled like old socks, saw the room shimmy.

Quickly she was on top of him on Claude's filthy bed. She shoved the popper up his nose, and hers, she entreated, "Roll over. I beg you."

After another long snort on the inhaler, he rolled onto his stomach and Alice straddled him. Lubricating her fingers, she caressed his sphincter. He was pleasured until she began to duplicate what she had seen Ben do. Rather than let himself go, he pulled back. She was frightening him. Was she was trying to reincarnate Ben? He could not give in to her efforts.

271

She disengaged. After a few minutes, she sat up, shocked at her own aggression.

"Let's forget this. I must be out of my mind. I'm an old lady. Can I take you to lunch?"

Being with Alice meant being without Ben. He caressed her hair. Saying nothing meant saying no. Her eyes were not old at all, they were wet.

"Forgive me. All these years I've wanted to feel what Ben felt with you. Now I have, I can understand why he found you so exciting. Why didn't you or I get sick like he did?"

He had no reply. Unable to part, he changed his mind, went to lunch. They slept together in her townhouse that night.

When John left, Alice was still sleeping. He stopped at his apartment, filled a little bag with a change of underwear and a toothbrush, hurried to Claude's apartment. At Union Square he got caught in rush hour. He imagined people hurling through space when he saw bunches of bodies popping up from the subway step. Against his own will, he stopped in a liquor store and bought a case of vodka and a gallon of grapefruit juice. It was too heavy to lug, so he arranged to have it delivered. It would not hurt to test himself.

When the delivery arrived, he decided to have just one drink, see if he could stop at one. He mixed juice and vodka to a specific shade of yellow. He had two drinks and stopped, was relieved. Obviously he had regained control. That night, though Alice waited, he did not go back to her house. He slept curled up in a corner that was already cleared.

*

He rented a dumpster, had it parked at the curb in front of the building. When all the plastic packages of clothes were cleared, he found a 3-foot-high pile of papers and junk mail on a coffee table. He carefully went through the pile. At the very bottom of the pile lay the lease to the apartment. It was dated 1959. He napped for an hour then chopped up the old mattress with an ax. He chopped up the rotting furniture and carried the bits and pieces down to the dumpster. He filled black plastic bag after bag with fabric and old newspaper. If house dust came from dead skin, he had come to live with it. He was willing to be a cannibal.

There was another pile of unopened mail against the wall, this one shoulder-high. Again he went at it piece by piece. He found a slip of paper with what might be a bank account number. He did not throw away a scrap of paper the size of a postage stamp without considering whether or not it might be important. After a few more hours of work the day had passed. He mixed grapefruit and vodka to make a drink that was a shade of buttercup and curled up to sleep. When he woke, he swallowed a few hairs of the dog.

As the mounds against the walls diminished, filthy paintings were revealed. He uncovered a door and discovered that it was a closet filled with debris. There was a shelf with a pile of cocoa-brown towels folded neatly. He tried to unfold one of the towels but it broke in two, revealing that it had once been a snow-white terrycloth towel.

His work had become an archeological dig, layer after layer. He discovered a woodburning fireplace. Nothing he tried would clean the brick over the fireplace. Finally, he tried acid. It worked, revealed soft, charming, ochre bricks. He uncovered mildewed books, articles cut from old newspapers, a postcard written in all caps:

STOP BOTHERING US.
STOP LEAVING
PACKAGES AT MY DOOR.
ROY

He put one newspaper clipping aside. In it was a black-and-white photo of a slim, fair-haired young man with the face of a Great Dane holding a paintbrush with a long handle. The man was painting an abstract canvas. The subject matter of the painting was an abstract sailboat. Standing against him, looking over his shoulder, stood Claude. Her waist was cinched with a tight belt. She looked about 40.

The caption beside the photograph read:

Claude Foot watching her artist husband, Roy, putting finishing touches on one of the paintings he is exhibiting this month at the Little Gallery in Maple Road, Birmingham.

The text of the clipping read:

Foot Exhibits at Little Gallery

Two of Roy Foot's most prized possessions are a letter from the great French painter Henri Matisse and his autographed book of pencil, ink and charcoal drawings.

They came to him after a surreptitious inspection of the young artist's work by the master.

Roy says that as far back as he can remember he wanted to paint. He studied both before and after World War II. For four years he lived and painted in Paris.

That was when his wife, Claude, who posed for Matisse, persuaded him to look at Roy's work – with the resultant commendation. Now Foot has returned here from the current exhibit of his paintings at the Little Gallery in Birmingham.

He said, "The going hasn't always been easy. It's plain hard work."

Foot describes his work as semi-abstract. He "feels" his angles and curves and puts them were he "sees" them in the composition.

He's a young man of casual mien with eyes atwinkle or of somber pensiveness. It's the former mood that provides the whimsy in the birds he loves to paint.

Prefers Blues

For a long time he was interested in "pure" color, but today he works principally with cobalt blues, Mars green and umbers.

He discovered an "affinity" for one or another of those tones by shifting jars of permanent color about on the floor one evening. And that was it. As a result, he has completely discarded reds and similar flamboyant tones.

He's no novice at exhibiting. In Paris he showed at the Salon d'Automne and Salon de la Jeune Peinture. He has had one-man shows at Galérie Breteau and the Hacker Gallery in New York.

Now he is returning to their studio-home in Fernanina, Fla., which, incidentally, they built with their own hands. Roy grins when he tells about the 3,000 bricks Claude personally cleaned before the chimney could be built.

Fun at Home

Claude works in her garden and waters her banana tree, which was flourishing when he left. And he can't wait to see "my son," Toby, a formidable police dog his wife befriended. She'll be cooking her specialty Boeuf

Bourguignon, and as Roy puts it – "re-arranging her clothes."

And Roy will paint.

*

The case of Popov was half empty. John found bundled mildewed newspapers full of worms. He found something the shape of a book wrapped in what must once have been a crinkly citron scarf. When he unwrapped it, the silk fell apart. Inside, in a small framed print, the glass smashed, a Matisse painting – *Woman in Blue Gandurah*. Another small painting in a frame had been crushed beyond recognition. There were more bags of clothes and fabrics. There was a set of partially constructed glass shelving. He found quantities of kitchen equipment, more tan shopping bags filled with crumpled dollar bills.

He found a letter from the French government certifying that in 1919 Paule Boule had been made a ward of the state. He found a bundle of letters with Japanese stamps tied with lilac ribbon. He found a small blue velvet pouch. Inside, rosary beads and bits of torn paper. He made a puzzle out of the bits. He was able to piece together part of what must have been a letter written in French:

... my mother would be glad if you would send back the watch chain that had belonged to her mother. You have apparently worn it for a long time.

Pierre.

There were more bits in an envelope, but his hands were not steady and there were too many to puzzle out, so he stuffed them back into the dusty pouch.

He found grocery bags brimming with envelopes that contained uncashed checks written by students at the Art Students League – years old, some for two dollars, some for $5, a few for $10. Stuck between the pages of a swollen, mildewed book of prints from the Louvre were two envelopes addressed to Claude. The return addresses – *H. Matisse, 132 Boulevard du Montparnasse, Paris.* These he carefully put aside.

The most disgusting job, the refrigerator, he left for last. When he pried open its door, it was frightful. It obviously had been unplugged for a long while. There was a solid mass inside that was no longer organic. There was no way of knowing for how long it had been unplugged. To tackle the refrigerator, he put on thick plastic gloves, closed his eyes and broke off large handfuls of the mass. He began to gag. Rapidly he filled a plastic bag, then ran the bag out the door, down the stairway, to the dumpster.

He leaned against the dumpster and vomited. Back upstairs, he shut the refrigerator door. The next day he hired someone strong from the neighborhood to help him carry it downstairs and hoist it up and into the dumpster. On the street he found a phone booth, dialed Alice's number. When there was no answer he went back upstairs and drank half a bottle of vodka in one go, decided, even though he was no longer a young, hard body, to go down to the river for some rough sex.

*

He got down to the bare floor and simply shoveled. Wearing rubber gloves up to his elbows, he pulled the plug in the bathtub. His hands were not steady because he was hungover. Ginger-brown sludge was caked on the bottom, so he bought strong chemical cleaner from an industrial hardware store. He plastered around the tub. He redid the bathroom walls. He hired someone to install a new shower apparatus, bought lavender soap, a toothbrush, shampoo and a nail clipper. He had new red, peach and yellow speckled linoleum laid on the kitchen floor. New shelving and a new cabinet were installed for the kitchen things.

He hired another carpenter to build permanent floor-to-ceiling shelves leading into the little alcove, sectioning off the shelves, adding two long racks on which she could hang clothes. The plasterer noticed there were minute green growths on the dead ficus tree, proclaimed, "There's some life left there!" and cut off the rest of the dead branches, leaving only the small green shoots.

Using a broken kitchen knife, John cut up the dead branches and tossed them into a black bag. New gray-green carpeting was put in. He had the clothes he had not thrown away dry-cleaned and hung them on the racks. Other clothes he took to the neighborhood laundromat. He folded and piled them on the new shelves. He had new window blinds installed after removing stiff, liverish-brown, stinking rags from the window. With newspaper and blue Windex, he washed the fudge-colored coating from the window. He ordered a new refrigerator and new furniture from a place on Canal Street.

*

In the course of the renovation, he threw out over 200 black, industrial-strength garbage bags. He was sipping a beer, trying to get over the shakes, get the taste of dusty human skin out of his mouth, when the new blue and white striped convertible couch was carried up the stairs by two hunky men. When one of them remained behind to help him assemble the couch, John knew at once that he was being cruised. He and the moving man got it off against the wall, then assembled the convertible couch.

Once it was assembled, his helper left and he unwrapped a new set of bed sheets decorated with a violet and red harlequin pattern. He made up the bed, and then he assembled two new blue and green striped canvas director's chairs; a new radio-cassette player was still in its box, so he pulled it out and plugged it in. He found a station playing Barry White, sat down on one of the director's chairs, leaned back on two legs. The music evoked the disco nights with Ben and Alice. He leaned over in order to look for another station, for something else, but changed his mind and stayed with Barry White. He did nothing to ward off the aching heartbreak that would probably never leave him.

He did not stanch the tears. Once shed, he got horny. He rubbed himself, laughed and sang along as he and Ben had always done when they heard this song. When it ended, he looked around, saw a charming, brightly colored, clean and fresh-smelling little rent-controlled New York apartment with a small window that opened on a purplish-blue airshaft. He hung Roy's large framed painting back on the wall, then counted the odds and ends of found money. It added up to $6,000. He put $800 into a ceramic bowl and the remainder into an envelope.

He waited until the locksmith had installed a new lock on the front door, then he broke down the cardboard box in which the radio-cassette player had arrived. He put the cardboard under his arm, closed the door behind him, put a copper-colored key onto a

281

ring with a furry monkey at the end and locked the door.

At a neighborhood bar, he eyed the brick-brown rum bottle, then the rusty-silver vodka bottle, then ordered a crème de menthe on ice. The liquor was a shade of silvery jade green. The bartender looked like someone he had been with in Vietnam.

"Are there other green drinks?"

"Yeah. There's green Chartreuse."

"What's that?"

"An apéritif. There's also yellow Chartreuse."

He ordered green Chartreuse. It came in a thin brandy glass with a side of ice water and left his lips sweet and sticky. He left the bar, stopped at a liquor store and bought a bottle of Galliano, went home and drank it. When it was empty, he washed out and saved the bottle. There was no more alcohol in his apartment. He laid low for three days, then walked the many blocks up to the nursing home.

The moment he walked into Mr. Walter's office, a barrage began.

"She's got to have a health care proxy, a guardian. She needs a power of attorney, a keeper of her living will. Social Security needs a representative payee to deal with her SSI checks, her bills, her rent, her...."

Mr. Walter paused to exert more pressure, but stopped when John said, "All right. I'll be her guardian."

*

John handed Claude a sweater that Ben had given him. It was made of a synthetic fabric that looked like confetti – cornflower-blue and marine-blue spots against black cashmere. She had been waiting for him, was dressed and made up with rouge and dark red lipstick. He had bought her a wooden cane that was painted hunter green, and she did not resist. On the street there were no cabs in sight. While they waited for one to pass, she pointed up at a first floor window where a white Angora cat sat. Finally a taxi passed and he hailed it.

In her building, she laboriously climbed the three flights with the help of the new cane. Reaching her door, she pushed, but it would not give. He handed her the key on the brown monkey key chain. She handed it back, so he unlocked the door, pushed the door wide. She looked inside, glared at him.

"Where is all my stuff?"

"Some of your stuff had deteriorated so I threw it away. I saved anything of importance."

"What's done cannot be undone."

"Not always. I found a bankbook. I was able to go to the bank and update your account."

She sat down on the couch, put her face in her hands, mumbled what sounded like an invocation of Jesus Christ. He sat next to her. When she looked

283

up, she patted his leg. He showed her the maroon and black bankbook.

"I deposited most of the cash here and the uncashed SSI checks. There was $32,000 in the account but Social Services took $10,000 out."

"Why?"

"To pay for your stay at the nursing home."

"Such cheapness in the richest country in the world ..."

She hesitantly walked around the apartment, looking and touching. There were copies of *Marie Claire* in French on the couch, a pile of *Art Forum International Magazines*, and a book of Matisse drawings; two he had done of her were included. The book of Matisse drawings was placed on top of the new coffee table. Noticing the original plant, she went into the kitchen to fill a glass with water and poured it into the dirt. Again she wandered through the room. When John began to speak to her, she stood still.

"While I was cleaning I found a paper the size of a postage stamp. It had a number. I went to the bank and discovered that 10 years earlier a bank account of yours had gone dormant, which meant that the State of New York had seized the money. What's in the account is the total of your accrued money in the account plus interest over the 30 years. I think this will clear up a few mysteries."

John handed her a sky-blue bankbook. Inside showed a balance of $196,000.

New York, 1989

New piles of detritus – magazines, used wrapping paper, newspapers – had grown. A bag filled with ribbon she had gotten for 10 cents from a trim shop on Eighth Avenue was stored under the fold-out bed. A pile of not-very-well-washed plastic containers, chopsticks and soy sauce packages from Chinese take-out rose against the wall beside the bathtub along with books found in a dumpster on 17th Street. When her attention was elsewhere, he would grab a handful or two of debris, put it into his gym bag in order to throw it away later.

He noticed a trail of bedbugs coming from Roy's painting above the bed and squashed as many as he could. They were filled with blood, Claude's blood. They left maroon stains along the wall. When he looked closely at her zinc-buff arms and neck, he saw minute violet bites – the bugs were feeding on her. She was dozing on the blue and white striped convertible couch. Her charcoal-gray hair – threaded with copper-colored strands and green streaks – was twisted back. Her ankles were swollen. She was wearing a kind of malachite-green smock and had thick, well-worn, fawn-colored cloth slippers on her bare feet. John sat down on a director's chair, saw she had awoken. She handed him a package wrapped with paprika-colored wrapping paper. Inside, a soft, furry white polar bear. She caressed the bear.

"I'm not good with people."

He had gone on the wagon – cold turkey – the day before.

"Me neither."

He stood up and removed Roy's painting from its hook, set it against the bookcase.

"I'll have to get the place fumigated."

She looked hard at the painting.

"My husband painted it. I was in Florida for a few years. He said his style was semi-modern."

"It looks Cubist to me."

She pointed her index finger up at the woman in the painting.

"Me. *La Madonna.*"

She pointed at the prone figure.

"My husband. Christ."

They both looked at the painting for a long while until she turned away.

"I need something new to look at. Maybe you could bring me one of your watercolors? Not your best one ... one you were going to destroy, maybe."

She closed her eyes.

"I want to end my life here, John. My home in France was not really a home. Why would they take a sick old lady back? On First Avenue is St. Bridget's Church. I want to end my life ... *une vie sédentaire* ... Do you hear me?"

"I do."

He got a sponge and Ajax and washed the bloody stains off the wall as well as he could. She turned on the radio. A sad look passed across her face as she listened to bassist Charlie Haden play a moody riff. When John opened the refrigerator door and began to clean out the old food, she snapped at him, "That food is good! You must not waste food, *chéri.*"

"It's green!"

"It's what?"

"It's green!"

"Don't waste! I can take the green off the white rice and save the bottom part."

"I'm sure you can. But you don't."

"*Peut ... etre ...* maybe I can. I'm *énervée.*"

She got up and unscrewed the light bulb from the one lamp in the living room and left him in the dark when she took it with her into the bathroom and screwed it into the empty socket. It lit the bathroom with emerald-green light. She did not entirely close the door while she made peepee and re-pinned her unruly hair.

*

Claude watched as he tore off brown wrapping paper from what must have been a painting. John lifted a 2½-by-4-foot wooden frame and turned it in her direction. Under glass was a blown-up black-and-white print of a Matisse charcoal, the body of a woman. Along the bottom edge was written – *Claude 1950. H. Matisse.* He lifted another piece of art, a framed watercolor. It was a realistic watercolor of Claude, a black crow at her window. Claude held scissors in hand, was sitting on a bed in a red room taking cuttings from a magazine. It was signed – *Lightfoot 1989*. He hammered nails into the wall and hung one, then the other.

While she watched him the color of his face changed from caramel to putty white. She took hold of his arm as he began to slither toward the floor. She broke his fall but was not strong enough to catch him. She bent down and wiped his face with a wine-stained sapphire-green silk handkerchief. His coloring changed again, from putty white to blue spruce. With an open palm, she slapped him, first one cheek, then the other. His eyes opened, glinted like stainless steel.

"I stopped drinking alcohol, Claude. I shouldn't have stopped abruptly."

"For today or forever?"

"I drink too much."

"If people drink too much, they should just not drink too much. In France everyone drinks. You need to paint. You need vocation."

From one of her shopping bags she lifted a plastic flower pot labeled "Country Dancing Flowers, ages 6 and up – motion-activated". She punched a button and a fiddle played "Cotton-Eyed Joe". Four daisies with green stems made from artificial fabric squaredanced to the music. He raised himself onto

288

his elbow and watched the dancing daisies; he was shaking. She mixed a packet of chocolate-flavored Instant Breakfast in what looked like a laboratory beaker with buttermilk, handed it to him. Her nails were long, either discolored a kind of citrus yellow or painted strangely. She was wearing black tights, a black blouse, shoes made of red leather.

He pretended to take a sip from the beaker, afraid he might vomit, sat up, braced himself against the pile of magazines. She brought him a pair of his socks. They had been mended with tomato-red thread. His body was trembling so much that she bent and slipped first the newly mended socks and then his worn leather boots onto his feet. He had come apart. He let her assist him when she strained to pull him up.

"Now we go to the museum with a taxi. See paintings …"

She colored her lips harsh pink and tied her hair up in a knot on the back of her head, inserted long black hairpins to fasten it, then put on her lambswool coat. She handed him his faithful brown leather bomber jacket. In a minute, he unsteadily got up and put it on. She picked up the monkey key chain from the coffee table and guided him out the door, down the stairs, outside, toward the Polish place on First Avenue. The Moslem Temple and Community Center on First Avenue was having an event. Moslem men, mostly somber and young, were coming from all directions toward the entrance.

When they were seated in a booth at the Polish place on First Avenue, she told the young Polish waitress, "Bring us soup, please."

"Meatless borscht or with meat?"

"With meat. We are carnivores."

It was not clear if she had said carnal or carnivore. There was an ivory and black pendant around her neck that he had never seen before. He asked, "Is it a horse?"

She fingered it.

"I'm *Sagitaire*."

"What day?"

She had not heard him. He repeated his question, more loudly.

"16 Decembre. The day of ...,"

" ... of?"

"The day of ... Beethoven."

She pushed a homemade envelope across the table which he cut open with a table knife. Inside he saw a folded piece of old peach-colored paper. On it a cut-out of a giraffe glued to a photograph of the New York skyline glued against a Moroccan design. The caption was handwritten:

A giraffe visits New York.

Inside, on the card, in green ink:

Without you I would not be alive. I owe so much to you though I don't often say it in words.

290

When the soup was served, he was still too shaky to hold a spoon. He reached inside his leather jacket and took out a silver flask and loosened the lid.

"Eat, *chéri*."

"I only eat when I don't drink."

She gripped his wrist, kept him from tipping the flask to his lips.

"If you continue like this you'll die. After death there's resurrection, transmigration of his soul, divine eternity. I know you're not Catholic but this is what we Catholics believe. If you die, I'll have no one again."

She grabbed his chin with her hand.

"*Rien? Rien, chéri.*"

She took the flask out of his unsteady hand and poured the contents into her water glass. Spoonful by spoonful she fed him the contents of the glass and then the soup. After she had fed him, she drank her own soup. When the waitress returned to take the bowls, Claude told her, "Two omelets with Polish sausage, also bacon and ham."

Abashed, the waitress asked, "Bacon? Sausage? And ham? Are you sure?"

"I'm sure. Once I lived on sour milk and black bread. If they gave us meat five times a year, it was a lot."

"She's sure."

He looked at Claude.

"I hope you've taken your heart pills ..."

Her sharp nails had cut into his skin. She shook her finger at him.

"You no more *boit* alcohol, *chéri*. Please!"

"I can't. I've tried and tried. Sometimes I can go a few weeks, sometimes a few days. But ... I forget my resolve ... "

He snapped his fingers.

"Like that, I drink and can't stop. Death is not such a large thing. I saw plenty of it in Vietnam ... it happens in a blink."

"It's whether or not we go to heaven or hell or stay in purgatory that matters."

She released her grip.

Aujourd'hui you ... stop. I'll ask God to help you. You're an artist. You must work. You need an idea."

"I have an idea."

The normal caramel color of his face returned; he brightened.

"It's true. On and off for years I've been thinking of a series of paintings I'd like to do."

"*Qu'est-qui se?*"

"I've been thinking of doing a series of paintings with Biblical themes set in contemporary settings."

The omelets were set on the table on white plates. As soon as the waitress had turned away, John whispered to Claude, "I can't eat this."

"Neither can I."

She pulled a large, folded square of aluminum foil from the pocket of her coat and spooned eggs and meats into it, then she twisted the top closed as the waitress returned with two cups of coffee. The waitress soon brought an aluminum pitcher containing milk and a wire holder for packets of sugar and Sweet'N Low. She prodded him, "Tell more about the Bible."

The palmed packets of artificial sweetener disappeared into Claude's pocket.

"I've made some drawings for the first painting; it's nothing like Leonardo's *Last Supper* but is a painting of the Last Supper. It's set in a coffee shop."

He was finally steady enough to pick up his cup and take a sip of slate-black coffee. His voice scorched her with excitement.

"Everyone at the Last Supper is at a separate table."

"*Intéressant!*"

"It is interesting. None of us know when we'll be eating our last supper."

A RISING URGE TO STRANGLE SOMEONE

New York, 2000

Realizing that it was insane to start up with John Lightfoot, that, doubtlessly, given the promiscuity of men like him, she would come down with AIDS and that she did not want to fall any more in love with him than she had always been, Alice Goldwyn left New York. She went to live in Oslo, Norway, from where her father's family had emigrated and where she still had two cousins – Marianne and Jan Christian. While she lived there, she bought art, attended a grief group, had a love affair with a young performance artist. She had her eyes and face done in Prague in 1998 and in 1999 had her breasts reduced in Bucharest. She returned to New York in 2000 when her father turned 90 and was diagnosed with macular degeneration. She wanted to be close to her father in his final years, to make sure that her brother did not get his hands on her share of her father's money. She wanted a new neighborhood, a new life, and bought an apartment in Chelsea in a glassy high-rise across from one the best art galleries in New York.

Once she was settled, regardless of her intentions, the urge to phone John Lightfoot was irrepressible. She tried his old number. To her surprise, he picked up the phone. She asked for news. He told her that he was enmeshed with the old French woman he'd met at the Art Students League long ago, in fact, had reluctantly become her

297

official health care provider. She was now quite old, in her 80s. A while back a doctor found that an untreated cancerous lump in her breast had grown to be as large as a chestnut and decided to do a lumpectomy. The surgery had been scheduled, cancelled, scheduled again. In the meantime, another large lump had formed on the inside of her right cheek. The dentist thought this meant that the cancer was spreading. An internist suspected that the lump was an abscess caused by the recent extraction of most of her remaining teeth. It hurt her to eat and it was becoming harder and harder for her to walk up and down three stairways to her apartment, took about an hour each time she did.

Alice asked him about himself. He told her he had been earning his living by working on the Upper East Side caring for a rich old man with Alzheimer's. He had not been painting. Between the old man and the old French woman – sandwiched between geriatrics – he had no time for himself. He admitted that intoxicants still had him by the throat though he could often go several days with nothing in his system. Also, he had gotten into crack cocaine.

"Can't you just stick to alcohol?" she suggested.

"Although I've gone on the wagon a number of times, I always relapse."

His rapid style of speaking was different than she remembered. His voice had turned slightly loutish. They met for a drink at a bar on Eighth

Avenue. His once lamp-black hair had been dyed bright copper with rose madder highlights, cut close to his scalp. Still sexy although youthless, his hairless skin was the color of good cognac. He reminded her of Ben. She realized that Ben had been about John's age when they began their *ménage à trois*. While she drank a Calvados, he drank a double bloody mary, passing it back and forth from one restless hand to the other. She told him she wanted to meet Claude. After all, she had helped him clean the disaster zone that was her apartment. He was hesitant but she persisted.

In November, she offered to invite Claude and him to lunch. John said, "Okay. You can meet her ... but I can't promise that she'll be friendly."

She suggested an expensive lunch at Il Botino in Chelsea but John picked a Polish place downtown on First Avenue. When Alice got there, he and Claude were eating scrambled eggs and toast. Claude was a handsome old woman, with a head of thick gray-green-coppery hair. Entirely silent as she ate, she held onto a small oval mirror made of silver or stainless steel. The mirror had a long handle, like a dentist's mirror. It was aimed to reflect what was in her mouth. John explained as if Claude was not there:

"Claude had a little stroke. She can't feel that side of her face and she's self-conscious about food because it sticks to that side of her lips. She doesn't like to talk because she can't remember words."

Between bites, watching herself in the mirror, Claude pushed peach-colored scrambled eggs that hung out of the corner of her salmon-gray painted lips inside her mouth with her fingers. Because John had mentioned that Claude liked to read the *New York Post*, Alice had collected a plastic bag full. Also copies of *Flash Art*. She set the bag down beside Claude, who did not acknowledge it, or her.

*

Hoping to make a better impression, Alice asked if they could all lunch again. John said okay and he told her when and where to meet them. Alice waited for John and Claude at a coffee shop on First Avenue for a second meal in a booth that had torn scarlet plastic seats. She was determined to get Claude to warm to her. It was the middle of January. Though the sun was shining, it was bitterly cold. She waited a half-hour and no one arrived. She was gathering her things to leave when John dashed into the restaurant, sat down, ordered coffee. He was agitated.

"Claude's in a state. I had to convince her to go to the dentist. She said she's not in pain, but, when I finally got her to go, the dentist said she must be suffering. He wants to pull the last two teeth out from her lower jaw and fit her for dentures. She's adamantly refusing. She's driving me crazy, I took time off from my job with Freddee to take her to her appointments."

He gulped half a cup of coffee that the waitress set down, went on ranting.

"Now the lump in her breast is the size of a ping pong ball, a solid mass, too. And ... she's got bedbugs in her room again. I'm not supposed to tell you. I had the place fumigated. I thought they got them all but I saw a trail coming down toward her bed from under the painting above the bed. It is a painting done by her husband. The bugs have infested it again. They've been feeding on Claude while she sleeps. She should be here in a minute."

"Isn't it a bit cold for her to come down?"

"As much as she hates the cold, she's dressing. She wants to meet you again. Did I tell you she calls you The Lady? She said, 'I owe my life to The Lady Alice.'"

Alice was surprised. She ordered a fourth coffee from the waitress, a very young woman recently arrived from Ghana. A half-hour passed before Claude hobbled by the steamy window and through the door. She sat across from Alice, was carrying an old black lambswool coat across her arm. Her hair was tied up at the back in a knot, held together with long pins, and she was wearing cobalt-blue stretch pants; her Nike shoes were not laced; her lipstick was bright blue. Alice handed her a Saks Fifth Avenue shopping bag full of copies of the *New*

York Post, also this month's *Vogue* and *Flash Art*. Claude whispered in Alice's ear.

"Thank you, *chérie*."

When the young waitress hovered, Claude whispered in John's ear what she wanted to eat.

"She'll have an omelet with bacon, Polish sausage and ham."

Because the waitress did not understand much English, the owner came from the kitchen to translate. Soon the waitress brought the food and Claude ate robot-like, holding the mirror so she could push morsels of egg that dangled at the corner of her mouth inside. When her plate was empty, she handed Alice a cylindrical package wrapped in pink, gold, silver and white Christmas paper encircled by silver lamé yarn. A red and white striped candy cane and a little Styrofoam ornament painted with leafy green watercolor paint had been attached to the yarn. John put his hand on top of the gift.

"Claude doesn't like her gifts opened up in her presence. Take it home and open it."

John went to the men's room. When he returned to the table his eyes were shining, he was more agitated than before. They gathered their things, left and walked north on First Avenue. Claude walked slowly, leaned on her hunter green cane with one hand and held onto John's arm with the other. It was bitter cold. The Nexus gallery on 12th Street had an exhibition called "Surreal Moments in Oil" by an artist named Ellen Goldring.

Also, "Pencil Drawings of Rodin Sculptures and Comic Book Superheroes" by Mark Lerer. Inside, Claude warmed up near the radiator against the wall in the dry, static-filled storefront space. She held onto the wall with one hand, leaned on the cane with the other. John and Alice left her there in order to wander through the gallery.

In a little while Claude began to move, too, carefully bracing on her cane each time she took a step, stopping to look at each of the paintings. When she had examined everything, she sat in the window seat studying a surreal painting on the wall opposite. Painted clumsily in oil was a line of evergreen trees that bent to form an arch. At the end of the arch was a bushy chartreuse tree. When John and Alice joined her, they stood on either side. She pointed at the arched tree painting. Her fingers were crooked with arthritis, the nails long, discolored, painted citrus yellow. Still buttoned up in their winter coats, all three looked at the painting in silence.

When Claude laid her head on Alice's shoulder and closed her eyes, Alice stiffened. John was getting restless.

"Do either of you hear someone gargling?" he asked.

Forgetting about Alice, John guided Claude out the door. Hurt because, in years past, he never would have dismissed her so rudely, Alice knotted her crinkled dun-colored scarf, left the gallery. She walked west avoiding the last bits of buttercream-colored slush from last week's blizzard. When she turned the corner she opened her gift. It was a small black umbrella.

Paris, 1952

Lydia handed him his long rod made from bamboo that had a thick stick of black charcoal inserted into the tip. With it he did not need to stretch his arms at all. Because he had so little energy and used what energy he had for work rather than for dressing and undressing, he wore his blue and white tea-planter's pajamas throughout the day. When his nurse had asked him if he would like a bath, he had huffed and told her that the great kings of France hardly bathed but used fragrances of fruit instead. He was having shortness of breath. Soon after the arrival of his model, Claude Boule, who continued to impregnate him, he said to her, "Even if I survive the day, I doubt I have much longer to live. Death doesn't faze me. I don't have an iota of fear of dying. There's no need for you to continue your prayers for my longevity ... I'll take my chances."

Two hours into the sitting a pinching pain in Claude's neck began to inch down into her shoulders and back. It seeped into the top of her buttocks on the right side. The more painful it got the more determined she was to hold her pose because she, like Lydia, was willing to do anything for him. No one else before or since had really looked at her, all of her, had seen inside. After another hour Matisse asked Lydia to tell the cook to bring *pommes frites* and beer, sausage for his model. She left and returned with his requests. He tasted a *pomme frite*, chewed carefully, washed it down with a glass of beer. He remembered that Claude's mother had committed suicide. Curiosity got the better of him. He asked, "You once told me that your mother died by her own hand. Would I be out of order if I asked why and how?"

"I would not be ashamed to tell you. When I was nine, my mother drank lye. It took two days for her to die. She died in agony. It was, as you can imagine, something a child should not witness."

"Was there a reason?"

"My father was sent far away to Devil's Island for stealing money. She did not want to live without him. Her world revolved around him ... nothing else."

They were silent after that. Once Claude had finished eating the sausage, he told her that she should stretch her legs.

*

Lydia listened as he described what costume he wanted for the next drawing. She went through the pile of fabrics and costumes, found the bright red, blue and black Russian blouse, as well as dark brown pasha-type pantaloons he had requested. While Claude undressed and redressed, Matisse sorted through various bits and pieces of pencil and charcoal, picked out a fresh chunk of pitch-black charcoal. Despite the pain it caused, he worked standing for about 20 minutes, making precise strokes. An image took shape. When the pain spiked, he sat down in the wheelchair.

His reverie deepened. After another quarter-hour five sheets of good paper had been tossed aside. On the top half of the sixth sheet an image he liked had taken shape. Because it was cold, the fat little stove was burning, hot and gray ash drifted from it, settled on everything. Suddenly he put down the charcoal.

"I need time for mental fermentation."

He asked Lydia to erase the lower half of the drawing. He said to Claude, "Would you be so kind as to return in two days time for another sitting? If I'm still alive."

His light eyes were blurred behind the thick glasses. While she went behind the screen to dress, he told Lydia to make a note that he wanted to book Claude for the next week, Sunday included. Again, as she had on and off for the past three years, her being had penetrated him. Elated as always, Claude ran a comb through her hair. Her heart beat as if it was a motor purring, a top tilting. Lydia handed her an envelope filled with cash.

After the week was up he booked her for another two days. At that point he had used her up. When she told him she was about to marry an American, a painter whom she had been living with, she asked if he would look at his work, give a critique. Matisse said he would, and did. He saw some talent in the American's work. When she told him she and her husband would be sailing for America, he and Lydia were anxious and offered words of advice. Matisse thanked her for their many productive sittings. He told her to send her address when she was settled so he could send her a wedding gift, a sketchbook of drawings he had done of her. He said he would keep in touch with her.

Early the next day Lydia went out to look for a fresh model, someone who had not had such a hard life. She found a set of twins, dark-haired girls from Bordeaux. He chose the smaller of the two to pose, the one with a wart on her ear. By now his assets had been divided between Amélie and the children; there was enough for all. And more. He had given Lydia many works. He had no anxiety about her, either. She would be the authority on his late-in-life work.

There was a new thumping pain in his temples. Even when he was laying down, he was not relaxed. The damp always reached his feet. The pain was making him cross.

"Why, after six decades of insomnia, can I still not get a full night's sleep? Is it because I need even more time to finish my work? Is it that we'll soon make the journey back to Le Midi? This journey south will be my last, I have no doubt."

Lydia reached her warm hands under the duvet and felt his feet. She laid the panther skin across the bottom of the duvet because they were like blocks of ice. He took off his glasses, cleaned them with a light brown square of silk for probably the hundredth time that day. He guessed that the reason everything appeared smudged was because a film of grease or grime must be coating the glass lenses. The truth was that his blue-gray eyes were clouding over. He propped himself up and made a series of what he called "rapid" drawings." If he made a mistake, he never worried because Lydia was a very good eraser.

Cimiez, 1953

Though the widow bird's plumage was black, Matisse had never warmed to it as he had his pigeon that was as white as bleached bone. It was a miracle that they had made it back to Cimiez. He was ashamed that he needed two nurses to accompany him on the train. Between the nurses, the housekeeper, the cook, Madam Lydia, crates of work, valises, trunks, bolts of cloth, he and his entourage took up an entire Portman. Once back in Cimiez, he resumed his normal life, saw friends, wrote letters to his children. Whenever his wife came up in conversation, he was taken by an overwhelming feeling of fatigue mixed with guilt mixed with longing. Hearing or saying her name brought on the sensation of fainting, which was what he did at one point when Amélie was mentioned just after the pigeon flew across the room.

When he opened his eyes he saw Lydia's face and the pang of Amélia caught in his chest. Lydia still had fair hair. Like Amélie, every single model and woman in his life had been dark. It was the exotic, the dark, that interested him, had always interested him. Lydia was the exception. She held the cigarette away from her face between thumb and forefinger as a conductor would a baton. The mandarin-orange-colored drapes had been drawn. Someone must have drawn them after he lost consciousness.

She took a final draw, let out a whip of mustard-yellow smoke, put out the cigarette in the saucer of a teacup that was on his nightstand. They must have had tea, but he could not remember. Lydia pulled the chair up beside him, sat down and flipped the duvet away from his feet. This time her hands were burning hot on his cold feet as she rubbed the ball of each foot with each of her thumbs. The leg cramps were eased by the massage. He whispered anxiously, "If I close my eyes, maybe I'll never open them again? Wouldn't you think that Amélie would want to see me one more time?"

Against his will, his eyelids drooped and he dozed, but, sleep was, as always, elusive. After an interval he became pensive.

"What was it that Brancusi said about the color blue – ' ... the sky that men believe to be blue is not. It is black beyond.' Something like that. My first love affair with the color blue was the dots my mother made on porcelain vases and bowls. Young as I was at the time, my dark mother let me stir paint while she decorated those porcelains with various lines and patterns and dots."

*

Lydia's fingers increased their pressure. She could hardly believe she was 42 years old. Her hands continued to be as strong as they were when she was 19. These same hands had once facilitated her survival as masseuse working on all manner of bodies and feet, some washed, others unwashed, at the spa near Pyatigorsk, one step from starvation. She once told the Polish cook when she was asked that remembering Russia meant revisiting hunger and body lice. She could hardly bare to recall the many ways as a young woman she earned the bits of money that took her, step by step, across Russia, across Europe, to France, stopping finally in Nice where the sun eased everything. She had more than a pang of nostalgia for the language of her birth.

The only keepsake that survived Russia was her father's deck of cards with which she had played so many games of Patience that many of the red and black indices were worn away by the oil on her fingertips. The only good memory she had of childhood was when the high Caucasian mountains turned green at sunset. As the years passed, she wondered if she had seen correctly, if the sunset was really green.

He was wide awake, implored, "Get me a cigarette, I need to calm down."

*

Because it was winter, the damp during the night permeated his bones. Lydia brought a pot of tea that was burning hot, the way she liked it. She spread the plaid mohair blanket across his legs. A storm was approaching Nice; there were rumblings of distant thunder. He spoke quietly.

"During the hours of insomnia, scenes keep burping up even though I have no wish to take stock of the long ago. Against my will my mind reconfigured the long-gone past, the hawthorn trees that were heavy with orange and red berries. At night the berries glowed in gaslight."

"Shall I take down your comments?"

"If you think what I say needs noting. I'm not sure anymore."

"I'll take them down. Later I can decide what is important and what isn't."

She was fibbing. She doubted there was much that was not worth preserving.

"During winter in Paris in those days, the berries really did glow in the gaslight. I was always dashing because of the cold, crisscrossing Montparnasse past the gardens that grew vegetables for the many markets."

The sound of thunder drew nearer.

"I gauged my mood by the quickness or lack of it in my step. In winter the black soil in the gardens was coated by a skin of frost. Académie Colarossi was on the rue de la Grande-Chaumière. The large studio where we gathered to sketch nude models was warmed by a woodstove so hot that we artists as well as the models dripped perspiration."

There was a look of damaged marble about his hands.

"What year was this? 1897? 1898? I didn't mind the smell of sweat nor the tinny Chopin played by the hired piano player because I was entirely focused on the body of the model on the platform. The memory of the night of the terrible fire at the opera house was still fresh; I was still guilty about abandoning my cousin to the flames and my concentration was easily interrupted. Outside the studio was the courtyard that was bordered on both sides by large, gloomy trees. Whether or not I was ready, the model was instructed to change poses at the end of 15 minutes. Fifty centimes bought two hours of drawing time, eight different poses. It was never enough."

They heard a crackling rumble followed by explosive thunder above them, a deluge of rain poured from the sky.

"At the end of the two hours, I was fatigued but elated, would walk to the Café de Versaille across from Gare Montparnasse which was usually filled with Norwegians shouting at each other in a language that sounded like they had stones in their mouths. With my cache of newly born drawings tucked under my arm, like a new mother, I drank a glass of beer and looked over my night's work. If I had a few extra coins, I'd make a short visit to the brothel. I was never asked, *'Pour la nuit ou pour un moment?'* Because *'Pour un moment'* was written all over me. By the time I left the red, mirrored room, I would be relieved of all vestiges of fatigue."

His voice was fading.

"I'm not sure what happened with all those drawings from those years. Only Amélie would remember. I can't believe she hasn't come."

The mention of his wife's name had the usual effect of bringing a pallor to his face. Shaky from loud thunder cracks, Lydia refilled her cup with tea. She lit a fresh cigarette from the last one, laid out another line of cards.

"Camille loved thunderstorms. As for me, I worship the thunderclap. Not literally, but as my *coup de foudre* ... Mademoiselle Inspiration."

Flashes of lightening illuminated the drawn drapes. Forceful rain beat heavily against the building. His voice was fading.

"Once I married, instead of visiting a brothel, I stopped at the delicatessen on Boulevard du Montparnasse for a treat to bring to Amélie and Marguerite. I saw tomatoes as small as grapes and, of course, could not resist bringing home a few. When the proprietor asked if I wanted to taste Hungarian stew flavored with pepper and paprika, I, of course, said yes. The evocation of that taste does not seem 54 years old but the same now as it was then."

A smash of thunder. Lydia crossed herself in the Russian way. Matisse ran his fingertips through his beard.

"I'm near the end. Much will be written about my work, about me. Among the commentary and biography and analysis of my work and long life, you will remain a fair-minded, intimate eyewitness of these past 20 years. In this late part of my life, you have come the closest to understanding and accepting all of me, the good and the bad, the warm and the cold. You know what holds the minutes of every day together. We both know that the work of these past years will not be viewed as important as my earlier work."

"We'll see."

He half smiled.

"Will anyone remember what Mademoiselle Stein said of me? That ' ... Henri Matisse doesn't know how to have fun. He wears a tie when he paints! He wears a tie when he screws!'"

His smile was erased by the pain in his calves. When he shifted his legs, he made it worse, not better. The sound of his voice was almost inaudible.

"The interest in my personal life irritates, has always irritated me. I'm deadly dull. So what if I once visited a brothel for an hour in the afternoon? I don't think anyone should know that I can identify a syphilis canker from across the room? Why should a need to ejaculate fluids before they became stagnant and bred bacteria be explained? Who wouldn't wish to flush out his plumbing, often and thoroughly? Will people think better or worse of me if I reveal that the thing that drove me to paint was a rising urge to strangle someone?"

The thunder withdrew into the distance, the rain became steady, soporific. Lydia smoked. Matisse unclenched his fists.

"I think I may be able to sleep for a few hours."

*

Lydia took the tray with the teapot and cups when she left, setting it in the pantry to be washed.

315

Hoping to perk up, she poured a full water glass of vodka from the bottle in the cabinet. She carried the glass inside, sat down at the desk with pen and paper before her. The time had come to put her thoughts in order, to think about herself. By occupying a space that adjoined his immortality, she had avoided any quandary of decision-making. She swallowed some of the liquid in the glass. The time to draw on the large stock of material she had gathered from 20 years as his eraser and sponge was now. Of course the biographers would write about her, too, would speculate about whether or not she and Matisse were lovers. She would never help them solve this mystery. This secret would die with her and would die with him, too. Only they knew the truth. Let the lascivious busybodies keep guessing.

What would they say of her Siberian mother? Probably nothing because no one was alive who had known her. No one would ever know that her mother had seen exotic crystallized grapes dipped in a strong sulfur bath that afterwards retained the shape of grapes though they became stiff with sulfur crystals. In a wavering voice only she would remember, her mother had described the relic of a nail from the cross on which Christ was crucified.

Her mother had seen a swatch of fabric from Christ's shirt in a glass box during a pilgrimage to the Uspensky Cathedral in Moscow. These oft-repeated tidbits were told before bedtime prayers, before her mother rose up, made the blessing over her.   Whenever her mother spoke of crucifixion, Lydia became sick with the thought of what it must be like to have a nail hammered into one's palm. When she would squeeze her mother's cottony hand, she tried to imagine a nail going through both hands, making it so that they could not pull apart from each other.

The Russia she remembered was not the Russia of white birch trees, black bears, balalaika strings.   The serene, unruffled exterior Lydia exhibited gave no clue of the typhoid and cholera she had lived among, of the bedbug-bitten little girl scratching the skin off her body like a dog. If she was noticed at all in these past 20 years, she was seen as a silky, efficient swan, or sneered at, called a designing whore.   No more than two people remained alive who knew that she had been married once, and had survived more than one affair that had gone bad with men who gambled and debased her.

Like everything else, her erotic history would go with her to the grave. Few who met her would guess that beneath the water the swan's sap-green legs were paddling frantically. There had never been news as to what the Soviets had done about Christ's nail and the cloth from Christ's coat.

Cimiez, 1954

Lydia sat in the red and white striped armchair with papers on her lap while Matisse shuffled from plant to plant, testing if the soil was moist, deadheading geraniums. Of course she was smoking. As he had requested, she was reading to him from a just-published biography written by an Englishman:

... He could do headstands and cartwheels. Every day he practiced to be an acrobat in back of his family seed and hardware store that also supplied fertilizer and fodder to the local farmers who grew beets in the area of northeastern France that melted into Flanders where they lived. He was a disgrace because he had ended his lower school career by leaning over a stairwell and spitting directly on the top hat of his teacher.

She looked up.

"True or false?"

He was bent, riffling through the trash bin, bracing himself with one hand against the wall, amused.

"Quite true."

He had rescued a handful of bits of charcoal that Lydia had thrown into the bin. His corset cut into his ribs. He said with a scolding voice, "You must not throw charcoal away, even if it seems like only a fragment. Go on."

... He spent two months in bed. The overt reason was a vague stomach and bowel disorder but, covertly, he needed to buy time to stave off his father's directive that it was time he went to work. But what work would be right for him? He was such a poor student. Such a clown. His ...

"I wasn't that bad a student! Lazy, yes. Stupid, no. A clown? Ha."

Everywhere were objects, things he had picked up at secondhand shops and flea markets – cherished swatches of fabrics, scraps of embroidery, tobacco jars, vases, both glass and ceramic, fishbowls, a pewter pitcher, cups, saucers, plates, some chipped, some not, chards of French faience. He took a green apple from a fruit bowl. It had been balanced on top of a pyramid of apples. He could no longer bite into anything that firm because of his teeth, so he returned it to the top of the pyramid. Lydia continued reading.

... His father sought the advice of the family priest, who suggested that perhaps the boy could become a pharmacist and the family could set him up in a chemist's shop ...

Matisse interrupted, "It was the family doctor, not the priest."

Lydia made a notation with a pen. Woozy from exertion, he sat on the side of his bed, tried to clean his glasses.

"I've been called a hypochondriac. If I felt symptoms, who is to say whether they're real or imagined? A pain is a pain. These biographers are molding me into a neurotic, eccentric, when essentially I'm neither."

He folded his glasses, placed them on the revolving bookshelf that held his sketchbooks just as the white pigeon landed on the edge of the lamp and spread its wings. It had been a painful day and it was turning into a pain-filled night. His skin was grayish-yellow. His eyes burned.

"I think you should ask the nurse to bring the thermometer."

When the nurse walked in he complained, "If I can't work, I can't exist."

"Try to sleep for a little while. I will mix a sleeping powder into brandy for you if you like."

He called, "Lydia, bring my scissors."

The nurse smoothed down tufts of hair, looked for the sleep medicine among the many pharmaceuticals on the tray. Lydia handed over the scissors, then went out onto the terrace for a breath of air. All of Nice was spread below. The copper dome of the Orthodox Church was on fire.

*

Lydia told him that she had read that his old friend Pierre Courthion claimed that his first drawing teacher had derided him. That he had once told Courthion:

... during my first lesson Bourguereau called me on the carpet for using my finger to smudge a charcoal sketch and failing to center a drawing on my sheet of paper.

As his eraser for these many years, she was amused. It was she who wiped out his mistakes, cleaned up his smudged charcoal marks. He said he would think about what she had read, closed his eyes.

She went into the kitchen and filled a glass with vodka, then cut a thick piece of bread with a long knife, spread it with butter and sprinkled salt over the butter. She carried it back to the desk and laid out the cards. It was good vodka made in Nice by an émigré who also made face cream. She abandoned the game of Patience, held the bread with one hand and picked up the book with the other, read what Félix Vallotton had written:

The second shop window was the best: 12 glass bottles, drawn up in battle order on a stand and filled to the brim with colors whose very names made me feel proud. They were in order, pale chrome yellow, dark chrome yellow, cadmium, cobalt blue, ultramarine,

Prussian blue, milori green, English green, rose madder, Austrian vermilion, Turkey red and pure carmine.

Beside it, she noted in pencil:

He doesn't remember the window of his family's shop in any detail – he told me when I read this to him.

She put the book down on top of the incomplete Patience game, scattering cards. People had warned that his family would have her out within hours after he drew his last breath. She had better start thinking about her future, how to go back out into the world after 20 years in the aura of greatness. Had she outgrown her attraction for gamblers? She noticed that it had gotten dark. She saw the first glinting citrine-colored star of evening. In childhood, Uncle Bora said that if she made a wish on this star, it would always be filled. She made two wishes: One was that bedbugs would never again crawl over her flesh. The other was that the monstrous husband of her youth would never come to look for her.

New York, 2001

John disappeared, could not be reached by phone. Alice's old father took much of her time. He was having more eye trouble, had blocked arteries,

322

emphysema, early signs of dementia. She hoped that by showing up, which her brother never did, she would make points with her father, who was redoing her will. While thumbing through the *Daily News* she read an article titled "Christie's Draw: Matisse":

Half a century ago, Denise Arokas, a 19-year-old French girl, arrived at a Paris address to look after an elderly artist whose name was unfamiliar to her.

The name was Matisse, and he was so taken with his nurse that he asked if he could draw her. She agreed.

Next month, the seven pencil drawings he did will be auctioned at Christie's in London.

Christie's expects the drawings to bring 210,000 pounds, roughly $306,700. One on which he wrote a note to her may fetch 60,000 pounds.

Arokas, now 69, would like to use the proceeds to establish a foundation for artists in the French countryside.

Last fall, a Matisse drawing in charcoal fetched $2.7 million at Christie's. A year ago, a Matisse pencil study drew $830,750 at Sotheby's.

Arokas fondly recalls her patient, who was then over 80.

"He was very harmonious and not demanding," she said. "Even when he needed something in the night, he would not wake me. He was very charming."

The artist, considered a giant of 20th-century painting, gave Arokas drawing lessons and also started her on a successful modeling career.

Matisse died in 1954 at age 85.

She phoned John Lightfoot and left a message but did not hear back from him.

Two months after she left the message, he phoned at eight in the morning, spewing apologies. He was not usually up until noon, so it was odd to hear his high, nervous voice so early in the morning. Nervy or not, the voice still roused the lust she thought was gone but was not.

"I'm moving Claude. I've gotten her an assisted living place on the Upper West Side, near me. I've been trying to get her into a place for five years. She doesn't want to go but I told her she has to, that if she gets sick I will be able to look after her. It's got an elevator. She can't walk up those stairs anymore. It takes her an hour now. Could you spend the day with her, the day I move her things?"

"The thought of being alone with her makes me anxious."

"Can't you gird your loins?"

"All right."

In early April, as promised, Alice walked west on Christopher Street to a senior center on Greenwich Street. Amidst two dozen geriatrics, she found Claude wearing black tights, a black blouse, red leather shoes; her hair was tied back with a Prussian-blue stretch band that took the hair off her face; her cheekbones protruded. She was in the dining area eating a lunch of chicken legs, peas,

324

carrots and applesauce. She was separating the peas and the carrots – an orange pile, a green pile – with her fork, did not look up. Beside her on the floor, a mesh tote bag crammed full and zipped closed. The attendant leaned over, whispered in her ear, "*Chérie.*"

She looked up, saw Alice, was unresponsive. After a few seconds she reached out her hand for Alice to clasp, as the Pope might with a supplicant. She motioned for Alice to sit with her while she finished eating. When the plate was half empty, she pushed it away and the attendant gave her a firm arm, helped her stand up, told Alice, "She's sleepy."

"I'm not sleepy. I just want to end my life in my own apartment."

Alice picked up a sweater made of a synthetic fabric that looked like confetti and helped her put it on. The attendant handed over the cane. John had recently repainted it cobalt blue, given it a coat of lacquer, added a pommel to the top that he had covered with gold leaf as Claude had requested, giving it the look of a king's scepter. Bracing herself with the strong stick, she climbed down the steps to the sidewalk while Alice hailed a taxi.

At 24th and Ninth they got out. For 10 minutes Claude stood in reverie in front of a black wrought-iron fence that surrounded a blossoming tree. She ogled the pure-carmine grass and the small chrome-yellow shrubs ringing the area. She tried to reach through the bars to pick a pistachio-green blossom but could not reach far enough. Alice tried,

325

too, but could not catch hold. After a while, Alice took her arm and led her past the uniformed doorman who stood at the door of a tall, tinted glass and chrome building.

They got off the elevator on the 12th floor. Alice had made up the bed so Claude could lay down but Claude dropped her tote bag beside the lizard-green rattan chair in the living room and sat down on it. From there she could view the rooftops, skyline and sky. Claude removed a faux terra-cotta flowerpot from her tote, set it on the white enamel art deco table that had cobalt-blue glass. She punched a button and called Alice's name. A fiddle played "Cotton-Eyed Joe" and the top of the box popped open. Four yellow daisies with green stems did a squaredance to the music. When the music stopped, she punched the button again. After the third time, Alice excused herself.

Holding onto the wall, leaving dirty prints from her hands on it, Claude walked around the apartment viewing the many paintings and prints and drawings. She saw that the ruined silkscreen Warhol had given her was hanging on Alice's wall. So Alice stole. Had she also stolen the sketchbook Matisse had meant for her? She noticed a painting of a man's genitals done with pale pastels – pale gold, king's blue, Indian yellow. It was framed in wood that was painted gold and held the place of honor centered above the white brocade couch. She told Alice, "The man who made this, I knew his mother."

326

"Andy's mother?"

"You know Andy's mother, too?"

"No. I knew Andy."

"I don't know what happened to his mother after he died. She may have died from grief for him. Could you find out? I would like to see her again."

Alice promised she would try. Claude glanced at the penis painting. So Alice was not a saint. She was glad to know it. When she glanced into the bedroom she saw a painting made up of dozens of green dollar bills. Another Warhol. Where were John's paintings? They should be on her walls, too. Alice's bed looked like St. Nicholas' sleigh. On it a blood-colored bedspread.

Claude sipped mint tea, ate chocolates, dozed, thumbed through copies of *Flash Art* and *Art in America* while Alice sat to her desk and paid bills. At one point Alice telephoned her father to check on whether or not the results of the test that he had done to assess the damage to his optic nerve had come back. It had not. Every time Alice went into the living room to check on her, Claude was dozing in the rattan chair. When Alice said her name she opened her eyes and said in a thin ribbon of voice, "I'm sorry I'm no good at talking. I'm 87 years old. Do you keep real butter in your house?"

Alice shook her head. John was supposed to arrive at four but had not. A worm was gnawing at her insides. She put on various CDs – Pablo Casals playing "Saint-Saëns", Schumann, Boccherini,

327

Campagnoli from 1915, and Catalan folk music "El Cant dels Ocells" from 1950, Amália Rodrigues singing Fado from Portugal – all of which Claude seemed to enjoy though she kept her eyes closed.

At seven the doorbell insistently squawked. When Alice opened it, John rushed into the living room, breathless. The move was complete. He was ready to take Claude to her new home. Alice was relieved because, in recent years, John didn't always show up when he said he would. She feared that one day, lost in the crack world, he would never show up again. As he gathered her things, Claude gave him an angry look. He told Alice, "She's angry at me for moving her. But ... " he flashed the palms of his hands in frustration, " ... if she got sick, I couldn't promise to keep her at home ... care for her ... downtown ... "

Claude turned the milori green palms of her own hands heavenward in renunciation.

*

Alice phoned the gallery that was handling Warhol's estate and explained that she would like to have the three Warhols she owned appraised. A Swede who worked for the gallery was sent to take photographs. Nikon camera in hand, he snapped dozens of photos of each of the works.

"I wonder if you know anything about what happened to Andy's Czech mother?"

"I know plenty. Of course, as you'd imagine, she got old. She drank. I mean, really drank. She had a stroke or something. Heart gave out. After that her mind wasn't ever right again. She would roam the neighborhood, forget to lock the door to his house. Finally he sent her back to Pittsburgh so that his brothers' wives could care for her. But she was too much of a handful. She kept running away, tried to find Andy ... tried to go to church by herself, tried to get back to New York. She would get lost. She shouted at people that they were fat cows, so they put her in a home. She died of a heart attack. Of course it was an expensive home, and she was given an expensive funeral because Andy paid for everything."

"Did his mother know him when he visited?"

"He never visited. But she should be satisfied, he's buried beside her."

He removed a last roll of film from his camera.

"We'll get back to you with estimates. Are you auctioning or selling?"

"I'm evaluating my estate. But ... I am interested in buying, too. Has the estate catalogued all the photos Andy did of men's cocks?"

"Yes."

"I'd like to buy the photo of one particular cock. I can give you the name of the man."

"I don't think they're catalogued by name."

"Not to embarrass you, but I can identify the cock I want if I saw a photo."

"I don't handle photographs.   I'll have someone phone you who does."

*

Alice brought yellow tulips to Claude, took the elevator to the sixth floor of the assisted living facility on West 54th. John had just come from his night job, his eyes were encircled with plum-colored rings.   He let her in and pointed out newly assembled shelves. Dozens of his watercolors, other prints and paintings filled the walls.   There were dirty plates in the sink. He whispered, "She's having the biopsy next week. She's refused a mammogram but has agreed to have a needle biopsy. This way, if it's bad news, I can nurse her."

Claude emerged from the bedroom wearing black and red stripes. She held onto the wall for balance, walked to meet Alice. She took her hand, navigated her over to look at the mechanical kitschy toys, to show off a jack-in-the-box that popped up and gave Alice a fright.   John left to fill a prescription, promised he would be back in 10 minutes. Not trusting him, Alice began to perspire.

She put down the shopping bag full of "soft" foods from the local Gristedes – macaroni and cheese, meatloaf, California roll, beets, cornbread, chocolate cake, a tub of Danish sweet butter. She smelled a fetid odor near or in the kitchen sink. Claude was subdued, inscrutable, her cheeks were swollen. She reached out her hand for Alice to take as Alice laid out the plastic containers in a row on her little kitchen table and then slowly crossed the room, sat down on the daybed. Claude's hair was twisted back; her legs, especially the ankles, were swollen, bruised black and blue. Over the plum and azure striped pedal pushers she wore a malachite-green smock, thick, well-worn fawn-colored cloth slippers were on her feet. When Alice sank down into a green easy chair beside the daybed, Claude handed her a soft, stuffed animal – a white furry bear.

After a few moments of silence, Claude spoke slowly, as if she were speaking to a child.

"I'm not social. I'm no good with people ... My marriage was no good. I thought we would be like Gauguin and his muse."

"Gauguin abandoned his wife."

"Then we were like Gauguin. I should never have modeled after the war. I could have lived out my life in a convent. But, if I had not modeled, I would never had sat for Alice, or Matisse, or your Warhol. That I don't regret."

Had Claude modeled for Andy? Flames rose in Alice's cheeks. She realized that she had forgotten to hide the Warhol she had let John, in his foolishness, give her. Best to change the subject, try for Claude's sympathy.

331

"My marriage was not what it looked like from the outside. My husband died of AIDS. He wasn't really heterosexual when I met him but he tried hard to be."

Alice admired the 4-foot-high black-and-white blow-up copy of Matisse's drawing – *Claude, 1950* – that dominated the north wall.

"He was 80 *ans*. In bed. You can have it when I die."

She took a manila envelope off the bed and handed it to Alice. Inside, two yellowing envelopes, both addressed to Madam Claude Foot. The handwritten return address on both was *H. Matisse. Le Regina. Cimiez, Nice.* Inside postcards on which notes written in French signed by Matisse were also handwritten. After a reverential interlude, Alice said, "These must be priceless."

"Why don't I put these in my safe deposit box for you. I'll Xerox them and give you copies. That way you'll know the originals are safe."

Claude got up, stood before Roy's painting on the eastern wall.

"Yes, if you insist, take them for safety. Everything that is mine is for John after my death. You will not forget this?"

"No."

Claude stood close to Roy's painting.

"My husband. We were in Florida for some years."

She pointed her index finger up at the woman in the painting done in Cubist style.

"Me. The Madonna."

She pointed her finger at the prone figure.

"My husband. Christ."

"Do you like it here?"

"I don't like the elevator. I'm not social. I like artists, *chérie*. But bourgeois people, I don't like."

"Do you miss the old neighborhood?"

"I wanted to end my life in my little place on First Avenue near St. Bridget's Church ... with a comic steeple. There's no St. Bridget's here. No spires of Sainte Chapelle, no Franciscan convent, no park."

Perhaps food was the way to Claude's heart? Though it made her queasy, Alice searched the kitchen area and found two unmatched gunmetal-green ceramic plates in the dish drainer. She placed the California roll and some macaroni and cheese on the plates.

"I have a sedentary life at last ... a nun's life without scrubbing hard floors with a bucket of ammonia burning my eyes."

Claude bit into a piece of the California roll. Though Alice wondered if it was wise to eat off the plate, wanting to please her, she did. What looked like a flea jumped from macaroni to California roll. She put the plate down as John burst back in. He was nothing like he had been when he left; he was manic. The cheeks that were cognac-hued had

333

become bright opal, his dark brown eyes were wide, as if he had glimpsed something astonishing. He spoke in staccato.

"Sorry I'm late. I was getting Claude's medicine ... "

He sat down in the second easy chair, caught his breath.

"Oh hell, I'm always late."

Claude laughed. John looked at Alice.

"Claude's got a bladder infection. That's why they've postponed the lumpectomy. They did a urine test, found E. coli, her hygiene's pretty awful ..."

He sounded like a hyena.

" ... they want to do another one. Another urine test."

He took off his blue and white Yankees baseball hat and laid it on the daybed, then emptied out a bottle of pills from a paper bag.

" ... antibiotics ... "

Claude bolted forward, "Never put a hat on the bed ... very bad luck in France."

He grabbed the cap from the bed, tossed it onto a kitchen chair. The day had darkened, gloom pressed against the window. He filled a plate with food and began stuffing it into his mouth like a man who was starving. Claude showed him the small, blank diary that had a Matisse painting of a blond woman on the cover.

"The Lady gave ...," and pointed to the painting of a blond woman on its cover, "Lydia. The Lady help me like Lydia help Monsieur Matisse."

Alice began to scratch herself. Big splats of rain dropped out of the afternoon gloom.

New York, 2002

More dates for the lumpectomy in Claude's breast were cancelled. When Alice's phone rang, John shouted.

"Good news. We had the lumpectomy. She came through. We're on 17th and Eighth Avenue. Claude's hungry. Want to meet us at Bendix in Chelsea? I think it's around 22nd or 21st Street."

Alice put on her shoes, gift-wrapped some silver jewelry from Thailand that she was saving for Claude and ran down Eighth Avenue to the coffee shop. At a booth, Claude was eating Thai coconut soup and brown rice. John had a big bowl of chicken noodle soup on the table in front of him, was devouring it. Claude regally reached out her hand. Alice had not planned to kiss it but did. Between gulps of soup, John explained, "She's ashamed to see you. She's not wearing makeup or lipstick."

Claude was wearing a somber dark brown blouse, black trousers. John spoke in a rant.

"I'm so happy. Listen to this. Claude was in the hospital. She opened her eyes and told me that she couldn't have the juice on the side table because she was waiting to have the surgery. I told her she'd already had the surgery. She still doesn't believe me ... doesn't believe that she had it. It's true, she ... " He laughed, slurped soup, pulled off a chunk of bread and stuffed his mouth, " ... did but it was so painless, she still doesn't know. They didn't even put in stitches. I'm telling you she doesn't believe they did it."

A minute flea circled Claude's rice. Alice began to itch. Claude ate with one hand, opened the gifts Alice had put in front of her with the other, examining the various pieces of silver jewelry. Then she re-wrapped it all carefully. She continued eating.

"She has quite an appetite, regardless."

"Oh, nothing ever interferes with Claude's appetite ... though it isn't what it used to be. I don't know when I got one, but I've got one now, too. I'm hungry all the time."

*

It was a humid, sick-making day in February; the temperature went into the 70s. Alice's father was suffering from a new array of illnesses: gout, tremors in his hands, inability to recognize people. There was no reply to her knock, so Alice left the brown paper bag that contained the *New York Post*, a copy of *Vogue*, a container of coffee and a piece of marble fudge cake in front of Claude's door and punched

336

the down button on the elevator. She was just getting on the elevator when she heard the lock on Claude's door release, saw Claude peeking out, leaning on her cane.

Alice let the elevator door close and Claude drew her in. Alice put the fudge cake on a plate. She poured coffee into a mug, sat down across from Claude at the kitchen table. Claude was wearing a cotton nightgown, the TV was on. She looked angry.

"I'm not American, even though I've been here 40 years, I'm still French. We take life ... gravely. McVeigh ... "

Found guilty of the Oklahoma City bombing, Timothy McVeigh had been executed that morning. The cake was melting. Alice ate her slice. Claude cut hers into little squares, speared one with a small steak knife, put it into her mouth. Scraping the melted fudge from the plate with the sharp blade of the knife, she gathered fudge, then inserted the knife into her mouth, licked fudge from the blade. Alice winced. Square by square, Claude speared, scraped and licked brown cake and icing.

"Putting to death is murder. I want to see your magenta glass table again ..."

"You mean the coffee table with the cobalt-blue glass with the crack?"

"Yes. I said magenta but I mean blue."

"A stoned friend just put a boiling teapot on top of it and it cracked."

Claude handed her a stuffed monkey wrapped with watermelon-colored paper, also a small tin of tuna in spring water. On TV, the sound muted, was the 1950s film *The Robe*. Claude told her, "Victor Mature! I saw this in Florida with Roy's mother."

Victor Mature was being tortured by Roman soldiers. As they watched, Claude whispered, "I fell and hit my shoulder, *chérie*."

Alice touched her shoulder.

"Can you lift your arm?"

She lifted her arm, rubbed Alice's leg with her hand.

"Your father? His eyes? I've been praying for him."

"He's brave."

" ... Matisse was brave."

"The doctor diagnosed dry macular degeneration rather than wet MD. The former is the slower-progressing form. My father remarried, you know. She's my age."

"And his eyes?"

"He won't go blind. He had a cataract operation this week that left some edema and has caused him to see all people with long heads and large noses. Since the surgery, my father periodically walks over to his new wife to feel her nose, to make sure it isn't long like it looks to him, but is the same little nose he remembered."

Splayed and tied to a rack, being tortured, Victor Mature glistened with spilled blood. Richard Burton lurched on screen with a band of Christians to rescue him. Alice's ankles itched and sweat was dripping down her back.

"We didn't have TV in Florida, no phone, no TV ... nothing. Do you like black people?"

"It depends on the person. Do you?"

"We have not so many in France. John has a new friend who is black."

"A good friend?"

"They're like husband and wife."

Alice stiffened. On the screen, Richard Burton and Jeanne Simmons were reunited.

"Please take me to see the film *Moulin Rouge*."

"I will ask John."

"You must buy John's work. You're rich, you have rich friends, you must make them buy, too. He must believe more in his work. If he continues working for sick old men and women, he won't paint anymore. For the sake of your soul you must care for John. Lydia cared for Matisse. John cares for me. You must care for John. Maybe somewhere someone will care for you ... "

*

Claude had her remaining teeth removed. Her face turned black, blue, lavender. A new tumor had developed on the side of her jaw. At the coffee

339

shop on Ninth Avenue she rearranged the food on her plate – green peas on one side, orange carrots on the other. She swallowed a large forkful of meatloaf and began to choke.

John shouted, "Spit it out!"

Her nose turned black and blue. John reached his fingers into her mouth and pulled out the food. The normal color returned to her face.

That night he telephoned Alice. As ice cubes rattled he slurred his words.

"She would rather have died than spit out food. I'm at my wit's end with her. Oh ... I was in a street fair and sold three paintings. I'm painting again. I hadn't mentioned it because I was afraid it wouldn't last but it's lasting. Not a lot but enough to scratch the itch. I won the blue ribbon, too. Claude said you wanted to buy some of my new work. I'll bring some to show you one of these days. If Friday is okay we can take her to see *Moulin Rouge*. Claude thinks we should get discounts on the tickets. She said, '*Chéri*, You're an artist, I'm a model, Alice collects and protects. Tell them at the movie theater to give us discounts.'"

At the wheelchair-accessible movie complex on 42nd Street, John wheeled her into the theater and across the lobby in a borrowed wheelchair. Alice sat beside the wheelchair and John beside Alice. John was fingering a pink St. Christopher's metal. When the film opened with a fantasy view of the rooftops of Paris, Claude waved one hand in greeting.

Cimiez, 1954

A cigarette between his lips, he was wearing his favorite old gray sweater, a green-blue wool scarf around his neck, sitting in the wheelchair cutting figures from paper that Lydia had painted periwinkle and navy. On the floor on all sides, also on his lap, periwinkle and navy cuts and scraps and spirals of paper. The spasms he was having in his eyes all afternoon had finally abated. Lydia and Matisse were assembling a list of his many models. She would worry about chronology later. She was trying to smoke less but could not keep her resolve.

He recited:

"Zita comes into my mind. A Hungarian gypsy named Wilma Javor. There's Lisette Lowengard, Hélène Galitzine. Lily. Loulou. Rosa Arpino. I used her often. Bevilacqua, a male model I liked very much. He was very good. Jeanne Thiery who married my brother. Jeanne Vaderin whose bust I made. Greta Moll sat for me for at least a week. Greta Prozor ... ah, how she leaned on the back of a chair. Mistinguette, Paule Brebion, Gabrielle Lang. We paid 50 centimes for three hours, we each had a cherry brandy to warm ourselves, the studio was unheated. Antoinette. Jeanette. Zorah. Germaine Raynal ... *Woman on a High Stool* ... have I mentioned her before?"

"I don't think so."

"I remember Micheline Payor."

341

He pointed to a sheet of magenta paper Lydia had painted.

"Is it dry?"

She handed it to him. The scissors cut into it. He curled and bent his wrist, turning the paper round and back with the other hand. The figure of a magenta woman's body in motion emerged.

"I remember Zulma well. Antoinette. Princes Galitzin. Many Negro models all in a row. They were like cathedrals. Lorette. Those many art students and film extras during and after the war."

Lydia lit a new cigarette from the end of the last one, rubbed out the old one in a dish decorated with gold geese.

"There was Elena. I used women at the Cirqúe Medrano in Montmartre. There was Tamara. Micheline. Graciella was Guatemalan. Henriette Darricarrére. Ah ... a great source of inspiration. I used her again and again in the '20s and also her young brothers ... her daughter, too. There was Monique Bourgeois who cared for me during the war and remained as a studio assistant, assisting in preparation of materials, gouaches. Like Sister Paule, she read to me at night. I made some drawings of her, and then she called on me as Sister Jacques Marie, the Dominican nun, and convinced me to design the chapel in Vence. One of my models leaves the convent, the other joins. Amazing. But you were there, forgive me, you know all this. Do you think it mattered to them that I am not a Catholic, that I have no religion except the work that I do, my love of creation, my love of absolute sincerity?"

"They would never say so if it did."

"If it wasn't for their prayers, I'd probably be dead. They had enough religion for both of us. I am satisfied with my little chapel in Vence. I remember Nézy-Hamidé Chawkat, the granddaughter of the Sultan of Turkey. I once used a peasant's daughter in Brittany to make a study of a girl holding a pig on a string. You must not forget to make note of Lily the sheepdog."

Lydia looked at her watch.

"In a few minutes your Indonesian acupuncturist is arriving to treat your eyes."

"There was Clotilde. Pignatelli. I used her for years. At least three years running. She must have sat for me hundreds of times. Oh ... Antoinette, I don't remember her surname ... from Provence. Antoinette Arnoux. We joked that she had breasts like two liter bottles of Chianti. She was exceptionally tall ... and ... very young ... 15 or 16. Her sister modeled, too. Janie Michels. Mabel Warren. Of course there was my blond Russian who left fields of rye, fields of sunflowers and giant watermelons with only an icon and a kopek."

He stopped cutting and stared at her. "What will you do when I'm gone, Madam Lydia? You're too old to become a doctor."

"I'll study the piano. I'll learn to play Ravel."

343

Was she serious? He raised an eyebrow. He had given her various drawings and other work for years but knew she could not use them for her upkeep because she was sending them to the Hermitage Museum in the U.S.S.R. What would happen to her? She was no longer young. He would go to his grave worrying about her, unable to repay her for what she had given him, given freely – the best years of her life.

"*Eh bien.*"

He started on a new sheet of painted paper, a long magenta curlicue swirled toward the floor. He was cutting out the figure of a dancer. There was silence; finally he spoke.

"And of course I cannot forget Caroline Joblaud. She was 19 when I met her, the first true odalisque I ever saw."

It was unusual for him to speak of Camille, the mother of Marguerite.

"She worked in a hat shop, when she left me she regretted it ever afterwards. I painted Camille wearing black, Camille facing forward, turning, half turned, her back toward me, wearing a poppy-patterned dress. Camille sewing. Camille reading. She modeled while she was pregnant …"

He was silent, carefully turned the paper with one hand and wielding the scissors that was growing heavy with the other. Lydia put down her notebook, left and returned with a pot of tea. Each thinking his own thoughts.

*

"Marguerite was my model many, many times. In Bohain I painted old Mother Massé and her grandson Capella and her daughter Lili. In Bohain there were many peasant girls working in the fields who became subjects of my work. Amélie Parayre looked like a Spanish queen. After we were married I painted her in her black hat. I painted her in costumes, at the window, by the water's edge ... I painted her with pink roses, in mauve, April green, blue shadows, lemon yellow, orange ... but never in deep crimson, ornamental gold, absolute white, cold emerald green, cherry red, or Veronese green, except for her nose."

He swung the wheelchair round to the window.

"Amélie pawned her emerald ring so that I could buy Cezanne's *Three Bathers*."

"I didn't know that."

"Amélie should be here now. There was room for both of you in my life. I'm sure she knew this in her heart. Why did she jump ship? In my heart she never did. You remember Katia?"

"I do."

"And all the mussels, oysters, shrimp, dates, all my birds, even mosquitoes, that have modeled for me as well."

345

"I do because they bit me and not you. And I remember not being allowed to eat the oysters when there was nothing else or almost nothing else to eat."

His heaviness was lifting. He picked up the scissors from his lap, pointed to a sheet of paper that she had painted a light shade of opal as he'd asked. After she handed it over, he began cutting a bird.

"I remember Marie Vassilieff, Olga Meerson, Joaguina, Claude Boule, Fatima, Pauline Chadourne ... a waitress from the Tiaré ... the sublime Tahitiennes. Princess Nézy, plump Doucia Retinsky maybe 12 or 14 years old. Oh. Carla Avogadio, Mme. Franz Hift, Jeanne Marin, Victor Crosals, Denise Arokas, my grandchildren, a thousand others. Figs, pomegranates, myself ..."

He raised his voice.

"Cook?"

The cook heard him and came to the doorway.

"What do we have that would appease my sweet tooth?"

Cook smiled, left and returned with a fancy box of marzipan that she pressed into the old man's upturned hand. He pulled off the top of the box. Inside were little animals – a fuchsia cat, a lilac fox, an olive-green pig, a chromium-yellow duck, a mustard-colored cow, a slate-blue sheep. Matisse put down his scissors and took off his glasses. He looked down at the various pieces, unsure for a long time. He reached into the box, hesitated, then chose the cobalt-blue rabbit.

"Ah. Good colors sing!"

He took a small bite, chewed with pleasure.

"Each color in its own way is a stick of dynamite. And ... my models ... I've had hundreds ... maybe thousands. Just think, penetrated and impregnated thousands of times, pregnant, conceiving and then giving birth thousands of times. A fertile life indeed. Ecstatic. Enough creation to fill every seat on the train from here to Paris. Bring me my stick."

He roughly bit the blue rabbit in two. Lydia handed him the long stick and a choice of charcoal pieces, then pinned a fresh sheet of paper onto the wall beside the others. His hands were black before he finished inserting the piece of very black charcoal into the tip. He sighed contentedly.

"Without work, I simply cannot exist."

The Japanese nightingales must have woken because they began to trill. After a few seconds they abruptly stopped. Lydia went looking for a clean rag so he could wipe the black dust off his fingers. She did not hear him when he spoke.

"I'm 82. I have not changed. All this time I have looked for the same things. My models are the principal theme of my work. I've depended entirely on my models whom I observe at liberty and then I decide on the poses that best suit their natures."

Because additional help was needed, a hard-up young woman, Jacqueline, who had been modeling and acting as a studio assistant, was offered a live-in position. Once she was settled, if he felt well enough in the afternoon, he invited her to join them for a glass of Alsace wine. He did not complain when the summer heat began; hot or not he continued wearing the gray sweater. He started modeling something small with clay and agreed to let Alberto Giacometti, the not-so-young Swiss artist and sculptor, do his portrait.

When Giacometti arrived at the first session, Matisse told him, "Work quickly. I'm surely at the end."

There was a vase filled with rhododendrons on the work table surrounded by shards of broken crockery, swatches of embroidery, a marbled bowl filled with charcoal bits. The large puppet with yellow and white feathers attached to the wooden head hung from the wall, its various limbs attached to the body by heavy twists of rope that had unraveled through the years. The limbs that had been painted various bright colors had faded completely.

*

The Great Colette had died. All of France was in mourning. When Lydia picked up the telephone, it was a newspaper reporter bringing news that Matisse's first love, Caroline Jobaud, called Camille, had died.

"It's being said that Monsieur has returned to his Catholic upbringing since he designed the Vence chapel, that old age and ill health, maybe despondency, has sent him back to God."

"Oh?"

" ... the Catholic writer Henri Daniel-Rops said when he visited the chapel, 'The Christian finds here nothing between himself and God.'"

Spots of jade and scarlet appeared on her face. As if she was speaking to a child, she explained, "Whenever Monsieur Matisse is asked this he responds in the same way and I quote: 'My only religion is work. I made the chapel to express myself completely and for no other reason.' Nothing has changed him. He was and is an agnostic."

"He was once a Catholic."

"True. By the way, he's not despondent."

"Has a priest been to visit him?"

"No."

Matisse had given Camille a fistful of violets when five of his earliest paintings were included in an exhibition at the salon of the Société Nationale des Beaux-Art. One had sold. Later Camille left him because he changed his painting style, had abandoned the – as he called them – blisters and earth colors of his early work, began going wild with color. It did not seem to her that any good would come of deranged Technicolor madness. Lydia went into his room, told him about Camille's passing.

*

Lydia said to Jacqueline, "Change? People think things change, but they don't change."

In his blue and white striped pajamas, Matisse had been in bed all day, hardly doing more than making a few drawings with pencil. Giacometti was with him for three hours. When he was leaving, Lydia walked him to the door.

"He says that he cannot see."

In early evening Jacqueline cooked cod and potatoes and brought the tray to his bed. When she returned an hour later, the food was untouched. When she nagged he put up his hand.

"Stop. I'm not hungry. Please take it away."

She took the tray. Hoping to tempt him, she returned with a plate of his favorite pastries – palmiers. He took a few bites.

"Save the rest for tomorrow. Perhaps I'll have an appetite then."

He called out to Lydia, "Please bring fresh paper and a pencil."

She had been inventorying sketchbooks and stray drawings. Before he began to sketch, she held sketchbooks one at a time.

"This?"

"Lisette."

"This?"

"Claude."

"This?"

"Zorah."

*

After the doctor left, he tried to get out of bed but could not. Lydia went to take a bath because it was All Saints Day, November 1st. Later he told her that the sound of rushing water from the other side of the apartment was the last thing he remembered hearing, and the last feeling he remembered was being crushed by his corset. He later told her that when he opened his eyes he saw but did not feel the doctor puncturing his forearm with a sharp needle.

When the drug began to take effect, he was less groggy, got talkative.

"Renoir wasn't kept from painting in old age by the agony of rheumatism. He painted regardless. Even if his deformed hands were swathed in bandages, he worked. Once I painted a mischievous sequence of monochrome blue nudes. I would like to do another series of blue nudes before I die ... if I'm given one more tiny reprieve ... if one of my saviors is praying somewhere today. The new series will have no mischief."

The doctor returned in the evening. Matisse tried to push himself into a sitting position but the doctor held up his hand.

"You must not."

He scrutinized the doctor's oval head, champagne-colored moustache, teal-blue eyes. He would have taken up a pencil if he could pick up his hand, but he could not. He looked at Lydia.

"I've always known that one day I would be right, that one day would be the last day of my life. Now it has come."

*

November 2nd was All Soul's Day, the Day of the Dead, the day of white flowers. After the doctor told Lydia that he had had a cerebral embolism and would not last long, she gave up the idea of going out to the cemetery to look at the graves decorated with asters and chrysanthemums. She told Jacqueline, "There'll be other All Soul's Days."

Matisse slept. Lydia poured a glass of milori-green vodka, lit a cigarette and sat down at the English-green wood desk picking up her pen. She described the early part of the day before his embolism in her diary:

I washed my hair. With my hair wrapped in a towel, turban-style, I came to see him. I laughed and said, 'Any other day, you would ask me for some paper and

352

pencil.' 'Bring me some paper and pencil.' he said. I brought paper and a ballpoint pen. He began to draw me. He made four sketches of my head and shoulders, about six inches high with a fresh sheet each time. He gave me the sheets, then asked to see the last drawing again. He held it at arm's length. Looked severely. 'It's good,' he commented.

She drank the vodka. The time had come to pack the yellow suitcase. She could not put it off any longer. He would die either today, All Soul's Day. Or tomorrow. She poured more vodka to fortify herself.

By afternoon she had organized her possessions and left a small pile of what didn't fit in the suitcase on top against the wall of her room. Marguerite would arrive shortly, would surely be the one with him when he breathed his last breath. Lydia sat at his bedside, could detect his eau de cologne among the smells of old age and sickness. There was silence except for the sound of a fly beating its wings against the window glass, trying to get out. The red room was suffused with cast-iron flecks of light.

He was conscious but either could not or did not care to speak. The bells of the churches began to ring. The special mass for All Soul's Day was beginning. After a few minutes the sound of singing floated into the room and a clear light splashed across the pale pink floor. Lydia peeled the pearl-yellow coating off her face before she turned and left him alone in the room.

Alice opened her front door, saw John crying. His words came through a closed throat.

"When I got to the hospital they asked me, 'Who are you?' When I told them, they told me she hadn't been well cared for."

Alice took his wet overcoat and sat him down at her glass table. She made fresh coffee and piled doughy white cookies onto a plate, filled a blue and white bowl with Spanish olives. She had not put on makeup, was looking ordinary, aged. But so was he. He would be 60 soon. She was well into her 70s. She did not stop herself from caressing his hand. Tears rolled down his cheeks; he wiped them away with the back of his hand.

"She's becoming obstinate. I'm quitting as guardian."

Claude had fallen down in her apartment, lain on the floor for a day until she was found and taken by ambulance to St. Vincent's Hospital. John could not be located for 24 hours, had gone on a crack binge. When he finally got the messages, he rushed to the hospital.

"She fell in her own poop. When I got her home she was still wearing the clothes that were

354

smeared with poop. I had begged her to change since the visiting nurse was coming to interview her. She'd promised she would, then didn't. I couldn't be there because I had to work. When the nurse came she was wearing clothes that were crusted with feces."

The pupils of his eyes were wide as windows.

"That's why they think she isn't well cared for."

He walked over to Alice's window. His shoulders were shaking. He sat down on the couch and blew his nose.

"She's just obstinate. I've given her a good quality of life. I've spent the last years seeing to it that she got her teeth removed, got the lump in her breast removed. I've made her happy by painting again. She's the one who was nagging me to start painting again. They said that, when the nurse came, Claude stood in front of the door and physically kept her out. I'm not surprised that they put her in restraints in the hospital."

He ate the entire plate of oyster-shaped cookies, drank two more cups of black coffee and leaned back on Alice's milk-blue couch and shook his head. Alice wondered why he was not eating any of the Spanish olives.

"It was terrible to see her in restraints when I got to the hospital. She wouldn't look at me. She only wanted her rosary beads from France."

When he stood up he noticed the two cock paintings in gold frames hung side by side above the couch.   Since   Andy   Warhol   had   died   of complications after gallbladder surgery, he could never see his work without regretting that he had not taken over as his medic's instinct had urged him to. Perhaps Andy would be alive if he had. Here was one more life that had slipped through his fingers. He spoke to the paintings.

"R.I.P. Andy."

He gazed at the one on the right.

"Hello goodbye Ben."

*

Alice phoned and left a message on his machine:

"How is she?"

He did not return the call until a week later.

"She's in the hospital. She's fallen so many times she can't go home again. She can't eat regular food anymore. She has a brain tumor, maybe that's why she's been falling …"

"Why can't she eat regular food?"

Alice sipped from a large crystal glass of red wine.

"Because she chokes on food. That's why she passed out. She fell and probably that was what dislodged the food. Maybe she had a little stroke. Did I tell you that the lid of her eye is swollen shut?"

"No."

"She got pneumonia. I kept telling her, I know you're young inside but you have the body of an old lady."

"Can I visit her?"

"She's ashamed to be seen. She's incontinent, too …"

"Her birthday's coming."

He swore he would let her know when she could visit, and she waited, heard nothing from him for a week so she left two more messages on his machine. While she was uptown having her legs waxed, he called back and left a message but it was so slurred that she could not make head nor tail of it. Again she waited. A few days later he called. His voice was clear, sober.

"I got her into a nursing home on East 79th Street, the DeWitt Nursing Home."

On her birthday, December 16th, the city was covered with ice from rain that had frozen. Alice hired a car to take her across the slippery city. She told the driver to wait, then navigated the icy sidewalk to the front door of the nursing home. She had with her a tub of strawberry ice cream, a furry brown stuffed bear wrapped in blue and white striped paper, French perfume, had put everything inside a buff and black Saks shopping bag. Claude was in room 1111, a two-bedded room. An indigo-colored curtain separated her from the unseen person on the other side.

She was in the bed beside the door, supine, her face in fixed repose. A black eye-patch was covering her left eye. Alice pulled up a chair and sat beside her. When Claude opened her right eye she showed no surprise. She let Alice squeeze her hand. Alice bent and kissed it; she looked up and saw that Claude was wearing new, too-white false teeth.

"The food?

"You must speak up, *chérie*, I don't hear well on this side."

"Is the food good?"

"I detest it."

"The staff?"

"They're not patient."

A tray of pureed food was rolled in. Claude was indifferent to it. She searched for the button to raise herself up, could not find it. Alice looked, found it and raised her to semi-sitting position. She went into the bathroom, got a white washcloth, ran it under hot water, soaped it and came back to wash Claude's hands and face. She sat down on the chair and watched as she unwrapped her birthday gifts. It took her 30 minutes to remove eight pieces of Scotch tape from one package that was wrapped in velvety yellow paper. It took her another half-hour to unwrap the rest. When she had removed the last piece of tape, she folded all the wrapping paper and put it under the bed cover, just as John rushed in.

"Ah, *chéri.*"

He was bony, unshaven, shaky. He kissed Claude.

"Happy birthday."

"Don't tell The Lady how old I am."

He laughed.

"It's on your chart, Claude. It's too hard to keep a secret."

She was 88 years old. She made wiggling motions with her hand and he laughed again.

"Oh, sorry. I forgot."

He looked toward Alice.

"She wants me to bring in her snake. It's a toy ... don't worry. She wants the snake so she can scare the old people here."

Claude brought John's hand to her lips, kissed it repeatedly, making little pt-pt-pt sounds with her lips, leaving smudges of tomato-red lipstick on his knuckles. John lowered the bed to its original position while he told Claude about a new painting of his new black friend he had begun. Alice touched his back with her free arm. He was a sack of bones.

"Claude said you have a new 'friend' in your life. Is that who you're drawing?"

"Yes."

"A lover?"

He turned his back on Claude, spoke so Claude could not hear.

"Yes, if you must know. I don't talk about my sex life in front of Claude."

He turned back to Claude, handed her his gift that was wrapped with aluminum foil. She shook her head.

"You open it, *chéri*."

John unwrapped a framed print, then hung it over a monitor meant for oxygen on the wall where she could see it. It was a reproduction of a painting of Christ by Rouault. Claude made the sign of the cross, then shut her good eye.

*

Claude went on oxygen. Two days before Christmas Alice stood in the doorway of her room. The walls were painted pale avocado, the bedding was navy blue, the side table was painted a soft shade of oyster gray and had been varnished. Claude saw her, raised two fingers. Alice went in and sat beside her on a vermilion straight-backed chair, took her hand. Claude's cocoa-gray eyes met hers.

"Did you find out about Julia Warhol?"

"Yes, I did."

"Where is she? She must be very old."

"I don't like to be the bearer of bad news."

"Is she dead?"

"Yes."

"By her own hand? I would not like to think of her stranded in purgatory for all eternity like my mother."

"I don't understand?"

"Never mind. Will you light a candle for her at her church, the ugly gray one on 15th Street?"

"Yes."

"No."

"No?"

"Not one. Light many, *chérie*. She would like more than one."

Claude dozed. Alice sat for an hour. Ben's ghost walked up behind her, buried his fingers in her hair. Warm currents streamed from her scalp into her neck, radiated out toward her tense shoulders. Ben's voice was lively. He told Claude that he and Alice would watch over John when she died. Before that, though, he would spend Christmas with her. Alice wondered, *What about me? Who will spend Christmas with me?*

"I'll come to visit you on Christmas Day."

Claude whispered, hardly moving her lips.

"I forbid you to come on Christmas."

Her tomato-red lips sucked on the oxygen nozzle. Alice sat down again, trying to decide what to do about Christmas.

*

On December 28th Alice purchased one burnt-orange-colored rose at a Korean grocery, also a coffee in a cardboard container decorated with blue and white. She had not been able to find a taxi so had taken the subway, walked through the bitter wind to the DeWitt Nursing Home, passed buildings like gold and black blocks in the winter sun. It took forever to get an elevator. She was irritable by the time she got off on the 11th floor.

Passing a dayroom, she saw a dozen geriatric men and women slumped in wheelchairs, propped up like puppets. At the idea of Claude scaring them with her snake, she had to laugh. At the door to 1111, she saw a rippled pink rubber mat lying on top of the mattress, a tan and brown suitcase at the foot of the bed. As usual the indigo curtain was drawn around the second bed. She walked down the hall, looked into a room with 20 old people in wheelchairs placed in a circle. Claude was not there. She stopped at the nurse's station and asked where Mrs. Foot was. The nurse looked at another nurse sitting alongside her. That one asked Alice, "Are you family?"

"In a way. She has no legal family."

"Are you close to her, like Mr. Lightfoot?"

"Not really."

"She passed away this morning. She went into respiratory arrest and her chart said D.N.R... . "

" ... what's D.N.R?"

"Do not resuscitate. So we didn't."

The nurse's amber eyes asked for Alice's approval.

"That was her wish. I would have wanted to be resuscitated. I'm surprised she didn't."

"Her chart said that she was a Catholic. We sent for a priest who came and prayed for her soul until the porter took the body downstairs to the morgue. The priest did not like it that she had asked for D.N.R."

Alice laid the burnt-orange rose across the desk.

"This is for doing a hard job."

In the elevator was a woman in a wheelchair. She had robin's-egg-blue eyes. One of her feet was in an opal-colored plaster cast. She was saying to no one, "Thank God I put my fur into storage. Yes, I fell 19 steps. On the 20th my foot caught ..."

On the main floor was a staff room that was almost empty except for a bright white Formica table at which three Philippine nurses in white uniforms ate slices of heather-colored cake. Alice opened her coffee container. The wallpaper on the back wall was an enlargement of Seurat's painting *A Sunday Afternoon on the Island of La Grande Jatte*, painted in 1884. Among the people Seurat had painted was a woman who reminded her of Claude, a woman wearing a black hat, holding an umbrella.

Alice scanned the print looking for someone who reminded her of herself. There was no one except perhaps the little girl with the straight back wearing a white dress and white hat holding her mother's hand, or the little brown monkey with his ass sticking into the air. When she looked hard, it seemed like the monkey was not brown, was actually cranberry-red, or claret-red, she was not sure which.

John arranged for a Mass to be said at the French church. The night before the Mass, he telephoned Alice and confided.

"The night Claude died my niece in Troy dreamed of her. Claude walked up to her and said, 'Make sure John paints. Make sure he paints flowers. He must paint three orange flowers, milkweed pods.'"

There was the sound of ice clinking in a glass, his voice was slightly shrill, he was speaking rapidly. He added, "A little miracle has happened, I've been hired to supervise a mural being done by art students on West 44th Street."

"Have you ever done a mural before?"

"Yes. I painted 57 birds on an upper floor of the Sherry-Netherland Hotel long ago. Don't you remember, you and Ben arranged the job for me?"

They never had, but she did not correct him.

AUTHOR'S NOTE:

Several years ago in New York I met a French woman who had modeled for Henri Matisse in the early 1950s. By the time I met her she was already quite old. I last saw her the day before she died at age 88. In the few years of our acquaintance, I got to know her as well as was possible although she was generally unknowable throughout her life. She is called Claude Foot and Sister Paule in this book but was born Paule Boule, in 1914. When she married an American GI who was studying painting in Paris on the GI Bill in the 1950s she became Claude Boot. Her husband wanted to bring her to the Florida Everglades where he would paint and she would be his muse. Against her better judgment, she went with him.

As the marriage wore thin, according to her sometimes-varying versions of events, her husband began going to New York in search of new stimulation. Following him there, Claude discovered he had begun living with and painting a new muse. She knew she was used up. She was not prepared to be self-sufficient and broke down. For 20 years, after her marriage ended, anyone who attended classes at the Art Students League in New York remembers Claude sitting in the school's lobby near the statue of Pegasus with full shopping bags at her feet. She might have had on green striped pantaloon-like

366

trousers, perhaps a white and dark blue, mauve and black scarf. Usually her eyes were outlined in black like an Egyptian cat.

This narrative, real and invented, stretches Claude's life between Matisse and Warhol, between France and New York, between pre-war Europe and century's end.

John Elderfield, once the director of the New York Museum of Modern Art's Department of Drawing, a Matisse scholar, described Matisse's use of models like this:

... he (Matisse) confers on his models an unsettling aloofness. It is one that conflates a sense of momentary withdrawal into the self ... It is an aloofness at once serene and disquieting, both sensual and cold. ... it (the body of the model) withdraws into its surroundings. It also withdraws into itself. By this, I do not mean only that it withdraws into paint. I ... mean that a vast psychological interval opens between viewer and model. She (the model) seems unwakeable, unreachable, so deep in her preoccupation that she can never return from it.

And:

... The absorption of the model has the effect of rendering her oblivious to the viewer's presence, as if the proscenium curtain of this theater had never been raised. Thus she does not invite our gaze, but is merely subject to it. ... While her absorption – including, especially, her not

seeing us – makes her actually more physically, including sexually, vulnerable to us, it also forces us to pause for a moment at least, both to acknowledge her vulnerability and to wonder at the cause of the absorption which makes her so vulnerable. What if the picture depicts that exact moment of pause?

The supporting armature on which this construction of fictions hangs is based on actual people and events. In some cases real names have been changed. The whole is a crumbling, strong-smelling, Roquefort cheese veined with green and blue mold. To shape and refine it, I have drawn on the scholarship of many and gratefully cite the following: Patricia Albers, Aurora Art Publishers, Stephen Barber, Rosamond Bernier, Richard Bernstein, Mona Bismark Foundation, Victor Bockris, Franco Carco, Bob Colacello, Paul Courthion, Jacqueline Duheme, John Elderfield, Raymond Escholier, Jack Flam, Kennedy Fraser, Francois Gilot, Pat Hackett, Robert Beverly Hale, Philip Hamburger, Bob Hay, Wayne Koesten, Alexander Liberman, Fran Mollnow, Jean-Bernard Naudin, Vera Nolan, Frank O'Hara, John Russell, Muriel Segal, Hilary Spurling, Pat Whitcomb. As this novel has been ripening for quite some time, regrettably, some attributions may have been unintentionally overlooked.

In the same way a smear of Roquefort cheese was once used to heal infected cuts and suppurating sores, I wish to acknowledge and thank the following who provided succor in one form or another: Alex Calothis and Oneiro Press (U.K.), Editor Helle Valborg Goldman, proofreader Amber Bryant, John Connors, the artist based in Troy, New York and New York City, whose kindness and generosity kept Claude going for the last 10 years of her life and who became the model for a vastly fictionalized John Lightfoot in this book. Thanks to: readers of various drafts – Brenda Currin, Danielle Durkin, Louise Fishman, Ingrid Inyeboe, Sheelagh O'Connor, Aine O'Healy; to eyewitnesses for their reminiscences – Niki Hale, Rita Kallerhoff; to players who participate either factually or imaginatively in larger or lesser degree, or are quoted in this book – Charles Baudelaire, Claude Boot, Constantin Brancusi, Lydia Delectorskya, Alberto Giacometti, Robert Beverly Hale, Alice Hoska, Wasily Kandinsky, Fernand Léger, Gerard Malanga, Amélie Matisse, Henri Matisse, Pierre Matisse, Kiki de Montparnasse, Gertrude Stein, Fëlix Vallotton, Andy Warhol, Julia Warhola, Barry White; to the bright star who cast a dazzling glow across more than four decades of my life – Ane Marie Torp Albertsen.

During these grim years it has been a balm to spend hours looking at Matisse's art; sticking Band-Aids of his heart-stopping color across bitter reality.

This novel's first publication coincides with and celebrates what would have been Claude's 100th birthday. It has been written as an homage to those who, like Claude, serve as inspiration to others, but for reasons unknown, are not treated kindly by life.

About the Author

Alison Leslie Gold has published fiction including *Clairvoyant, The Imagined Life of Lucia Joyce*. Jay Parini said about it: "A vividly written book that plays daringly in the no-mans-land between biography and fiction." A reviewer in the *New York Times* summed up another novel, *The Devil's Mistress: The Diary of Eva Braun, The Woman Who Lived and Died With Hitler*, as follows: "It's hard to forget a novel that spreads across the imagination like a mysterious and evil stain." This book was nominated for the National Book Award.

Alison Leslie Gold's nonfiction writing on the Holocaust and World War II has received special recognition. Among those who have singled her out as a protector and chronicler of Holocaust experiences has been Elie Wiesel, who said of her: "Let us give recognition to Alison Gold. Without her and her talent of persuasion, without her writer's talent, too, this poignant account, vibrating with humanity, would not have been written." Her works include *Anne Frank Remembered, The Story of the Woman Who Helped to Hide Anne Frank*, written with and about Miep Gies, who hid Anne Frank and rescued Anne's diary, and *Memories of Anne Frank: Reflections of a Childhood Friend*, written for young people about Hannah "Lies" (pronounced "lease") oslar, Anne Frank's best friend. Both books have been international bestsellers translated into more than 18 languages. Neither Miep nor Hannah had been willing to tell their entire stories until meeting Alison. Also for young people, *A Special Fate*, about Chiune Sugihara, the little-known Japanese diplomat who saved 6,000 Jews and others during the war. The adult nonfiction book *Fiet's Vase and Other Stories of Survival, Europe 1939–1945*, 25 interviews with survivors, is her farewell to that subject matter. She has published a short work in the Cahier Series, American University of Paris/Sylph Editions "Lost and Found."

Her nonfiction work has received awards ranging from the Best of the Best Award given by the American Library Association, to a Merit of Educational Distinction Award by the ADL and a Christopher Award for affirming the highest values of the human spirit, among others.

She divides her time between New York, an island in Greece and a hide-away in British Columbia.

information can be obtained at www.ICGtesting.com
'n the USA
's1909050315

BV00001B/27/P